Praise for

DEMOCRACY DERAILED

"Lucent and fair... Broder is utterly convincing."

—*The New York Times Book Review*

"Broder's argument is a worthy corrective to the recent enthusiasm for instituting national initiatives and referenda to make government policy.... A very useful book about an important issue."

—*The Washington Post Book World*

"[Broder] addresses the fundamental issue of what is meant by representative democracy and raises troubling questions about a growing phenomenon.... A highly valuable starting point for thinking about the implications of this side-stepping of democracy and should be of national interest as well as receiving the attention of all thoughtful Californians."

—*Los Angeles Times*

"A concise, cogent political analysis...This alarm-bell of a book deserves—and is likely to command—wide attention."

—*The Baltimore Sun*

"Broder stands almost alone among Washington-based political columnists in pursuing matters beyond the latest game of gotcha in the capital, or the newest tidbit of campaign bus gossip. And examining the modern initiative trend, which began with the Proposition 13 property tax revolt in California 22 years ago, is certainly worth the time and effort."

—*San Francisco Examiner and Chronicle*

"A must read for anyone who cares about our government and the direction in which it is headed at the start of a new century and the cusp of a revolution in communications."

—Judy Woodruff, CNN

"Broder's book is important... it turns [an] abstract argument into troubling specifics."

—*American Journalism Review*

"Well-argued and often chilling... As tensions rise between direct democracy and representative government in America, this book gives a provocative critique of the initiative process as a panacea for democracy's ills."

—*Publishers Weekly*

"The knowledge, experience, and perspective of one of America's best political commentators combine in an intriguing and provocative manner to blow the whistle on what has become another bastion for the special interest groups and monied causes."

—*Library Journal*

"Broder offers solid evidence that the initiative process, with its up-or-down simplicity and potential for manipulation by deep-pocket funders, is no solution to the nation's problems."

—*Booklist*

"Could money and technology actually hurt not help our democracy in the 21st century? David Broder lays out an insightful, compelling, and sobering scenario."

—Tim Russert, NBC's *Meet the Press*

"David S. Broder is one of America's hardest working, most thoughtful and even-handed political reporters."

—*The Seattle Times*

"In this intriguing book guaranteed to raise controversy, *The Washington Post's* revered political reporter David Broder argues that, like Pogo, we have met the enemy and he is us. . . . An informative, concise appraisal that should be placed in the hands of every citizen."

—*Nashville Tennessean*

"Broder's book is a startling, well-documented exposé."

—*Providence Journal*

"Good read, Good book."

—Britt Hume, Fox News Network

DEMOCRACY DERAILED

ALSO BY DAVID S. BRODER

The System: The American Way of Politics at
the Breaking Point *(with Haynes Johnson)*

The Man Who Would Be President: Dan Quayle
(with Bob Woodward)

Behind the Front Page:
An Inside Look at How the News Is Made

Changing of the Guard:
Power and Leadership in America

The Party's Over

The Republican Establishment
(with Stephen Hess)

DEMOCRACY DERAILED

INITIATIVE CAMPAIGNS AND THE POWER OF MONEY

David S. Broder

A HARVEST BOOK
A JAMES H. SILBERMAN BOOK
HARCOURT, INC.
San Diego New York London

www.harcourt.com

Library of Congress Cataloging-in-Publication Data

Broder, David S.
Democracy derailed: initiative campaigns and the power of money/
David S. Broder.—1st ed.
p. cm.
Includes bibliographical references.
ISBN 0-15-100464-1
ISBN 0-15-601410-6 (pbk.)
1. Referendum—United States. 2. Democracy—United States.
3. United States—Politics and government. I. Title.
JF494.B76 2000
328.273—dc21 99-054190

Designed by G. B. D. Smith
Text set in Melior
Printed in the United States of America
First Harvest edition 2001
A C E G I J H F D B

In memory of Meg Greenfield,
a friend and colleague for forty years,
whose love for this country and whose
understanding of its politics were unsurpassed

CONTENTS

Dr. Franklin, what have you given us?

A Republic, if you can keep it.
—Benjamin Franklin

DEMOCRACY DERAILED

A REPUBLIC SUBVERTED

At the start of a new century—and millennium—a new form of government is spreading in the United States. It is alien to the spirit of the Constitution and its careful system of checks and balances. Though derived from a reform favored by Populists and Progressives as a cure for special-interest influence, this method of lawmaking has become the favored tool of millionaires and interest groups that use their wealth to achieve their own policy goals—a lucrative business for a new set of political entrepreneurs.

Exploiting the public's disdain for politics and distrust of politicians, it is now the most uncontrolled and unexamined arena of power politics. It has given the United States something that seems unthinkable—not a government of laws but laws without government. The initiative process, an import now just over one hundred years old, threatens to challenge or even subvert the American system of government in the next few decades.

To be sure, change is the order of the day in the United States and elsewhere in the advanced countries of the world. The computer and the Internet are revolutionizing the economy. The speed of communications and the reduction in barriers to trade are making national boundaries less and less meaningful. The end of the Cold War has brought an outbreak of ethnic warfare and has heightened awareness of the dangers of terrorism by extremist groups on every continent.

Amid these changes, American life looks like an island of strength and stability. One reason—in addition to the vitality of our business and entrepreneurial culture, the incredible productivity of our farms, the quality of our great research universities, and the energy and vigor of our people—is the time-tested solidity and flexibility of our system of government. The United States Constitution, in this third century of our national life, continues to provide a durable foundation for our governing institutions. The presidency, Congress, the Supreme Court, the federal system, the rule of law, have been tested by many challenges. Twice in the twentieth century we fought world wars. Twice we faced efforts to impeach and remove our chief executive. We overcame the Great Depression and led the reconstruction of Europe. Repeatedly we wrestled with the terrible legacy of the almost indelible moral stain left by slavery. And we have managed to absorb and integrate waves of immigration from lands far distant from our European roots, giving this nation a richer variety of ethnic and racial groups than ever before.

But even as the system of government invented by the founders—a system based on the separation of powers and a complex matrix of procedures designed to require the creation of consensus before the enactment of laws—has proved its worth in crisis after crisis, public impatience with "the system" has grown. Some argue that the science of public-opinion sampling and the speed of electronic communications make the political arrangements of the eighteenth-century Constitution as out-of-date as the one-horse shay. With journalism focused on the foibles in the private lives of political leaders, disdain for those in government has mounted with each new scandal. Political campaigns have become demolition derbies, in which even the winners emerge with ruined reputations. The trust between governors and governed, on which representative democracy depends, has been badly depleted. Polls consistently show an alarmingly small percentage of Americans believe the government in Washington will do what is right all—or even most—of the time. With the end of the Cold War, that distrust of Washington has brought about a significant shift in political power. Fewer of the decisions that determine the quality and character of our lives and communities are being made in Washington, D.C. Responsibilities are being transferred to state capitols and city halls. Except for Social Security and Medicare, federal spending is smaller than that of state and local governments. Only 13 percent of public employees are on the federal payroll. And states have become the innovators in vital areas of domestic policy, from welfare to education to growth policies.

In half our states—including the giant of them all, California—and in hundreds of municipalities, from New York City to Nome, policies are being made not by government but by initiative. In a single year, 1998, voters across America used the initiative process to pass laws or to amend state constitutions, achieving a wide variety of goals. They ended affirmative action, raised the minimum wage, banned billboards, decriminalized a wide range of hard drugs and permitted thousands of patients to obtain prescriptions for marijuana, restricted campaign spending and contributions, expanded casino gambling, banned many forms of hunting, prohibited some abortions, and allowed adopted children to obtain the names of their biological parents.

At the local level, things were even busier. No less than 226 conservation measures—for parks and greenways, open space, zoning, land-use and "smart growth" regulations—were on local ballots, and 163 of them were approved. That was a 50 percent increase over 1996 and committed more than a billion dollars in local revenues. Voters in New York tried to force a referendum on building a new Yankee Stadium, and Cincinnati voted on the location of its own new ballpark. The ballpark issue was also put to a vote in Round Rock, Texas, while Kenosha, Wisconsin, voters decided on a proposed gambling initiative. Nude dancing and thong bathing suits were the issues in Seminole County, Florida. And in August of 1999, voters in Beverly Hills decided on an initiative promoted by animal-rights advocates that would have required fur shops on Rodeo Drive, and other swank venues, to place on each garment a tag saying it was "made with fur from animals that may have been killed by electrocution, gassing, neck breaking, poisoning, clubbing, stomping, or drowning and may have been trapped in steel-jaw leghold traps." Backers, including Sid Caesar, Jack Lemmon, and Buddy Hackett, raised $75,000 and distributed 5,000 videotapes of hidden-camera scenes in which merchants assured customers the animals had died humanely. But the fur makers, bolstered by the city council and the Beverly Hills Chamber of Commerce, spent even more—$81,000. It was the only issue in an election that cost the city $60,000, and it failed, 3,363 to 1,908, with barely more than a quarter of the registered voters participating.

Not one of these decisions was made through the time-consuming process of passing and signing bills into laws—the method prescribed by the Constitution, which guaranteed the nation and each of the states "the republican form of government." Rather, they were made by the voters themselves—or whatever fraction of them constituted the majority on Election Day. This is the new form of government—an increasingly popular one.

Government by initiative is not only a radical departure from the Constitution's system of checks and balances, it is also a big business, in which lawyers and campaign consultants, signature-gathering firms and other players sell their services to affluent interest groups or millionaire do-gooders with private policy and political agendas. These players—often not even residents of the states whose laws and constitutions they are rewriting—have learned that the initiative is a far more efficient way of achieving their ends than the cumbersome process of supporting candidates for public office and then lobbying them to pass or sign the measures they seek.

The process had its roots in the beginning of the last century, when Populist and Progressive reformers promoted the initiative—along with its cousin, the referendum; popular primaries; direct election of senators; and recall of errant officeholders—as a remedy for the corruption rampant in the legislatures, the state capitols, and the city halls of their day. The initiative let voters, by petition, place legislation or constitutional amendments of their own devising on the ballot. The referendum made enactments of the legislature subject to up-or-down votes by the public.

A spate of reform legislation resulted, including measures regulating business practices and working conditions, and laws anticipating the federal constitutional amendments for the enfranchisement of women and the direct election of senators. But after World War I, interest in the initiative lagged. In 1977 Laura Tallian, a publicist for the People's Lobby, headquartered in Los Angeles, could lament that the school texts of her day "scarcely mentioned direct legislation, when they should have taught it as a democratic process important as the right to vote. The history of direct legislation, which lies unnoticed in the clippings from old newspapers of seventy years ago in the Haynes collection at the University of California in Los Angeles, should have been recited as a rich legacy.... An entire generation must learn again what these early reformers taught."

A year later the lesson Tallian so passionately desired was taught. The modern-day romance with the initiative began on June 6, 1978, when two old geezers restructured California government and arguably changed the course of public policy across the nation. Howard Jarvis, described by the *San Francisco Chronicle* as "a choleric seventy-five-year-old gadfly who saw taxes as government-licensed theft," and Paul Gann, a retired, sixty-six-year-old Sacramento real-estate man, started and ran a successful campaign to roll back and cap property taxes in California.

The battle over their Proposition 13 cost each side almost $2 million—exceptional at the time, but small change in California initiative fights—but the victory was lopsided. A remarkable voter turnout of 69 percent, testimony to widespread public frustration with the legislature, approved the initiative by a 65 percent to 35 percent margin, despite the opposition of Democratic Governor Edmund G. (Jerry) Brown Jr.; the two Republicans who would succeed him in office, George Deukmejian (then minority leader of the state senate) and Pete Wilson (then mayor of San Diego); and virtually the entire political establishment of the state.

Jarvis and Gann had no formal power base. But they had available to them a tool Hiram Johnson and the Progressives had written into the California constitution three quarters of a century earlier as a device that would let the people override interest groups (especially business) that controlled the legislature in Sacramento.

Prop. 13 struck some people as the antithesis of Progressivism. As the University of Denver's Daniel A. Smith, one of the students of this celebrated initiative, has written, "Prop. 13 can be better understood as a faux populist movement.... Using direct democracy, populist entrepreneurs, such as Howard Jarvis, offer citizens populist-sounding solutions as antidotes to societal problems.... Populist entrepreneurs seize an opportunity, tap into an ill-defined public mood and couple their pet solution to it. The role of the populist entrepreneur is to craft a popular message, place it on the ballot via the initiative process, and put it forward as *the* solution to a widely perceived public problem."

Whether true or false populism, Prop. 13 revived interest in the initiative process. After Prop. 13, use of the initiative became much more frequent in the twenty-four states, plus the District of Columbia, where it is available. In the decade before the United States entered World War I, there were more than fifty initiatives per two-year election cycle. In the next decade the average dropped below forty, held there through 1936, then dropped to thirty-two, and in the decade ending in 1966, to twenty-nine. Then it fell to under twenty. But it revived late in the 1970s, and from 1976 through 1998, the average has been an astonishing sixty-one initiatives per cycle. In 1997–1998, the number was sixty-six. And thirty-nine of the sixty-six became law, boosting the success rate for the decade to 50 percent—by far the highest for any period since the initiative was introduced.

The initiative game has become a big—and very lucrative—business for those who collect petition signatures and run the ballot campaigns. And it also has produced great controversy, with some praising it as the purest form of democracy and others taking the view expressed in the headline on a 1998 *San Francisco Chronicle* series, marking the twentieth anniversary of Prop. 13: DEMOCRACY GONE AWRY.

I was agnostic on the subject myself when, in 1997, I made a West Coast reporting trip for my paper, the *Washington Post.* I started in Oregon, one of the pioneer states in use of the initiative, and the state with the largest number of ballot propositions in the 1990s. In late summer of 1997, Oregon voters were preparing to cast ballots—for the second time—on the deeply divisive issue of physician-assisted suicide. In the first vote, on Measure 16, held in 1994, physician-supervised access to a lethal mix of drugs for terminally ill patients was approved by the narrowest of margins, 51 percent to 49 percent. The legislature, responding to pleas and pressures from the losing side, ordered a second ballot on the identical proposition, Measure 51, in a vote-by-mail special election in November of 1997.

As I interviewed activists on both sides of the issue, I came to understand the depth of the moral, ethical, and religious beliefs that brought them to their opposing positions. For some, the sanctity of life meant that no one but God should determine the date of anyone's death. For others, the individual's freedom to choose to end suffering when there is no hope of recovery was as fundamental a right as freedom of speech or freedom of worship.

Doctors felt the dilemma intensely. Their mission is to heal and to reduce suffering. Now they were being asked to make judgments that would permit some of their patients—though not the doctors themselves—to administer lethal chemicals. In many instances, inevitably, the doctors would be asked to supervise and witness the process. Some saw it as a final service they could render. More found the prospect repugnant.

Interviewing leaders on both sides of the issue, I found myself asking, toward the end of each conversation, "Is this a good issue to decide by majority vote of the people?" Almost without exception, they looked as if it were the most stupid question they had ever heard. The response was some variation of the same two rhetorical questions: "Who better than the people? You want to leave it to the politicians?"

My private reaction to their responses was that in any legislature I had ever covered, politicians who sensed (or learned from the polls) that their constituents were so closely divided on an issue of that weight would find some convenient way not to make a decision. Simple self-preservation, to say nothing of the checks and balances built into the legislative process, would keep them from imposing a judgment so deeply offensive to such a sizable minority of the people—whichever way it went.

But in Oregon, I quickly learned, the legislators were seen as interlopers, busybodies who had interfered with the sovereign right of the people to make their own laws. A flyer distributed by Oregon Right to Die said, "Three years ago, over 600,000 Oregon voters passed Measure 16 [the 1994 physician-assisted suicide initiative]. This year, 52 legislators voted to send it back to the ballot. It was a bad vote. A wrong vote. Almost every Oregon newspaper said so. But still we have to vote again. Much is at stake." Along with the question "Who controls end-of-life decisions?", the flyer said voters must ask, "Can the legislature usurp our initiative process with such impunity?"

For many people, the second question was at least as important as the first. Governor John Kitzhaber, himself a physician who had opposed assisted suicide during the 1994 fight, because of his personal doubts, came out against Measure 51, the 1997 repeal measure, in large part because he thought the legislature had overstepped itself.

I saw something else in the 1997 initiative campaign that disturbed me. While the debate covered much of the same ground as the earlier battle, there was an added element of religious antagonism and prejudice. An article in *Willamette Week,* a widely read "alternative" paper in Portland, talked about how "church dollars flowed in" and almost defeated assisted suicide in 1994. It was particularly critical of the Portland *Oregonian*'s handling of the issue. It found fault with the reporting of Mark O'Keefe, described as "a clean-shaven Episcopalian who attended Pat Robertson's Regent University school of communications." It noted that "longtime *Oregonian* publisher Fred Stickel, a Catholic, has strongly opposed Measure 16 since the beginning and has used his editorial page to push his crusade against assisted suicide." The *Week*'s article blamed "Catholic and Right to Life activists" for instigating lawsuits against Measure 16 and for the lobbying that led to the legislature's sending it back to the voters.

I went on to California, where an arresting spectacle was unfolding. In previous elections, the people of California had approved three ballot initiatives that fundamentally recast the political and governmental structure of their state. One imposed some of the strictest term limits anywhere on members of the legislature—six years in the assembly, eight years in the state senate, and never again. A second initiative put the tightest controls anyone had seen on campaign contributions to state and local candidates. And the third changed the system of nominating candidates for state offices. Instead of having separate primary ballots for Republicans, Democrats, and the minor parties, it placed all candidates of all parties on a blanket primary ballot, allowing any voter of whatever persuasion to pick anyone from any party for any particular office. All three of these initiatives were being challenged in federal court; two of the cases were being argued before district judges in Sacramento; the third, before an appeals court panel in San Francisco.

Interviewing in the state capitol, I was struck by the frustration of both Republicans and Democrats waiting to learn whether they could run for reelection or would be term-limited out; whether they could raise money, as they had in the past, or would be severely constrained; and whether their nominations would depend on their appeal to their fellow partisans or be subject to the vagaries of influence by members of the other party—or no party at all.

In court the issue pitted the voice of the people of California, who had spoken through the initiative process, against the opinions of unelected judges, who had the power and the responsibility to measure the initiatives against the guarantees and protections of the Constitution. The only people who had no voice in the outcome were the elected officials of the state. They were mere spectators on the sidelines, waiting for the verdicts.

I filed news stories and columns about what I had seen, and when I got back to the newsroom, suggested to my editors that what was taking place in these states—and the many others with initiative process—deserved more examination than we had given it. This book is an effort to carry that discussion from the academic arena, where it has largely been confined until now, into the arena of public discussion and political debate.

The founders of the American Republic were almost as distrustful of democracy as they were rebellious against royal decrees. They were steeped in the writings of philosophers such as John Locke, who proposed a social-contract theory to justify representative government against the claims of absolute monarchy, and Montesquieu, who urged the separation of legislative, executive, and judicial branches as a safeguard against abuse of power in a democracy. As their disciples, the writers of the Constitution placed the legislative branch first in their document—and preeminent in power—with independent executive and judicial branches providing the necessary checks and balances.

The founders were not naive. They recognized the potential danger that those elected to the national legislature might abuse power. So they divided that authority between two bodies, the House and the Senate—the first, numerous and of short tenure, to reflect short-term shifts in public opinion, and the latter, at one remove from the people and with a longer term, in order to apply a prudent check on those instant judgments by the House.

Further, they created a role in legislative matters for the executive, by arming him with a veto power that could be overruled only by a two-thirds vote of the House and Senate. And implicitly, at least—or so John Marshall successfully argued—it empowered the Supreme Court to invalidate any legislation that contradicted the terms of the Constitution.

Irving Kristol, in an essay in his 1972 volume *On the Democratic Idea in America,* wrote:

> Although none of the founding fathers can be called a political philosopher, most of them were widely read in political philosophy and had given serious thought to the traditional problems of political philosophy. One of these traditional problems was the problematic character of democracies. The founding fathers were aware that, in centuries past, democracy—in the sense of the unfettered rule of the demos, of the majority—had been one of the least stable and not always the most admirable of political regimes.... In short, the founding fathers sought to es-

tablish "a popular government" that could be stable, just, free; where there was security of person and property; and whose public leaders would claim legitimacy not only because they were elected officials but also because their character and behavior approximated some accepted models of excellence.... They were partisans of self-government—of government by the people—who deliberately and with a bold, creative genius "rigged" the machinery of the system so that this government would be one of which they, as thoughtful and civilized men, could be proud.

In establishing such a popular government, the founding fathers were certainly under the impression that they were expressing a faith in the common man. But they were sober and worldly men, and they were not about to hand out blank checks to anyone, even if he was common man....They took it for granted that democracy was capable of bringing evil into the world, and they wanted a system of government that made this as unlikely as possible, and that was provided with as strong an inclination toward self-correction as was possible. And I should guess that they would have regarded as a fair test of their labors the degree to which common men in America could rise to the prospect of choosing uncommon men, speaking for uncommon ideals, as worthy of exercising authority over them.

These were the intellectual currents bubbling in the final decades of the eighteenth century—some of them already published, others still being formulated—when the delegates from the former colonies met in Philadelphia to frame a charter for the new nation.

Their struggles—intellectual and political—are familiar to most readers, and their conclusions, compromises, and solutions have served this nation extraordinarily well. They provided a framework of government so solid that it has proved adaptable, as America grew from a small set of Atlantic seaboard settlements, populated largely by northern European émigrés and African slaves, into a continental Republic of almost 300 million people, drawn from all corners of the world.

The great defense of that scheme of government can be found in the *Federalist* papers, written to persuade the states and their people to ratify the new Constitution. In *Federalist 10,* James Madison, one of the principal architects of the Constitution, gave the classic argument for its careful effort to balance democratic impulses with safeguards against heedless majorities.

He wrote:

> Complaints are everywhere heard from our most considerate and virtuous citizens, equally the friends of public and private faith and of public and personal liberty, that our governments are too unstable, that the public good is disregarded in the conflicts of rival parties, and that measures are too often decided, not according to the rules of justice and the rights of the minor party, but by the superior force of an interested and overbearing majority. However anxiously we may wish that these complaints had no foundation, the evidence of known facts will not permit us to deny that they are in some degree true.

Their reading of history had convinced them that the Greek city-states had failed because they had tried to govern themselves by vote of the people. Madison further wrote:

> It may be concluded that a pure democracy, by which I mean a society consisting of a small number of citizens, who assemble and administer the government in person, can admit of no cure for the mischiefs of faction. A common passion or interest will, in almost every case, be felt by a majority of the whole; a communication and concert results from the form of government itself; and there is nothing to check the inducements to sacrifice

> the weaker party or an obnoxious individual. Hence it is that such democracies have ever been spectacles of turbulence and contention; have ever been found incompatible with personal security or the rights of property; and have in general been as short in their lives as they have been violent in their deaths.

They also argued that while direct democracy might be appropriate for a small, compact civil society, it would be impractical, let alone inconvenient, in a nation the size of the United States. Yet, as children of the Enlightenment and believers in natural law, they were convinced that individual rights preceded the formation of the state and were superior to the edicts and laws of any ruler. Thus, they wanted the government they were creating to derive its powers from "the consent of the governed."

Translating that phrase into reality became the great work of the Constitutional Convention. No one there argued for direct democracy. Instead, their solution was representative government—based on election of officials who would exercise power within the limits set forth by the constitutions of the nation and the states and under the discipline of frequent elections, which would require them to defend their actions to their constituents and allow the people to replace them if they abused their power or exercised it in ways that did not meet public approval. As Madison said at the 1788 Virginia ratifying convention, "I go on the great republican principle that the people will have the virtue and intelligence to select men of virtue and wisdom."

In the *Federalist,* he wrote:

> A republic, by which I mean a government in which the scheme of representation takes place, opens a different prospect and promises the cure for which we are seeking. Let

> us examine the points in which it varies from pure democracy, and we shall comprehend both the nature of the cure and the efficacy which it must derive from the Union.
>
> The two great points of difference between a democracy and a republic are: first, the delegation of the government, in the latter, to a small number of citizens elected by the rest; secondly, the greater number of citizens and greater sphere of country over which the latter may be extended. The effect of the first difference is, on the one hand, to refine and enlarge the public views by passing them through the medium of a chosen body of citizens, whose wisdom may best discern the true interest of their country and whose patriotism and love of justice will be least likely to sacrifice it to temporary or partial considerations. Under such a regulation, it may well happen that the public voice, pronounced by the representatives of the people, will be more consonant to the public good than if pronounced by the people themselves, convened for the purpose.

Madison conceded that there was a risk that "men of factious tempers, of local prejudices, or of sinister designs, may, by intrigue, by corruption or by other means" come to office and abuse their powers. But that risk, he said, is reduced by the size and diversity of the American Republic. "Extend the sphere and you take in a greater variety of parties and interests; you make it less probable that a majority of the whole will have a common motive to invade the rights of other citizens; or if such a common motive exists, it will be more difficult for all who feel it to discover their own strength and to act in unison with each other.... Hence, it clearly appears that the same advantage which a republic has over a democracy in controlling the effect of faction is enjoyed by a large over a small republic... [and] is enjoyed by the Union over the states composing it."

Thus, the rationale for making the United States a republic, rather than a democracy, rested on a healthy apprehension of the dangers of direct democracy and the manifold risks of relying on simple majority rule. Direct democracy, Fisher Ames of Massachusetts wrote, "would be very burdensome, subject to factions and violence; decisions would often be made by surprise, in the precipitancy of passion.... It would be a government not by laws but by men." The threats, as the founders envisaged them, ranged from raids on the treasury and shifting of tax burdens from one constituency to another, to the infringement of civil liberties, the submersion of minority viewpoints and interests, and even the destabilization of the entire political order.

All of those effects except the last can be seen in a number of California initiative campaigns. Proposition 13, for example, relieved many businesses and almost all apartment owners of property taxes and shifted the cost of government on to those with more transient addresses. Other initiatives commandeered high percentages of the state budget for education, requiring stringent economies in health and welfare programs that might otherwise have competed for available funds. In 1994, Proposition 187 denied education and health benefits to the families of illegal immigrants, a relatively weak minority group. And in 1996, Proposition 209 ended affirmative action, or racial and gender preferences for minorities and women, restricting education opportunities for those groups and closing down job and contract opportunities for them.

What the founders never could have foreseen, however, was the growth of a lucrative initiative industry, in which a variety of firms make handsome profits from drafting the language, collecting the signatures, managing the campaigns, and creating the media that result in the passage or defeat of these ballot measures.

A review of records for the 1998 election cycle—not one of the busiest of recent years—discloses that more than a quarter-billion dollars was raised and spent on this unevenly regulated—and fitfully reported—arena of politics. Even more than candidate elections, initiative campaigns have become a money game, where average citizens are subjected to advertising blitzes of distortion and half-truths and are left to figure out for themselves which interest groups pose the greatest threats to their self-interest.

It is a far cry from the dream of direct democracy cherished by the early nineteenth-century reformers who imported this peculiar institution and installed it in this country, hoping it would cleanse our politics. They might be the first to throw up their hands in horror at what their noble experiment has produced.

Is it compatible with our form of government... or an alien growth? One answer comes from the distinguished historian Charles A. Beard, who was a great advocate of popular democracy in all its forms. In a book on the initiative, which he published with Birl E. Shultz in 1912, *Documents on the State-Wide Initiative, Referendum, and Recall,* Beard wrote that "it is idle to speculate whether [the framers of the Constitution] would have regarded a system of initiative and referendum, such as now existing in Oregon, as repugnant to the republican form. They were not called upon to consider any such proposition."

But Beard immediately went on to quote the warnings Madison and other Founding Fathers voiced in Philadelphia about what Elbridge Gerry called "the excess of democracy." Beard wrote:

> In the face of such evidence, which may easily be multiplied by citations from the records of the convention, the *Federalist,* and other writings of this period, no one has any warrant for assuming that the founders of our federal system would have shown the slightest countenance to a system of initiative and

> referendum applied either to state or national affairs. If some state had possessed such a system at that time, it is questionable whether they would have been willing to have compromised with it, as they did with the slave states, in order to secure its adherence to the Union. Democracy, in the sense of simple direct majority rule, was undoubtedly more odious to most of the delegates to the convention than was slavery.
>
> When the judges of the Supreme Court are called upon to interpret the "republican" clause of the Constitution as applied to a system of initiative and referendum, it is evident they cannot discover what was the intention of the Fathers, for the latter can scarcely be said to have had any intention about a matter which had not yet come within their ken in anything approaching the form which it has now assumed. If the court, however, wishes to apply the spirit of the federal Constitution as conceived by its framers, it can readily find justification in declaring a scheme of statewide initiative and referendum contrary to the principles of that great instrument.

Beard hastened to write that such a verdict "hardly seems possible," because in a number of cases the Supreme Court said that it was up to Congress, in exercising its authority to admit states to the Union, and not to the Court, to determine whether the state constitution was satisfactory. As early as 1912, in a pair of cases challenging the constitutionality of the initiative process, *Pacific States Telephone and Telegraph* v. *Oregon* and *Kiernan* v. *City of Portland,* the justices held this was a political question, not subject to judicial review. Over the decades courts have overturned numerous individual initiatives as violating rights guaranteed by state constitutions or the Constitution. But the process itself remains constitutionally protected. And Congress has admitted to the Union states such as Oklahoma and Alaska which had the initiative process in their original constitutions.

Some legal scholars have argued that the Supreme Court rulings do not relieve state supreme courts of the right or responsibility to weigh whether the initiative process is compatible with a republican form of government, but so far no court has taken up their challenge.

The growing reliance on initiatives in the half of the country where they are available is part of the increasing alienation of Americans from the system of representative government that has served this nation for over two hundred years. As the new century begins, the reputation of elected officials at all levels has rarely been worse. Our citizens always have had a healthy skepticism about the people in public office; the whole Constitution rests on the assumption that the exercise of power is a dangerous intoxicant; hence, those in authority must be checked by clear delineation of their authority and balanced against one another, lest anyone commandeer too much power.

But what we have in the country today goes well beyond healthy skepticism to a pervasive distrust of those we ourselves have elected to exercise temporarily the authority we have given them. As a young woman attending a session of the North Carolina Institute of Political Leadership—a wonderful skills-training program for community leaders who are preparing to enter elective politics—told me in 1999, "The reaction I get from people I've known for years is, 'You're such a nice person. Why would you want to go into politics?'"

The general disdain for politics and politicians is especially fierce when it comes to legislatures (including Congress) and their members. While many voters are prepared to exempt their own representative from the blanket indictment, the pervasive attitude is that our lawmakers are selfish, self-centered partisans, controlled by special interests and constantly on the lookout for ways to line their own pockets and pay off their pals and political sponsors.

One expression of that disdain has been the term-limits movement, which swept across the country during the last two decades, usually implemented by the mechanism of the initiative campaign. In that combination of initiatives and term limits, we have seen the clearest expression of the revolt against representative government. It is a command to "Clear out of there, you bums. You're none of you worth saving. We want to clean house of the lot of you. And we'll take over the job of writing the laws ourselves."

Many Americans—and presumably many of those who read this book—will heartily endorse those sentiments and shout "Good riddance!" to the ousted legislators. In every state I visited in my reporting, the initiative process was viewed as sacrosanct. In most of them, the legislature (even though term-limited) was in disrepute.

The argument of this book is that representative government is not something to be discarded quite so casually. We need to examine what really happens in direct legislation by initiative. And we must ask ourselves about the implications of a weakening of our republican form of government. Is California the model we want for the nation? Or is there enduring wisdom in the founders' design?

Chapter 1

POWER TO THE PEOPLE

In the minds of the nation's founders, the distinction between a democracy and a republic was clear-cut and important. Yet the democratic principle has coexisted with the republican from the very beginning of the nation and created a tension that has undergirded much of our politics for more than two centuries. During the first twenty years of the Plymouth Colony in Massachusetts, all its adult males met every three months to consider legislation. The New England town meeting was, of course, an exercise in direct democracy. In Massachusetts from 1715 onward, town meetings, under mandate from the colonial legislature, were required to place on their agenda any item supported by a petition of ten citizens. And there were some decisions—including fundamental issues of governance—that would be regarded as legitimate only if taken directly to the people. Massachusetts conducted a referendum in 1788 on adoption of its new constitution. Charles Beard notes that in 1821, New York became the first state outside New England to submit its revised constitution to popular referendum. Thomas E. Cronin, in his 1989 book *Direct Democracy: The Politics of Initiative, Referendum, and Recall,* writes, "By the 1850s it had become accepted practice for admission to the Union that state constitutions first be approved by the people.... At the end of the nineteenth century only a handful of states were governed by constitutions that had not been approved by popular referendum." Cronin also notes that in 1850, Texas held a referendum to resolve a conflict over the location of its capital.

It was not until the end of the nineteenth century, however, that the movement for direct legislation began to gain momentum in the state legislatures. During the last quarter of the century, the coincidence of two economic forces produced a political reaction with historic consequences.

Following the Civil War the scale of enterprise—particularly of manufacturing, mining, and transportation—exploded. The Industrial Revolution swept across America, and its economic efficiencies were captured by a generation of brilliant, ruthless entrepreneurs who built companies and fortunes that dwarfed anything ever seen on these shores.

As historian Gerald Gunderson noted in his book, *The Wealth Creators*:

> Until 1830, American businesses were almost always small and directed by a simple managerial structure. They were largely proprietorships, owned by one person, or partnerships of a few owners working together. Managers and owners were largely synonymous, except in limited cases where passive investors, called sleeping partners, supplemented capital. Managers seldom had anything like the leverage that modern corporations obtain by drawing capital from thousands of investors.

The change began before the Civil War and accelerated markedly after hostilities ended. As Arthur M. Schlesinger, Sr., wrote in *The Rise of Modern America,* "The actual process of absorption and consolidation was directed by men who, because of their boldness, creative energy, and relentless driving power, embodied many of the mythical elements of folk heroes."

Even today we think of those men as larger-than-life figures: John D. Rockefeller, J. P. Morgan, Andrew Carnegie, Jay Gould, Leland Stanford, James J. Hill, Cornelius Vanderbilt, and other businessmen and bankers assembled oil companies, railroads, steel mills, and banks on a scale never before imagined. In a sympathetic history of the Populist movement, published in 1943, Anna Rochester wrote, "The flaunting extravagance of the new industrial rulers and their Wall Street brothers covered depths of mass poverty and suffering. Both the crowded tenements and the scattered farms were cruelly exploited in this onward march of American capitalism."

Workers employed by these new industrial and financial giants found that as individuals they had little leverage to protest the meager wages, the miserable conditions, and the long hours of their employment. So they formed unions. The Knights of Labor came into existence in 1869, just four years after the end of the war. The American Federation of Labor was founded twelve years later. Employers responded with force. The Homestead battle and the Pullman strike saw private armies of strikebreakers reinforced by state militia.

At the same time that workers in many of the burgeoning urban areas found their wages were being eroded by waves of cheap immigrant labor, farmers were caught in a cycle of declining commodity prices and calamitous weather. The financial panic of 1884 wrecked their markets and was followed by a drought, which inspired a contemporary observer to write that "from 1887 to 1897, there were only two years in which the central and western areas of Kansas, Nebraska, and the Dakota territory had enough rainfall to insure a full crop, and for five seasons out of the ten, they had practically no crops at all." With banks charging usurious rates for their mortgages, many of the farmers went broke.

The political reaction to these twin economic forces took two forms: first, the Populist movement, a farmer-worker protest challenging corporate power; and later, the Progressive movement, a middle-class and intellectual movement bent on cleaning up governmental corruption.

Both adopted the initiative as a device for achieving their goals. The process had been introduced to American political thought by authors who had seen it used in Switzerland. One pamphlet, "Direct Legislation by the People," was published in 1892 by Nathan Cree. A year later J. W. Sullivan set forth in "Direct Legislation by the Citizenship through the Initiative and Referendum" the argument that as citizens took on the responsibility of writing the laws themselves, "each would consequently acquire education in his role and develop a lively interest in the public affairs in part under his own management."

The largely rural protest groups from the Midwest, South, and West came together at the first convention of the Populist Party, in Omaha in 1892. They denounced both Republicans and Democrats as corrupted accomplices of the railroad barons, who charged exorbitant freight rates; the banks, which set ruinous interest rates and cut off credit; and the industrial barons and monopolists, who profited from the labor of others and paid meager wages.

The thrust of the Populist platform was economic: free coinage of silver, a graduated income tax, and public ownership of railroads. But it also called for direct election of senators and "the legislative system known as the initiative and referendum."

The link between these last two items was the belief that the moneyed interests had taken control of—and thoroughly corrupted—the legislatures, that bribery had robbed them of their representative character and had made elections a sham.

This was the heart of the problem, as the Populists saw it, and a direct contradiction of the faith on which the founders had rested their hopes for the Republic they created in the Constitution. John Adams had written of a Republic where the lawmaking power is delegated "from the many to a few of the most wise and good."

In the minds of the Populists, the founders never contemplated what the country now faced: the systematic corruption of the nation's legislatures by money power, assembled and deployed on a scale unimaginable to those eighteenth-century planters and merchants.

The Progressives shared some of the same concerns as the Populists but had a distinctly different emphasis to their rhetoric and analysis. Many of them were successful and prosperous, animated by civic ideals. They were offended by the spectacle of corruption, even when they were not personally injured by the felons in government. Robert M. LaFollette, a founder of the Wisconsin Progressives, and a governor of that state, who also served as a Republican senator, expressed that sense of outrage when he declared:

> The forces of special privileges are deeply entrenched. Their resources are inexhaustible. Their efforts never are lax. Their political methods are insidious. It is impossible for the people to maintain perfect organization in mass. They are often taken unaware and are liable to lose at one stroke the achievements of years of effort. In such a crisis, nothing but the united power of the people expressed directly through the ballot can overthrow the enemy.

LaFollette was an attorney and prosecutor, and many of the other Progressives came from the learned professions—ministers, doctors, professors, and, notably, journalists. Lincoln

Steffens, perhaps the most influential journalist of the era, wrote scathingly of "the shame" he found as he traveled the country, examining how it was governed. "We are pathetically proud of our democratic institutions and our republican form of government, of our grand Constitution and our just laws," he wrote in the introduction to a collection of his magazine pieces. "We are a free and sovereign people, we govern ourselves and the government is ours. But that is the point. We are responsible, not our leaders, since we follow them. We let them divert our loyalty from the United States to some party; we let them boss the party and turn our municipal democracies into autocracies and our republican nation into a plutocracy.... Isn't our corrupt government, after all, representative?"

But Steffens, like the other Progressive thinkers, is quick to assert that the latent goodness of the people can be mustered to cleanse the system of its evils. Richard Hofstadter, in his 1955 book, *The Age of Reform,* characterizes their thinking this way:

> What the majority of the Progressives hoped to do in the political field was to restore popular government as they imagined it to have existed in an earlier and purer age. This could be done, it was widely believed, only by revivifying the morale of the citizen, and using his newly aroused zeal to push through a series of changes in the mechanics of political life—direct primaries, popular election of Senators, initiative, referendum, recall, the short ballot, commission government, and the like. Such measures, it was expected, would deprive machine government of the advantages it had in checkmating popular control, and make government accessible to the superior disinterestedness and honesty of the average citizen. Then, with the power of the bosses broken or crippled, it would be possible to check the incursions of the interests upon the welfare of the people and realize a cleaner, more efficient government.

The key word is *disinterestedness,* and the organizations that embodied Progressivism were notably altruistic. Hofstadter mentions the National Civil Service Reform League, the Pure Food Association, the Child Labor Committee, the Consumers League, the National Civic Federation. He quotes William Allen White, the Kansas editor and voice of Progressivism: "Democracy is, at base, altruism expressed in terms of self-government."

As Hofstadter says:

> At the core of their conception of politics was a figure quite as old-fashioned as the figure of the little competitive entrepreneur who represented the most commonly accepted economic ideal. This old-fashioned character was the Man of Good Will, the same innocent, bewildered, bespectacled and mustached figure we see in the cartoons today labeled John Q. Public....
>
> In years past he had been careless about his civic responsibilities, but now he was rising in righteous wrath and asserting himself. He was at last ready to address himself seriously to the business of government.... He would act and think as a public-spirited individual, unlike all the groups of vested interests that were ready to prey on him.... Far from joining organizations to advance his own interests, he would dissociate himself from such combinations and address himself directly and high-mindedly to the problems of government.... He would study the issues and think them through.... It was assumed that somehow he would really be capable of informing himself in ample detail about the many issues that he would have to pass on, and that he could master their intricacies sufficiently to pass intelligent judgment. Without such assumptions the entire movement for such reforms as the initiative, the referendum and recall is unintelligible.

The idealism of the Progressives was palpable. Even as it challenged the old politics, it influenced the rhetoric of both parties, the Theodore Roosevelt Republicans and the Woodrow Wilson Democrats. In his manifesto "The New Freedom: A Call for the Emancipation of the Generous Energies of a People," Wilson wrote that "the men who have been ruling America must consent to let the majority into the game. We will no longer permit any system to go uncorrected which is based upon private understandings and expert testimony; we will not allow the few to continue to determine what the policy of the country is to be.... It is our part to clear the air, to bring about common counsel, to set up a parliament of the people... to lift so high the incomparable standards of the common interest and the common justice that all men with vision, all men with hope, all men with the convictions of America in their hearts, will crowd to that standard and a new day of achievement may come for the liberty we love."

It was not just presidents and politicians who gave voice to such hopes. The Progressive movement enlisted many of the leading thinkers of the era and they, too, were true believers. Leon Fink, in his book *Progressive Intellectuals and the Dilemmas of Democratic Commitment,* wrote that philosopher William James "similarly offered a heroic view of the scholar-democrat. The constant danger of democracy, he advised, was that the people 'will choose poorly.' Yet the antidote to such democratic 'self-poisoning,' according to James, was just as surely available in the form of a leadership class drawn from the college educated; 'individuals of genius show the way and set the patterns, which common people then adopt and follow.'"

John Dewey, another of the philosophers of Progressivism, believed that education of the right sort could equip every citizen to exercise the franchise with great wisdom. At one point he even started his own venture in journalism, called *Thought News,* in an effort to bring the wisdom of economic and sociological analysis to people ill served by the penny press. At

Hull House, her Chicago settlement house, Jane Addams, another of the group, established the Working People's Social Science Club, to educate and mobilize the urban immigrants for political action.

The fervor and conviction of these advocates is vividly captured in a twenty-five-cent pamphlet published in November 1900 by Eltweed Pomeroy, the head of the Direct Legislation League, headquartered in Newark, New Jersey. Titled "For the People," it combines arguments and endorsements for initiative and referendum.

The pamphlet begins with a set of propositions familiar to the founders—that progress depends on uniting justice with the particular interests of those in government. Monarchy and aristocracy fail this test, because the interest of the sovereign or of the ruling class will often diverge from that of the mass of the people.

But then Pomeroy takes it a step beyond anything Madison or Hamilton or even Jefferson would have contemplated:

> Does justice coincide with interest in a representative government where the people choose, for longer or shorter periods, the rulers to govern them? The theory is that they choose the wisest and most trustworthy and that these officers, when chosen, retain and exercise these qualities.
>
> At first in this country, the answer seemed to be yes. The representatives elected frequently from a homogeneous and nearly equally wealthy people, and having comparatively few and simple problems to decide, responded readily to the popular will, and the beginning of a just and rapidly progressive government was made. But, as its functions became more and more varied and important and as the wealth of the country increased and concentrated, it soon became evident that the interest of the ruler after election did not coincide with justice to all the people. It either was or could easily be the interest of a

class, the corporations or organized wealth-owners. The tradition of an ideal legislator for a time hindered the rapid domination of class interest and injustice. The enlarged publicity of the newspapers and modern life partially stopped it. The frequency of elections retired the most gross and open corruptionists, but not the subtlest and most dangerous. This tradition is well-nigh dead and the legislators have thrown up a great cloud of laws and vastly increased the complexity of public business that they may hide themselves from this publicity.

Because of this corruption, we are fast progressing toward injustice and instability in our government. The evidence of this is the recent civil wars at Homestead, Chicago, Coeur d'Alene, etc. [Pomeroy is referring here to labor-management struggles in which scores of striking workers were killed.]

Then this stark conclusion:

Representative government has been tested on these shores for over a century. In many cases it is better than the older forms. It has been acclaimed a finality. But it has borne its legitimate fruits, and they are the dead sea apples of corruption and insidious injustice. Representative government is a failure.

If we pursue the path we now are treading, a strong government, buttressed by force, is necessary, and that will be followed by anarchy, death, retrogression.

Interest coincides with justice, not in government, but in self-government; not in any form of rule by others, but in pure democracy, where the people rule themselves. Where the people vote or are able to vote on every law by which they are to be governed, then interest coincides with justice....This can be attained through Direct Legislation, the Initiative and Referendum.

In later chapters Pomeroy sketches the multiple advantages of this form of government. "Transcending and embracing all questions of the finance, the tariff, taxation, etc." he wrote, "is this fundamental one, Shall the people rule or be ruled? Shall organized wealth, with its subtle corruption, govern the people or shall the people govern themselves through Direct Election?... Settle it and the solutions of all other questions will follow in time and with experience."

In support of that assertion, Pomeroy's pamphlet included praise from eighty notable Americans. The range of their backgrounds attests to the power this idea had attained among both Populists and right-minded reformers of the Progressive era.

The first testimonial came from Frances E. Willard, president of WCTU, the international Women's Christian Temperance Union: "The reign of the people is the one thing that my soul desires to see; the reign of the politician is a public ignominy.... Whether for weal or woe, I am now inseparably connected with direct legislation.... It will abolish the domination of bosses and corporations. These threaten the durability of our nation, as they are sources of corruption. Direct legislation will give greater freedom to the voter from the political mastership of these malign influences."

J. R. Rogers, the Populist governor of Washington: "I am in favor of direct legislation. The people are helpless against the bribery which is resorted to by the great corporations and interests which fear the people and deal with their corrupt officials."

Hazen S. Pingree, Republican governor of Michigan and four-time mayor of Detroit, as well as head of the shoe manufacturing firm H. S. Pingree and Smith: "Give the people what they want is my motto, and as I understand that direct legislation is only a means to do this, I most heartily favor it.... The representative system has developed some disastrous weaknesses.... From a choice of the ablest and best, indifference and ignorance have left the field to the shrewd, the unscrupulous, the vigilant self-seekers."

Samuel Gompers, president of the American Federation of Labor: "I have full faith in the people. The safety of the future as well as the interests of the present can safely be entrusted in their hands. The whole are most honest, more intelligent than the few. We must soon choose whether we are to have an oligarchy or a democracy."

John Wanamaker, former postmaster general, a "leading citizen of Philadelphia and one of the foremost businessmen of the world": "I heartily approve of the idea.... I am willing to trust public questions to the intelligence and conscience of the people."

William Dean Howells, "the great novelist, chief of living American litterateurs": "I am altogether in favor of the initiative and referendum as the only means of allowing the people really to take part in making their laws and governing themselves."

On and on the praise for this panacea rolled. It is hardly a wonder that the initiative movement spread like wildfire. Between 1898, when South Dakota became the first state to adopt initiative and referendum, and 1918, eighteen states installed both, four others referendum only, and one the initiative only. The high-water mark was 1912, with five states joining the list.

The Oregon story embodies the history of those Progressive reformers. In the early years of statehood, the Oregon legislature developed an unenviable reputation as the best that money could buy. An author named Allen H. Eaton, writing in 1912, the height of the Progressive era, said the legislators who assembled in Salem were "briefless lawyers, farmless farmers, business failures, barroom loafers, Fourth of July orators and political thugs." Much of their time was consumed with election of U.S. senators, although, as David Schuman, a University of Oregon law professor, noted in a 1994 essay, "the term 'election' dignifies a process that was apparently more akin to an auction. The bidders at these auctions, who bid as well for the votes and other services of legislators, were the state's major corporate interests: timber, railroads, utilities and banks."

The situation cried out for reform, and in the 1890s the center of a reform movement was located in the town of Milwaukie, a community outside Portland, where a family named Lewelling led a group of Swiss and German émigrés in discussions of topics ranging from spiritualism to the single tax—a proposal promoted by economist Henry George to finance government exclusively by property levies.

As the story goes, Alfred Lewelling came across J. W. Sullivan's book on his experiences in Switzerland, and became an enthusiast for the initiative.

Into this feisty mix of reformers came a man named William Simon U'Ren, whose personality and intellect proved the catalyst Oregon needed. U'Ren was a troubled figure. He had followed his father, an immigrant blacksmith and sometime preacher, on a restless journey across the Midwest and the Rocky Mountain states. U'Ren apprenticed himself to a lawyer in Denver, became a member of the bar and active in politics. He told Lincoln Steffens that he was appalled when the Republican bosses of Denver gave him what we would now call street money to buy up votes against opponents who were appealing to those same voters by attacking Chinese immigrant laborers.

In 1891, having moved to Oregon in search of a healthier climate, U'Ren brought his interest in spiritualism and reform to the Lewelling circle and quickly became its unofficial leader.

They formed the Direct Legislation League and launched a propaganda campaign, distributing almost half a million pamphlets and hundreds of copies of Sullivan's book, in support of a constitutional convention that would enshrine initiative and referendum in the charter of Oregon's government. They failed narrowly in the 1895 session of the legislature, in part because the *Portland Oregonian* labeled the reform "one of the craziest of all the crazy fads of Populism" and "a theory of fiddlesticks borrowed from a petty foreign state."

U'Ren won a seat in the 1897 session, but that legislature saw a two-month deadlock between rival factions of Republicans and a U'Ren-led boycott, when the leader of the main Republican faction reneged on a deal to trade a Senate seat for himself in return for his endorsement of initiative and referendum.

Steffens, in his book *Upbuilders,* has left us a vivid portrait of U'Ren, the "very quiet man" who fancied "he would be like Moses, the giver of laws that should lead the people of Darkness into the land of Promise." In that tumultuous legislative session—"a session of bribery, drunkenness, hate and deadlock," as Steffens described it—"men were bought, sold and bought back again.... Most of these men didn't know what they were doing, and they didn't care. They wanted something for themselves; U'Ren wanted something for the people. On that basis, William U'Ren went into every political deal that he could get into." U'Ren, who was nothing if not practical, told Steffens, "We helped through measures we didn't believe in, to get help for our measures from members who didn't believe in them. That's corruption, yes; that's a kind of corruption, but our measures were to make corruption impossible in the end."

The initiative and referendum failed to pass in that 1897 session. But after another grassroots campaign, U'Ren lined up enough support so that a constitutional amendment for initiative and referendum passed easily in 1899 and received the required second endorsement from the legislature two years later, with only a single dissenting vote. The voters ratified the amendment in 1902 by a margin of eleven to one, and it withstood a legal challenge that was carried all the way to the Supreme Court.

The years immediately following introduction of the initiative justified the reformers' faith in its power. Using the new tool, they levied the first serious taxes on railroads, utilities, and other big companies; regulated freight rates; introduced a presidential primary and direct election of senators; gave women the right to vote; and instituted the eight-hour day and workers' compensation.

Ironically, the first great setback came with the defeat of single-tax measures on the ballot in 1912 and 1914. That particular economic reform had been at the center of U'Ren's and the Milwaukie group's agenda. But this failure did not dissuade subsequent generations of Oregonians from cherishing—and frequently using—the initiative.

As Allen Eaton wrote in his 1912 volume celebrating the "Oregon System":

> From what has been said, it already must appear that the people of the state of Oregon enjoy a very wide political power—so wide that they may do anything in politics that they please to do. There are practically no restraints upon their power. From this standpoint, Oregon is without doubt the most democratic democracy in the world, if we mean by democracy a state where the people have absolute power....
>
> Through the initiative, the people have not only taken over to themselves powers which they once delegated to the legislature, but have taken even greater power than those originally set forth in the constitution. The people of Oregon can and do not only make laws independent of the legislature, but pass constitutional amendments at will. But this is not all: the governor cannot exercise his power of veto on any measure passed upon by the people....
>
> Notwithstanding the fact that the Supreme Court has held

> that the initiative and the referendum do not destroy the representative character of our government, it cannot be denied that they have set up another legislative branch of government with greater power and less restrictions than were originally provided by our constitution.

California, the state now most commonly associated with initiative campaigns, adopted the process in 1911, after more than a decade of intensive lobbying. The leader of the movement was a physician, Dr. John R. Haynes, who moved from Philadelphia to Los Angeles in 1887. A student of the Swiss success with direct legislation, Haynes, who made a fortune in Los Angeles real estate, organized other wealthy and influential citizens and formed the Direct Legislation League of California. He lobbied incessantly for the initiative, arguing that "from 25 to 40 percent of the income of our large cities is dissipated by extravagance, mismanagement and corruption." The initiative process is far more prudent, he said, because "in each case, the individual voter has considered a few questions for months, and votes upon those in the quiet of his booth alone, while the ordinary legislator often votes upon scores of questions at a single sitting, amid tumult and uproar, the appeal to party passion and to his private pocketbook."

In 1903 Haynes and his allies succeeded in making the process part of the Los Angeles city charter. After the California supreme court upheld the constitutionality of the provision in 1906, it spread to other cities. As in Oregon, the leading newspaper was initially deeply suspicious of the effort. The *Los Angeles Times* editorialized against "the ignorance and caprice and irresponsibility of the multitudes" and contrasted it with "the learning and judgment of the legislature."

Few others shared the journal's high estimation of the lawmakers in Sacramento, who notoriously had allowed themselves to be purchased by the Southern Pacific Railroad with free passes, bribes, and other considerations. Haynes made repeated lobbying trips to Sacramento, only to return in frustration. Laura Tallian, in her 1977 book, *Direct Democracy,* quotes one of Haynes's accounts of his Sacramento adventures:

> I was sitting by the side of a member who had been in the legislature twelve years, who was a member of the "ring," and who had introduced my measure, not because he believed in it but because I had been his family's physician for several years and he wished to oblige me.
>
> Turning to me, he said: "The man who is acting as Speaker pro tem is a $2,500 man," and he informed me of the facts connected with this man's getting a $2,500 bribe. He pointed to various other members as being $2,000, $1,500, $500, $50 men, and finally to one who purloined stationery, stamps and other Senate chamber appurtenances.

It was not until 1910, when Hiram Johnson was elected governor and a reform legislature with him, that Haynes's labors bore fruit. Johnson was the son of a Sacramento lawyer-politician and began his maverick career fighting against "the bosses" in his native city and in San Francisco. The renown he won in the local fights fueled his successful campaign for governor, in which he promised to break the influence the Southern Pacific Railroad had long exerted in the state capitol. After winning the governorship, Johnson became Theodore Roosevelt's running mate on the 1912 Progressive Party ticket and—from 1917 until his death, in 1945—a United States senator, best known for his isolationist views and his fierce battles against Woodrow Wilson's and Franklin Roosevelt's efforts to make this country a leader on the world stage. But nothing in his later life brought Johnson the acclaim he enjoyed during his first years as governor. Tallian quotes the lyrical account of Frederick O'Brien, in the March 28, 1911, edition of the *Los Angeles Record,* regarding the wonders of that first Johnson-controlled legislature.

> It made hope spring again in the hearts of men and women who had long been held in the chains of political lawlessness. It thrust from power the Captains of Greed. Of all the legislatures ever in California it alone represented the real majority of the citizens of the state....
>
> From the initial day of the session until its close, no taint of bribery nor political corruption was upon it....Most of the members of the legislature fought the good fight. Most of them acted up to their consciences and their lights. Most of them go back to their constituents—not like whipped hounds to live on the bounty of their master[s], the Southern Pacific or other corporations—but to take up again the common burdens of the citizen. They return having honored themselves and those who sent them....
>
> Like coyotes who shun the light, the horde of big and petty bosses and hucksters who, until this season just finished, openly marketed measure and place in the Capitol, kept in the dark. What orders they gave the wretched few who survived in the Senate and Assembly to do their bidding, were whispered elsewhere, and with small hope of their being carried out. For the first time since a railroad ran in California, its crooked factors and log-rollers have not cried their commands in the legislative chambers, and trafficked in votes there.
>
> For the first time in the memory of the old inhabitants of Sacramento, wine, women and gaming have not entered into legislation.
>
> The rightful business of the state was done in the open. Men came and went without fear. They knew their responsibility was but to the people who sent them, and in whose hands is today the vehicle to recall them whenever they do not stand for what they were chosen.

That 1911 legislature proposed amendments to the constitution for initiative, referendum, and recall, and after a vigorous campaign by Governor Johnson, they were approved by margins of better than three to one.

It was, they all believed, the opening of a glorious new era.

Chapter 2

THE INITIATIVE INDUSTRY

It did not last long. World War I—and its aftermath—shattered the illusions about the inevitable triumph of democracy on a global scale, and it ended the brief Progressive period in American politics. The era had its notable accomplishments. Laws for women's suffrage, direct election of senators, and presidential primaries were passed by the voters, and the new populist tool was used to impose wage and hour laws, end child labor, and regulate banks, railroads, and utilities.

But it was doomed from the start, in all likelihood, by the shakiness of its intellectual premises. As Leon Fink remarked, "the confidence of the Progressive intellectual generation [those thinkers who came of age between 1890 and 1918] would be sorely tested. On both intellectual and political grounds they would discover that it was one thing to mouth democratic principles and quite another to demonstrate that they could work in daily life.... Beginning before World War I and continuing through the decade of the 1920s, a cloud of disillusionment with the processes of popular self-government and even the very concept of the democratic will spread thickly over the centers of higher learning in America." Such developments as the success of wartime propaganda campaigns and the spread of press agentry "convinced many observers that public opinion was not the stuff of which dreams of progress could be made."

No sooner had the concept of popular sovereignty been implanted in the political system than clever politicians realized that the key to power now lay in the manipulation of public opinion. Ironically, some of the first to make the leap were the self-styled Progressives. When Teddy Roosevelt challenged William Howard Taft in the Republican primaries of 1912, he employed a press agent—a figure previously associated only with the world of entertainment. Senator Robert LaFollette, the patron saint of Wisconsin Progressives, enlisted the help of conservationist Gifford Pinchot, described as "a master and promoter of political publicity," and set up the original version of what Bill Clinton's campaign later called "the War Room," an instant-response center primed to wage propaganda war on his enemies.

The success of the Wilson administration's wartime propaganda machine generated civilian imitators, and the public-relations industry was born in the 1920s. One of the original geniuses of that business, Edward L. Bernays, wrote, "The mind of the people is made up for it by the group leaders in whom it believes and those persons who understand the manipulation of public opinion. It is composed of inherited prejudices and symbols and clichés and verbal formulas supplied to them by their leaders."

"In less than 25 years, American social science had become deeply disenchanted with the dream of an informed, rationally self-governing public," Fink writes. And yet the legacy of the early Progressives remains. It is embedded in our political system, where nomination of candidates from president to school board member is legitimate only if accomplished through primary elections. And it is embedded in the initiative process, where more and more states have opted for direct legislation, and more and more issues have been settled by that method.

California's Proposition 13 deserves much of the credit or blame for the renewed popularity of initiatives. What propelled the voter rebellion was clear. In the housing boom of the late 1970s, property values soared and local communities, reaping a property tax bonanza, were slow to reduce property tax rates. Many longtime residents, especially retirees, feared they would be taxed out of their homes. Adding to the frustration was the fact that the legislature in Sacramento, watching the budget surplus rise to $6 billion, fell into a partisan dogfight and failed to pass any state tax relief.

Howard Jarvis and Paul Gann offered a simple, sweeping remedy of immense appeal: No community could tax property at more than 1 percent of its assessed value. It rolled back all assessments to the 1975 level—wiping out three years of housing market inflation—and further decreed that whatever future inflation might be, property assessments could not increase by more than 2 percent a year. Instead of the biennial reappraisals most cities did, Prop. 13 decreed that property would be reassessed only when sold. It barred any new taxes based on property values; said any new taxes levied locally would have to be approved by two thirds of the voters; and for any new or higher levies imposed at the state level, it would require a two-thirds majority in the legislature.

The rhetoric of the campaign was as much antipolitician as it was antitax. The legislature and the governor became the whipping boys. As Jarvis wrote in his own book about the Prop. 13 campaign, *I'm Mad as Hell*:

> In plain English, what we were trying to accomplish was to put a fence between the hogs and the swill bucket. Virtually all of the howlers against Prop. 13 had their noses buried deeply in the public trough. They were on a gravy train provided by the taxpayers and they wanted to ride that train at the taxpayers' expense until they reached the promised land of exorbitant pensions for the rest of their lives. They were trying to use the taxpayers' money to bankrupt the taxpayers at whose trough they were gorging themselves. Prop. 13 was intended to forge a chain around the necks of all elected officials and their coteries of bureaucrats so that they could be dragged away from the feedbag. We wanted to put the politicians and their comrades in the bureaucracy on a permanent diet that did not include large portions of the taxpayers' money.

The effect of the vote was to reduce property-tax revenue in fiscal 1979 by two thirds, slashing the annual revenue of local governments by more than $6 billion. Surprisingly, surveys at the time indicated that the voters who approved Prop. 13 were not trying to shrink government. One poll showed a 38 percent plurality believed that services could continue at the same level, even if revenues were cut by two fifths, simply by eliminating waste and inefficiency. Jarvis assured them that "even after Prop. 13, the state would have plenty of money to pay for all the necessary programs. . . . The taxpayers have services coming out of their ears already. They don't use all those exotic services." Even those voters who told pollsters that they favored higher spending by government on schools, health, and other programs supported Prop. 13. They must have been shocked by the cutbacks that occurred.

Initially the state government used its accumulated surpluses to make up for the lost property-tax revenues missing from city budgets. That was fine as long as the California economy was booming, but when recessions came, Sacramento responded by slashing aid to localities. As a result there were recurrent crises in financing basic health, education, and welfare services.

The most dramatic effect was on California schools. What in the 1970s had been the nation's model school system—from the elementary grades through a system of junior colleges, colleges, and great research universities—fell into disrepair and disrepute. By the time the twentieth anniversary of Prop. 13 came around, California, which had consistently been in the top third of the states, had fallen to forty-second in per-pupil spending on its schools.

The long-term effects were far-reaching. Because Prop. 13 allowed reassessments to market value only when a property changed hands, the tax burden shifted from apartment-house owners and corporations—both of whom tended to keep their properties for long periods of time—on to the backs of individual homeowners, who moved with greater frequency. Although Prop. 13 was fueled by a revolt of homeowners against rising property taxes, two thirds of the initial savings went to corporations. The *Los Angeles Times* reported that in the first year alone, Southern California Edison saved $54 million; Pacific Gas and Electric, $90 million; and Pacific Telephone and Telegraph, $130 million. Twenty years later, the *Times* said, almost one third of the commercial and industrial property in Los Angeles County was still being taxed based on its 1975 assessment. The percentage of individual homes benefiting from that bonanza was 4 points less.

Individuals and families also bore the brunt of the scores of fees local governments imposed in an effort to recoup some of the lost revenue. The *San Francisco Chronicle,* in an article on the twentieth anniversary of Prop. 13, noted, "In San Bruno, for example, it costs $2 to play basketball in the city gymnasium, while South San Francisco charges $30 to reserve a public barbecue pit at Buri Buri Park. The San Francisco Zoo doubled its 50-cent admission fee after Prop. 13 passed and has raised it to $7 in the years since. San Mateo County now even charges local cities when it books their prisoners into the county jail."

A further result was that old settlers gained at the expense of younger people just starting out in life. A family that bought a house in the 1990s paid three or four or five times as much property tax as their next-door neighbor who had been living in an identical house since 1978.

Perhaps the biggest unintended consequence of Prop. 13 was to shift control of spending from localities to the state government in Sacramento. Capping local property taxes made the state responsible for funding what had previously been local responsibilities. It made local officials—the very ones the voters said they trusted most to make wise use of their tax dollars—figureheads rather than policy makers. By one estimate, the share of the Los Angeles County budget left to the discretion of its elected board of supervisors dropped from 17 percent before Prop. 13 to 3.3 percent in 1998. Ironically, as time went on, governors and state legislators also found themselves hog-tied. Ten years after Prop. 13 passed, school officials and the teachers' union, alarmed about the squeeze on schools, got together to pass Prop. 98, which mandated that 40 percent of the state's general-fund revenues must be spent on K–12 education. That was not enough to provide well for the schools, and it left other services—from higher education to health care—squeezed even harder. As urban planner William Fulton remarked in the *Los Angeles Times,* "Prop. 13 was supposed to change the relationship between people and their government. That was the goal. And that goal was achieved. But it was achieved in all sorts of weird ways that were never anticipated."

Nevertheless, a Field Poll (a highly regarded statewide poll started by Mervin D. Field) taken in the summer of 1998 on the twentieth anniversary of Prop. 13's passage found that it would pass again, though by the reduced margin of 53 percent to 30 percent—despite the fact that the poll found that 55 percent of those surveyed disapproved of one of its basic features—shifting the basis of assessment from the current market appraisal to the most recent sales price. These voters split almost evenly on whether they were satisfied or dissatisfied with the tax and spending changes that Prop. 13 had brought—40 percent, satisfied, and 38 percent, dissatisfied. Survey director Mark DiCamillo said voters were taking "a more sober view" of their handiwork, but noting the immutability of such a celebrated initiative victory, he added, "It's proven to be almost a third rail of California politics." Los Angeles County supervisor Ed Edelman told the *Times,* "People think it's the word of God, some kind of coming from the Almighty, and they shouldn't touch it."

While politicians have been loath to tamper with Prop. 13, it has been the subject of endless litigation—a fate that has befallen many of the other initiatives spawned by the success of Jarvis-Gann. "Through July 1985," according to Frederick G. Stocker, the head of the National Tax Association, "there were more than 81 court cases, 56 new statutes and resolutions, 21 attorney generals' opinions, 13 legislative counsels' opinions and eight amendments of Prop. 13 at statewide elections, all undertaken to make the new system run more smoothly or less abrasively." And that was just in the first seven years!

In 1992 the basic challenge to the constitutionality of Prop. 13 reached the Supreme Court. The justices ruled eight to one that, despite the fact that identical side-by-side dwellings might be appraised at widely differing amounts, depending on the date of purchase, the initiative did not violate the "equal protection" clause of the Constitution. The Court told Stephanie Nordlinger, a first-time home buyer in Los Angeles, that it was all right for her to pay $1,700 a year in property taxes, while neighbors in almost matching homes paid $400 or $500 a year. To reach that conclusion, the majority found that the state "had a legitimate interest in local neighborhood preservation, continuity, and stability," in effect, saying it was good policy to lock people into their current homes. The second rationale was that California voters could legitimately decide that giving current homeowners the promise of stable taxes was more important than assuring equal treatment of new and old home buyers. The lone dissenter, Justice John Paul Stevens, sarcastically saluted the majority for protecting "the Squires," those who had purchased their homes before 1975 and who could, under the terms of Prop. 13, deed them to children or other close relatives without increasing the bargain-basement assessments. An observer might well conclude that the justices were no more eager than elected officials to overturn what the voters had ordained.

Peter Schrag, the former editorial-page editor of the *Sacramento Bee,* argued in his 1998 book, *Paradise Lost,* that there was an implicit—and perhaps explicit—bias built into Prop. 13. Those "who bought their homes in the distant past, and the children and grandchildren to whom they can leave their homes with the low dynasty provision tax assessments, are, of course, disproportionately white," he wrote. "And those who tend to lose out in this arrangement, and who are sometimes shut out of the housing market altogether, are disproportionately young and Hispanic and Asian."

He argued that by forcing developers to build all the social costs—schools, roads, police—of new developments into the price of new homes, Prop. 13 permanently stunted the growth of the housing market and forced up the cost of living for newcomers to the state. With evidence from many business analysts, Schrag also argued that Prop. 13 created a bias toward shopping center and retail developments—which produce sales-tax receipts—rather than factories and firms, which might provide jobs but from which property-tax payments are limited in perpetuity.

Frederick Stocker saw additional problems. In appraising Prop. 13 ten years after its passage, he described an administrative nightmare. It is clear, he wrote, "that the unforeseen consequences of Prop. 13 were enormous. As the legislature, administrators, courts and the voters themselves in subsequent referenda sought to deal with these consequences, complexities were piled on top of other complexities to produce a system that defies understanding by any but the most determined specialist. Local finance in California has become an incredible maze."

None of this, however, diminished the reputation of Prop. 13 as the emblem of conservative populism, a nationwide tax revolt, the forerunner of "the Reagan Revolution," and the signal act of repudiation of the era of liberal big government. *Time* and *Newsweek* both did cover stories on the initiative. *Time* called it "a California earthquake, a Pacific tidal wave threatening to sweep across the country." Sweep it did. Between 1979 and 1984 more than fifty-eight tax-limitation measures popped up on state ballots—with a high rate of success. The movement spread clear across the country to "liberal" Massachusetts, which enacted its tax cap, Proposition 2½ (so named for its limitation on both rate and growth of the property tax) in

1980. On the twentieth anniversary of Prop. 13, the Heritage Foundation's Policy Review said, "Within two years of its adoption, 43 states implemented some kind of property tax limitation or relief, 15 states lowered their income tax rates and 10 states indexed their state income taxes for inflation. The widespread public backlash against high taxes that began in California contributed to Ronald Reagan's election to the White House in 1980 and pushed taxes to the top tier of national political issues."

As that article suggests, with the passage of time, Prop. 13 has attained even more mythic status. Robert Kuttner, a liberal journalist, has described it as "that rarest of political events, an authentic mass protest brought on by economic grievances." A conservative writer, James Ring Adams of the *Wall Street Journal,* agreed. "The vote for Proposition 13," he wrote, "was to the tax revolt what Bastille Day was to the French Revolution."

Prop. 13 and its progeny have spawned a huge industry devoted to the manipulation of public opinion. Campaign consultants, pollsters, media advisers, direct-mail specialists, and others have made themselves, in effect, the new bosses of American politics. Joe McGinnis put the spotlight on those working to elect candidates, in his 1969 book, *The Selling of the President.* But those who work with even fewer inhibitions and with markedly greater success in initiative campaigns have managed for the most part to avoid equal scrutiny.

The unique part of the industry—and the one that makes everything else possible—is the business of collecting signatures to place initiatives on the ballot. It sprang up within the first decade of the Progressive era—the first decade!—as if to mock the pretensions of those public-spirited reformers who brought the idea to America.

The volume by Beard and Shultz quotes from an article by one B. J. Hendrick, in the August 1911 issue of *McClure's* magazine, titled "Law-making by the Voters." It could almost have been written today.

> At all times these signature-gatherers keep busy, though they are most active during the April and May following a legislative session. They are found in practically every part of the state. They invade the office buildings, the apartment houses and the homes of Portland, and tramp from farmhouse to farmhouse. Young women, ex-book canvassers, broken-down clergymen, people who in other communities would find their natural level as sandwich-men, dapper hustling youths, perhaps earning their way through college... all find useful employment in soliciting signatures at five or ten cents a name.
>
> The canvasser bustles into an office, carrying under his arm a neat parcel of pamphlets, the covers perhaps embellished with colored pictures of the American flag. He gives his victim a few minutes to read the printed matter, and then, placing his finger on a neatly ruled space, says, "Sign here."
>
> Very likely the person approached will demur. The proposed law is foolish, unnecessary... the work of a group of harebrained cranks. Perhaps a protracted argument takes place, which may ultimately ramify into the fundamental principles of constitutional government. Everywhere the canvassers go there is a flood of talk. There is no state in the Union so perpetually argumentative and voluble as Oregon. This is especially true when the solicitors are not paid workers, but enthusiasts. And at times these workers do not receive a cordial welcome; there are plenty of Oregonians who regard the whole system as a nuisance and treat its representatives accordingly.
>
> In other instances people sign petitions thoughtlessly... sometimes without reading the measures or even understanding their contents. "I could easily get ten thousand signatures to a law hanging all the red-haired men in Oregon," one cynic on popular government remarked to the writer. It is not at all unlikely that he could. The business of getting names, as everybody

> knows, depends more upon the individual than upon the merits of the particular case at issue. This new profession in Oregon has its well-recognized experts; and not infrequently one group of canvassers will return disheartened, having absolutely failed in pushing a particular measure, only to have another group go out and return with all the signatures the law requires.

These days professional signature-gatherers do less arguing. They and their employers have found it is a waste of time. If they encounter any significant resistance, they simply move on to the next prospect, hoping to find someone more pliable. And the venues have changed. Instead of going office to office or farm to farm, the signature gatherers set up in a shopping center or on a busy downtown street corner and grab people as they come by.

A Sacramento auto salesman named Edward Koupal is often credited with developing a basic technique in the late 1960s. As described by author David Schmidt, "It's called the 'table method.'... One volunteer stands behind a card table covered with petitions, hands people ballpoint pens, and shows them where to sign. The other partner walks up to passersby asking if they're registered to vote, and if they are, tells them briefly about the petition and directs them to the card table to sign. If the voters hesitate, they are reminded, 'This is just to get it on the ballot.' When reassured, most will sign." Koupal told the *California Journal,* "If the table doesn't get 80 signatures an hour using this method, it's moved the next day."

Fred Kimball, the proprietor of one of the major signature-gathering firms, told me of a variant on the Koupal method he had seen, where the card table was placed next to an ironing board, on which were arrayed seventeen petitions. If the attendant found a voter with sufficient patience, he could collect—and be paid for—seventeen signatures at one swoop.

Another time-saver was described in the California Commission on Campaign Financing's report, which noted that "the most effective version of this technique is for a single circulator to work long, slow-moving lines of people waiting to get into a movie, play, concert or other event.... On one occasion, a paid circulator for the Kimball Petition Management firm gathered 700 signatures in a single day by approaching people who were waiting in line to see the King Tut exhibit at the Los Angeles County Museum of Art."

Most of the major signature-gathering firms have headquarters in California (or, in one instance, just across the border, in Nevada). That is no accident. California, because of its size, requires the largest number of signatures to qualify an initiative—5 percent of the total vote in the most recent gubernatorial election for statutory initiatives; 8 percent, for constitutional amendments. Currently that translates to 419,260 and 670,816 names. Add a substantial excess—30 percent or more—for erroneous or invalid signatures and it requires collecting close to a million names.

California also has the third-shortest qualification period of any state—150 days. So the "market" conditions are made-to-order for firms that can quickly deliver large numbers of signatures. Those firms can make their owners a very comfortable living.

According to the California Commission report, "the first firm to pay persons to gather signatures was established by Joe Robinson of San Francisco in the late 1930s," but it was not until thirty years later that the industry took off. Fred Kimball told me that Los Angeles County assessor Phil Watson was trying to qualify a property-tax-relief initiative for the 1968 statewide ballot. Kimball's father, also named Fred, was a Watson deputy and was handed the assignment of collecting the needed signatures. "So my dad organized a bunch of crews and went throughout the state and processed the signatures, and he realized he could turn it into a little cottage industry. He pretty well put himself out on the market to say, 'Look, if you need something qualified, I can get the signatures to get it on the ballot—paid signature-gatherers for hire.' And that's where it all started."

Young Fred and his brother Kelly were hired by their father to work after school and on weekends, entering the precinct number opposite each signature, for a nickel a name. "We were happy," Fred said. "We were making good money. Other kids were out on their bikes delivering newspapers, but we were being involved in the political process." After college Fred went into the army but came back to join Kelly in running the business their father had started.

The proprietors of two other signature-gathering firms learned their trade in the Kimball training camp. Back in 1978 Mike Arno was a young man of twenty-two, living in La Jolla, and became a volunteer with Paul Gann in the Prop. 13 campaign. When it was over, "I was thinking this was a very powerful thing," he said, and, at the suggestion of in-laws, got a job working for Fred Kimball Sr. He was there only briefly when he and another employee, who has since left the business, decided to strike out on their own. The first venture failed, and Arno turned to journalism, but late in 1982 he was asked by a staffer in California governor-elect George Deukmejian's office to collect signatures for an initiative that would strip redistricting power from the Democratic legislature. It qualified but failed—just as was the case with Fred Kimball Sr.'s first project. But Arno and his two brothers, William and Peter, have been running American Petition Consultants (APC) ever since.

The other Kimball spin-off is National Voter Outreach, owned by Rick Arnold. He spent twenty years in the army, retired as a major in 1979, moved out to California, and for most of the 1980s was a key employee of the Kimballs, eventually running their field operations. At the end of the decade, he and his wife, Geneva, set up shop across the border, in Nevada, and have developed a healthy business, mainly in states other than California.

Two other successful signature collectors came to politics, as the saying goes, to do good—and have stayed on to do well. Ken Masterton was a student at Drexel College in Philadelphia and joined with other liberals to fight against Frank Rizzo, the tough ex-police chief who became mayor of that city. Masterton moved to San Francisco after college, enlisted in the antinuclear movement, and helped collect signatures for a 1976 initiative banning new nuclear power plant construction. It lost, but Masterton, too, had discovered the rewards of direct democracy. He went on to do an antismoking initiative in San Francisco and another anti-nuclear-plant initiative (this one successful) in Bakersfield. With his wife, Sarah, Masterton runs the firm Masterton and Wright from a Marin County headquarters.

Angelo Paparella, who owns and runs Progressive Campaigns, is another transplanted easterner—raised on Long Island, educated at Notre Dame. He became active in Massachusetts with a Ralph Nader–sponsored consumer group. When he moved to California, he continued working in the Nader network on voter registration and political campaigns. In 1988, when Nader sponsored an auto insurance initiative, competing with others backed by the insurance industry and the trial lawyers, Paparella was the field coordinator. The victory Nader won over the more heavily financed rival initiatives gave Paparella the credentials to set up Progressive Campaigns in 1992. While Paparella retains his identity with liberal politics, his firm bids on work of all kinds.

I found these men approachable and reasonably candid when I interviewed them in the spring of 1998, though locating them was not easy. Their offices are usually hidden in nondescript suburban office complexes, or in Paparella's case, a warehouse district on the western fringes of Los Angeles. No big signs proclaim their presence. These bosses of the initiative process like to operate as anonymously as possible; the regulators in the legislatures, who resent their influence, would probably resent them even more if they became high profile.

They run low-overhead, mom-and-pop operations that consciously try to keep costs down in what is essentially a seasonal business. "We've taken nepotism to a new art here," Mike Arno told me. His wife has supervised the signature-verification operation since 1982, and his sister-in-law has also been in the firm for five or six years. "I can't really hire someone full-time, if we're a year-on, year-off business, so we turn to relatives," he explained. The permanent staff usually consists only of the owner-partners and a handful of administrative assistants. None of the headquarters I visited had room for more than a dozen people.

In petitioning season, I found large numbers of name checkers working in bare rooms near each company's office, spaced out at long tables, with piles of signature petitions before them and computerized voters' lists close at hand. Rick Arnold told me that when his father started the firm, "he lived in a mobile-home park that was mostly filled with senior citizens. They were looking for something to do, and they were the greatest workers we ever had. They were available. And they were very prompt. And they give it a lot of time and attention." The sons have continued that employment pattern, using what Arnold calls "one of the largest untapped resources in America, our senior citizens." The name checkers' work is tedious but vital. Most firms guarantee a validity rate of at least 70 percent, and they know their reputation—and future business—depend on meeting or exceeding that standard.

California officials do a random check of 3 percent of the names; the firms verify more to be sure the petitions are not invalidated. Arnold gave me a memo he had prepared for potential clients, emphasizing the importance of verifying the signatures. It notes that sixteen of the twenty-four initiative states "check each and every signature by comparing the signature to the actual voter registration card. It is a tedious process... frequently wrought with error. Numerous times validation errors at the state level kept issues from receiving ballot access in timely fashion." Because of the work involved, Arnold recommended that clients seeking a position on the November 1998 California ballot turn in signatures by February of that year.

Most companies contract out the actual signature gathering, as a way of keeping their own administrative burden simple. Because of that practice, in California a network of area coordinators and crew chiefs has sprung up—very much like the ones that organize migrant farmworkers to harvest the crops. Each coordinator controls the petition business in his own section of the state. Most of these field generals have alliances with several of the statewide firms.

"Let's say I hire someone here in the San Fernando Valley," Arnold said. "She's working for APC, she's working for Masterton and Wright, Bobby Glasser, and a few of the others. The only time we have a problem is when we have directly competing issues out there, and then we give them a choice: 'You can work ours or you can work theirs.'"

Arno told me there were about fifty such area coordinators in California, managing large or small territories, depending on their energy level and their financial ambition. "Our guy that we contract with in the San Joaquin Valley has San Luis

Obispo, Bakersfield, all the way up to Redding covered," Arno said. But more of them are part-timers or seasonal workers. "A lot of them have other businesses," Arno said. "We have real-estate agents, we have insurance agents, we have one woman who raises dogs. They're all pretty ingenious and enterprising."

The area managers have crew chiefs—usually people who have worked with them for a number of years—and they in turn recruit and train the people who are actually out on the street collecting signatures. "The business has evolved over the years," Arno said. "Now they all have cell phones and pagers. They have computers. It's become quite sophisticated." I met two of the managers from the Stockton area who had dropped in to talk business with Arno. Dave Vance and Tom Gray, both early retirees in their fifties, work with APC and its competitors. "On average, I'll be doing about five petitions at a time during the season," Gray said, "but I've done as many as ten."

The people who actually gather the signatures are a mixed crew—students, housewives, laid-off workers, and some who evade state residency requirements and follow the initiative trail from place to place, wherever they can pick up a paycheck. Gray said he looks for people who have "a salesman's personality. You have to be outgoing, ready to talk, you have to make people comfortable signing something they never had heard about." His partner, Dave Vance, added, "You have to keep 'em laughing when you have a lot of petitions. You tell them the next one they sign will guarantee they can sue you for keeping them so long."

One day in Portland, Oregon, I tagged along with a man who was working for the local firm that handles most of the conservative initiatives in that state. His name is Len Weisberg, and for the last ten years, he had been making a modest living, working petition campaigns across the country, from Massachusetts to Oregon. Weisberg, who is in his forties, was motivated more by ideology than by money, he told me. He is a Libertarian and he wanted to help get Libertarian candidates qualified for the ballot (which required petitions in the states where the party's previous votes were not large enough to guarantee ballot access). And he was happy to help any initiative that reduced the power of government.

Dressed in blue jeans and an open-neck sport shirt, he drove me out to a Fred Meyer supermarket in southeastern Portland, that he had picked for his afternoon's work. He was carrying only two petitions that day—both sponsored by Bill Sizemore, an antitax activist who was running for the Republican nomination for governor. One petition would abolish Metro, the regional government for the Portland area, and return its functions to local communities. The other would make it illegal for the state government to withhold union dues from the salaries of teachers and other public employees if any part of that dues was used for political purposes.

As we drove, Weisberg told me that the area we were working had been very productive of signatures a few weeks earlier, when he was working on an initiative to permit patients to get marijuana on a prescription from their doctors. But he was afraid these same young singles would be less sympathetic to abolishing Metro, which ran the bus and light-rail system many of them used to reach their jobs. "I'd rather be working fifty miles out from Portland on this initiative," he told me.

As he patrolled the sidewalk in front of the grocery store, his first question was, "Are you registered to vote in Oregon?" If the answer was yes, he said, "I have a petition here to abolish a big government bureaucracy. Would you like smaller government? I'd really appreciate your help. We just want to get this on the ballot so the people can decide for themselves what they want to do."

Most people had heard enough at that point to decide. Many walked on, saying they were too busy to stop. Most of those who stopped took a moment to sign their name and address. Infrequently someone would pause and ask for a fuller explanation. Weisberg was prepared with a succinct, if somewhat slanted, response. "About fifteen years ago," he said, "they set up something called Metro. There are seventeen board members, and they decide things for the whole region. We don't want to abolish the services—the zoo or the transportation—but we want to give the power back to the local communities." Very rarely, if they still looked skeptical, he would venture into the controversy over growth policy, where the Metro board has tried to channel development to the inner city and resist suburban sprawl. "They force developers to build high-rises," Weisberg claimed, "even if they don't want to. They pushed through light rail even after the voters said no. It's a yuppie service. It costs the taxpayers thirty dollars per rider in subsidies."

The spiel was not only dubious in content, it was too often unproductive. Confirming his fears about the neighborhood, Weisberg often was told, "I like Metro. I'm not for getting rid of it."

The second petition was never mentioned until someone had signed the first. Then Weisberg would add, "I have another one here that would stop the use of public funds for politics." Impatient to move on, most of the signers asked no more; they simply scribbled their name and address on the second clipboard.

In the hour I watched him, Weisberg collected sixteen pairs of signatures on his two petitions. He was getting fifty cents a name, he said, from Sol Klein, who had taken over the work for Sizemore after a firm previously working for him had pocketed payments owed to the signature collectors. Figuring he had made sixteen dollars in his first hour, Weisberg said, "I'm not gonna complain about that."

His "production," as it is known in the signature trade, was modest, I was told. Arno said a good worker (who normally would be carrying more than two petitions) can make twenty-five to fifty dollars an hour. Rick Arnold offered a similar estimate. "I'd say twenty to twenty-five dollars an hour is on the low side; a hotshot will do forty-five to fifty dollars." But in a crisis, they can do even better. "In Florida, in 1994, when gaming interests were paying $2.50 a name, some people were earning $750 a day," Arno said. Phil Keisling, then the Oregon secretary of state, said he had been told of canvassers making a thousand dollars a day, adding, "We've had reports of fist-fights between signature gatherers who claim a particularly good corner."

As good a deal as it may be for itinerant workers like Weisberg, it is a far more lucrative business for those up the line. Kimball said the area coordinators and crew managers usually split a fee of twenty cents a name, but when the season is at its height, late-starting initiatives may boost that override to fifty cents in order to be sure they get enough signatures by the deadline.

Arnold said some of the area coordinators "make more money than God. If their override is twenty cents and they're splitting it with the crew chiefs, at a time when there are five or six petitions out there, they're probably doing twenty thousand signatures a week. They're doing two thousand dollars a week on these things. That's pretty good money for part-time work. Most of 'em make enough money during the petition season to last them through the year." Arno said that some of the area coordinators with whom he does business "make six figures a year."

No one needs to plan a benefit for the owners of the

signature-gathering companies, either. Kimball said that in 1998, his firm was getting an override of twenty-three cents a name on most of its contracts. In California that would mean Kimball Petition Management collects close to a quarter-million dollars for its work on each campaign. Rick Arnold said his firm, which collected more than 1.5 million names in 1998, "probably makes 10 percent as a net profit." Ken Masterton said he and his wife charge differently, setting a consulting fee of four thousand to five thousand dollars a month for each of them for the six- to nine-month period the average initiative campaign lasts.

I heard varying opinions about how competitive the business is. Rick Arnold told me, "Not terribly. We're getting more firms, but the number of issues being circulated is growing." Fred Kimball said he was tired of the jockeying among the firms. "I'll give you an example. There is the horse-slaughter issue that's being circulated right now in California. The proponent goes to Masterton and Wright, and says, 'Give me a bid.' Then they come back to us and do the same thing. Then they go back to Masterton and say, 'Kimball says he'll do it for this.' And they'll say, 'Well, OK, I'll do it for two cents less.' And then they come back to me, saying, 'Well, he came down two cents. Do you want the contract?' Sure, I'll come down another three cents. And you play this Ping-Pong match back and forth. I've pretty much decided that I'm going to stick to what I consider my loyal clients and I'm not going to play the Ping-Pong match anymore. Our clients are basically the unions, gaming interests, trial lawyers, and people like that. We're very loyal to them. We do good work for them. And they pay our prices."

Most of the firms have carved out their areas of specialty. The Arno brothers, who were set up in business by Republican George Deukmejian when he was governor, have continued to handle issues favored by Republicans and conservative business groups. Rick Arnold has built a thriving business mainly outside California. Masterton and Wright, following up on their early contacts in the antinuclear movement, have done a great many environmental and public-health issues. Progressive Campaigns, a relative latecomer with a reputation for being an aggressive marketer of its services, has moved beyond its original liberal causes and has collected signatures for term-limits measures and for the initiative that effectively ended bilingual education in California.

Some firms play a political role beyond signature gathering. Mike Arno said his company also does grassroots political work, "organizing letter-writing campaigns, door-to-door canvassing, voter registration, get-out-the-vote, absentee ballot programs. We even organize rallies."

Masterton's firm is the only one that claims it mobilizes and utilizes significant numbers of volunteers in its work. In 1990, using two thousand environmental and animal-rights activists as volunteers, it qualified an initiative banning the hunting of mountain lions—perhaps the last time such an all-volunteer effort succeeded in California. And even then, the coordinators were paid staff members of Masterton and Wright. Masterton said, "It's fun to train middle-class people to go out there and be signature gatherers. It's a completely different dynamic. And they learn a hell of a lot about the political state of their community and about human nature." Masterton and Wright also offer campaign management services to candidates—something most of the other firms avoid.

Progressive Campaigns has yet a different structure. Paparella keeps a core staff of twenty or twenty-five people, year-round, he said, and hires them out as organizers, not just in initiative campaigns but in local elections as well. Paparella told me that the lucrative signature-gathering pays for a year-round program of community organizing—very much in the Naderite tradition. "When I started doing political work, I was hired as a door-to-door canvasser in Massachusetts, and from the very beginning, I loved the process. You actually went out and knocked on doors and talked to people, and said, 'Hey, this is what is happening. Why don't you do something?' Of course, most people say no, but so what? That's all the more reason to be out there. My own opinion, the more people you have out there sending that political message, that you ought to know about issues, you ought to try to be involved, the better off we're going to be.

"But to carry that forward," he said, "you have to build up skills in your staff. So we've tried to create a business where people can have a decent living, so they can do this [organizing] work for twenty years without burning out. That's the challenge, and we may not meet it, but we're sure-as-hell trying."

High-minded talk notwithstanding, I heard many complaints, from groups who had hired one or another of the signature-gathering firms, about practices that would draw the interest of a Better Business Bureau. I was told of cases where a firm made a lowball bid in order to secure the contract, then informed the sponsor just weeks before deadline that voters really didn't want to sign this petition—and confronted the sponsor with a choice between accepting a jacked-up price for the final weeks of the drive or writing off the costs already incurred and admitting defeat. In Washington state, the sponsor of an antiaffirmative-action initiative was embarrassed by newspaper stories recounting how black canvassers had been recruited from out of state by a signature-gathering company that told them they would be working on a civil-rights initiative. The sponsor blamed the company for the public-relations gaffe.

The efforts to regulate the industry have been sporadic and, for the most part, ineffective. Legislatures, which are often hostile to the initiative process as a threat to their prerogatives, have tried to require that circulators be registered to vote in the state. They have attempted to make them wear badges proclaiming they are being paid for their work, or to legislate that they be paid by the hour, not by the signature. The courts have been generally hostile to these regulations, finding that they seriously infringe on the First Amendment rights of the petitioners. In the most recent case to reach the Supreme Court, *Buckley* v. *American Constitutional Law Foundation,* a six-to-three majority ruled that Colorado could not require signature gatherers to wear name badges, be registered voters, or file detailed financial reports. That case followed much the same logic as a 1988 decision, also coming out of Colorado, which ruled as unconstitutional a ban on paid petition circulators.

The courts have upheld residency and age requirements for the signature gatherers and have said it is reasonable for the state to require them to put their names and addresses on the petitions they are circulating. They have also upheld state time-limits on signature gathering and financial disclosure for the sponsors of initiatives. Badges saying PAID or VOLUNTEER are permissible, but the petition-circulation executives I interviewed said that is no deterrent to collecting names. But they claim these regulations are designed to discourage use of the initiative by driving up the cost of signature gathering. The Supreme Court drew the line at regulations it said would diminish the labor pool from which these companies could recruit workers—including the registered-voter and name-badge requirements. Protecting the First Amendment rights of the signature companies, the justices said Colorado's claim that "today the initiative and referendum process is dominated by money and professional firms" might be valid but regulation and disclosure requirements should be limited to the minimum necessary to prevent fraud.

Even where residency laws are on the books, they have not been enforced strictly enough to become much of a barrier to the itinerant signature gatherers. Mike Arno told me, "California says it's illegal to circulate a petition unless you're a resident or have an intention to reside. That means you have to change your driver's license and pay taxes here or enroll your kids in school. It's not just putting a suitcase in a hotel room. But I will tell you that it is routinely violated." Referring to an Indian gambling initiative then on the streets, he said, "The Indians have probably brought in fifty people and paid their transportation from other states." And California, he added, is far from the worst. "The state of Washington probably has not had an initiative qualify without Californians in a long time."

In 1998 Oregon authorities opened another line of attack, which, at least initially, proved to be more nettlesome to the companies. Officials began prosecuting the signature-gathering companies for failure to pay workers' compensation and unemployment insurance taxes on the people out collecting names. The companies claimed those workers were independent contractors, not employees, and thus not their responsibility. But the Oregon courts held otherwise, and signature-gathering companies warned that if the ruling held, their costs would soar—and the financial barrier to getting initiatives on the ballot would become even higher.

As it is, that cost is so great that, with rare exceptions, only the wealthy can apply. I asked most of the proprietors I interviewed to tell me what they would say if I walked into their office carrying a proposal I wanted to put on the ballot in California. Mike Arno gave me the fullest answer. "The first question I've got to ask you is, 'Can you raise the money?' And not just raise the money for our services but raise the money to have a lawyer draft it, to do a poll to make sure you've drafted it correctly, and then you still have to think about the campaign. It would be at least half a million to get a statute on the ballot here; for a Constitutional amendment [requiring more signatures] I'd say, $800,000 or maybe $900,000 to be safe."

Fred Kimball put the figure somewhat higher. "Just to get it on the ballot, I would say anywhere from one million to two million dollars. That's everything. Initiative attorneys. Polling. Focus groups. Taking a look at what issues are going to be most effective for it and against it. And then having it drafted. Putting it through the attorney general's office. And then the signature-gathering process. I'd say you're looking at a million to two million."

As both these men said, there is a lot of lawyering in the first stages of an initiative campaign—enough so that there are firms in California that have made a specialty, and a good living, out of drafting initiatives. I talked with two of the practitioners of this specialized trade, Thomas Hiltachk of Sacramento and Barry Fadem of San Francisco.

Fadem, a New Jersey native and Rutgers graduate, won a fellowship from the Coro Foundation, a leadership-training program based in San Francisco that has produced scores of skilled operatives for both parties. After working in Governor Jerry Brown's administration and attending law school at night, he made his mark by writing the California lottery initiative of 1984. With a Republican partner, Peter Bagatelos, the firm has developed a clientele that spans the political spectrum.

Hiltachk, a fourth-generation Sacramento native, and his partners, Charles H. Bell Jr. and Colleen C. McAndrews, are deep-dyed Republicans. The attraction of this kind of practice, both Fadem and Hiltachk said, is the combination of political strategy and legal practice. "I tell my friends that I'm probably 70 percent lawyer and 30 percent political consultant," Hiltachk said. "Often my clients will ask me if something they want to do is legal, and I'll say, 'Yes, but it's politically stupid.' I think that sort of political sophistication is what distinguishes us from other lawyers."

The first step in the initiative process is "drafting the legal language as if it were a statute or a bill in the legislature," Hiltachk said. But because this is a bill that will not be redrafted by committee staffs or amended by legislators and will be voted on by average citizens after a political campaign, it must be written with an eye to probable opposition tactics. "You've got two goals to accomplish," Fadem said. "Since every initiative seems to be tested in the courts, it better be legally sufficient to accomplish the purpose. But politically, I've worked on the no side of enough campaigns to learn an initiative is only as good as its weakest part. If your opponents can find anything that's wrong, it's going to have a good chance of losing."

In California, once the initiative is drafted, it goes to the attorney general's office for an official title and summary. (The procedure varies from state to state, but all have some supposedly neutral mechanism for accomplishing this process.) This step, which is invisible to the public, is critical to sponsors and opponents. "Everything's basically behind closed doors until you go public with it," Fadem told me. This stage of the process was described to me by Hiltachk:

> The attorney general is required to summarize the main points of the initiative in about five hundred words. It goes on the ballot and in the voters' pamphlet. And it can have some important impact in terms of the sex appeal when the measure is being circulated on the street. As an opponent, you may want

> to make sure that it isn't that sexy, and so I'll sometimes be hired by the opponents to sort of lobby the attorney general's office as to why they should or shouldn't describe it in a particular manner.
>
> The statutes require that it [the review] be done in an impartial manner. They're not supposed to comment on whether it will work or not, whether it's legal or not. So we basically write a letter summarizing our analysis of what the measure is, and if we're representing the opponents, they'll [the reviewers] send our letter to the proponents for comment. And you will argue over the language.
>
> For example, some environmentalist has submitted five initiatives which would effectively eliminate the timber industry in California. Timber law is very complicated, and the attorney general's office has about thirty days to try to come up to speed on areas of the law they really don't have a lot of expertise in. So while they consult with some of the [land management] agencies, we took the opportunity to say, "If you overlay this on top of existing laws, they're effectively eliminating the harvesting of timber on four million acres. Just because they're not using the word *clear-cutting,* that's what they're doing and that's what you ought to describe to the voters." It's basically a political discussion.

Indeed, politics is so pervasive that the lawyers want the professional campaign consultants in the room right from the beginning. "It's not a game for amateurs," Fadem said, explaining why he insists that the proponents hire a pollster and a campaign consultant at the same time they approach him. "Many times the way in which we would draft an initiative would be influenced by the polling and the campaign consultant's input. You want them all at the table, because those who do the best job in phase one of the campaign are ultimately going to have the best campaign. And sometimes, when we have done phase one, we have to tell the client, 'Don't do this. We've tested this. We've put it in the best fashion possible, and you can't win this. Or if you are determined to try, it will take such-and-such an amount of resources.'"

That phase is not the end of the lawyers' work. They supervise the financial reporting and the contracts in the campaign, counsel their clients on the arguments between supporters and opponents about the effects of the initiative, and, as Fadem said, prepare for the almost inevitable day when the initiative, if approved, is challenged in the courts.

Phase one typically costs the sponsor of a California initiative about $100,000. Fadem said a typical budget would include about $30,000 for legal fees, an equal amount for a statewide poll, perhaps $15,000 for focus groups—small roundtables of voters asked to react to possible pro and con arguments about the initiative—and perhaps $20,000 for the first work by the campaign consultant.

Then comes the much larger expenditure for collecting ballot signatures. I have described that work in some detail, but I should add that groups flush with money or short on time or blessed with really reliable mailing lists of supporters, sometimes collect signatures by direct mail. Jarvis and Gann did this on Prop. 13, relying on lists they had accumulated in two earlier, unsuccessful tax-limitation efforts. But direct mail is several times more expensive per name than hiring a signature-gathering firm. Unless the cause is so compelling that the same letter can produce both a petition signature and a contribution, most groups find it prohibitively expensive.

When the legalities have been completed and the petition gathering is finished, the campaign is just beginning. At that point, control shifts to another group of consultants—the pollsters, the media experts, and the campaign managers. They, too, have been around for a long time. It was 1930 when

Clem Whitaker and Leonie Baxter teamed up to form a company that was the preeminent California-initiative consulting firm for the better part of two decades. Now there are many more. I talked with principals in two of the most prominent firms specializing in initiative campaigns.

Ben Goddard is a partner with Richard (Rick) Claussen in the California-based Goddard-Claussen firm, one of the prime movers in this phase of the game. In the 1990s the company managed twenty-four initiative campaigns in California and other states and won all but two of them. They became nationally famous for the "Harry and Louise" ads they created, not in an initiative campaign, but in the successful effort by the health insurance industry to defeat the Clinton health care plan in 1994.

Like many of the other operatives, Ben Goddard is an old-time liberal who has found this populist invention profitable. Goddard grew up in Idaho, where his godfather, C. Ben Ross, was a three-term Democratic governor. He worked for Jimmy Carter in 1976 and then started a campaign consulting firm in Arizona with clients like Representative Morris K. Udall and Senator Dennis DeConcini. He had a tumultuous year in 1988, working first for Gary Hart, until he was driven out of the race by scandal, and then for Bruce Babbitt, whose hopes collapsed in Iowa and New Hampshire, and finally for Jesse Jackson.

That year soured Goddard on candidate politics. In 1985 he had managed a county referendum campaign in Arizona and had discovered, "I loved it. You have so much more control" than is ever possible when it's a human seeking election. He hooked up with Claussen, who also came out of Democratic politics, having served on the staff of Senator Frank Church of Idaho, another unsuccessful aspirant for the presidential nomination. Claussen moved his campaign consulting company from Boise to Los Angeles in the early 1980s and in 1991 took on Goddard as a partner. They have worked for various groups—almost always on the business side—on health care issues, timber policies, gambling, insurance, nuclear power, and tort reform, and boast a 95 percent success rate on more than thirty initiative campaigns.

Without my even asking, Goddard explained how a liberal Democrat rationalizes his new affiliations: "My view of ballot issues is that, contrary to what the inventors had in mind, these are now usually battles between special interests. These are not white-hat versus black-hat issues. So we're pretty catholic in our clients. We have turned down the tobacco companies and people interested in restricting abortion rights. And we have stayed away from the gun issue."

Once the contract has been signed, Goddard told me, "We will bring in outside consultants with appropriate expertise to do a thorough analysis of the proposition—to see what the economic effects will be, the legal effects, the policy effects." Often, he said, the proposition has been poorly drafted, with ambiguities or overreaching language.

The content analysis shapes the arguments that go into the voters' pamphlets, used by many states to inform the citizenry about issues on the ballot. These pamphlets, which are mailed to every registered voter, contain the texts of initiatives and neutrally worded descriptive material written by state officials. But in most states they also contain pro and con arguments written respectively by supporters and opponents. "Your pamphlet arguments are doubly important," Goddard said, "because when you make your ads, you can say, 'The voters' pamphlet says such-and-such.' You don't tell them that it's your argument in the voters' pamphlet."

Once the content analysis is finished, "you start your research process to determine which arguments will push people's buttons," Goddard said. This can be a lengthy, painstaking process, requiring panels with different political and demographic makeups, and a constant refining of the arguments they hear. "When this qualitative research is finished, you do your broad polling to be able to quantify the results: This argument is likely to shift opinion by this percentage."

The next step is to decide "who are credible messengers," Goddard said. Often the answers are surprising. "Doctors do not have credibility on health care issues," he said. "Nurses do.

"Expert opinion doesn't count for much. People know you can hire experts to say almost anything you want said. Politicians have no credibility," although in a 1996 fight, where Goddard-Claussen was working for the high-tech industry against an initiative that would have facilitated stockholders' suits against companies, "our friends in Silicon Valley were able to get statements from both [Bill] Clinton and [Bob] Dole opposing the initiative. We ran an ad saying, 'These guys don't agree on much, but they agree this would be bad.'"

Generally speaking, Goddard said, "people trust people who seem like themselves—that's why the Harry-and-Louise ads were so effective." In those ads, actors playing a typical middle-class young couple sat at the kitchen table, discussing the Clintons' plans to reorganize the national health care system. The intent was to convince people who already had health insurance that their options would be reduced—not increased—by the legislation. The line was: "If they choose, you lose." Both Harry and Louise expressed concern about the cost and availability of medical services. But then they said to each other, "There's got to be a better way" than this complex proposal from the Clintons.

"So we get ordinary people, or actors who seem like ordinary people," he said. A Goddard-Claussen star was Andie Chapman, an amply constructed black actress who played the part of the proprietor of a small restaurant in an ad used in the health industry campaign against a 1992 California health insurance initiative. The script called for her to express her indignation over a proposal that would raise costs so much that she could no longer afford to insure her employees. "She was so convincing in her anger" that Goddard-Claussen brought her back as Louise's business partner in one of the 1994 Harry-and-Louise ads, and then found another actress to play a similar part in an Arkansas workers' compensation campaign. "Women have more credibility; they're thought to be more honest," especially on social issues like health and schools, Goddard said.

But the message and the tactic have to fit the particular campaign. In addition to the Clinton-Dole ad, Goddard-Claussen helped kill Prop. 211 for the high-tech companies by staging scenes of hordes of well-dressed lawyers leaving private jets and jumping into limousines to file suits against California employers. When proponents of insurance reform in California could not agree among themselves and put competing initiatives on the ballot in 1996, the most effective ad ridiculed them as quarrelsome twins, "and we made them a laughingstock," Goddard said.

In killing a 1998 Oregon initiative for increased regulation of timber companies, they used animated bugs rejoicing that they would no longer face the threat of pesticides. And despite their own California base, Goddard-Claussen ran a campaign warning against importing policy from the big neighbor to the west when Arizonans attempted in 1990 to pass a clone of California Proposition 103—a rollback of insurance rates.

The effectiveness of these ad campaigns is demonstrable. Polls showed the Arizona initiative was supported by more than 60 percent of the voters at the start of the effort but lost 78 percent to 22 percent. The California health insurance initiative went from 70 percent favorable to 68 percent against.

The shift on Proposition 211—the target of the Clinton-Dole and limousine-lawyers ads—was just as great.

"We operate on the premise that most people will vote their self-interest," Goddard said, "so if you show them they can best defend themselves by voting a certain way, they will move to that position in very large numbers."

I talked with a second initiative-campaign manager, Les Francis, one of the four partners in the firm of Winner, Wagner and Mandabach Campaigns, whose main offices are in California. Francis now works in Washington, D.C., but his roots are in California Democratic politics. A native of San Jose, where he once ran unsuccessfully for a seat in the state assembly, he became an aide to Mayor Norman Mineta and moved to Washington as his administrative assistant when Mineta was elected to the House of Representatives in 1974. One day in 1975, a former Georgia governor named Jimmy Carter came by to talk about his ambitions with Mineta. The congressman was out, so Carter settled for his administrative assistant, and the next thing Francis knew, he was working for Carter in the Pennsylvania primary. He handled California in the general election of 1976, moved to the White House to work on congressional liaison, and eventually became deputy chief of staff. In the 1980 campaign, he split his time between the Carter headquarters and the Democratic National Committee. And then, as he told me, "After I lost the White House, I went into the consulting business."

On his own for a decade, he joined forces in 1992 with his present firm, whose lead partners, Chuck Winner and Ethan Wagner, were themselves alumni of liberal Democratic politics, having met in Jerry Brown's gubernatorial campaign in 1974.

Although Brown was strongly antinuclear, Winner and Wagner hired out to the big utility companies opposing Prop. 15, the 1976 ban on nuclear power plants. It was the same fight in which Ken Masterton learned initiative politics while working for Prop. 15's proponents. When the utilities won, Winner-Wagner was launched, and since then, Francis said, the firm has done about 120 initiative campaigns, winning about 90 percent of the time.

In recent years the company—and Francis personally—has made something of a specialty of working for gambling interests, or, as the casinos would prefer, gaming interests.

The principles of initiative campaigns outlined by Francis were very much in line with those I had heard from Ben Goddard: Intensive opinion research, the vital first step; definition of the issue—an abstraction with no inherent character of its own—in terms that appeal to voters' self-interest; focused and repetitive advertising; and careful selection of endorsers.

What is intriguing is the way Francis and his partners applied those principles to selling an idea as controversial as casino gambling. He told me that gaming issues are particularly difficult, because "there's a hard core, probably of about 40 to 45 percent in most states, which is against expanding gambling for religious or moral reasons or for more secular reasons. And the pro-gambling side does not feel nearly as intensely about their position as does the no side. Even people who gamble don't feel that intensely about it. So if it becomes a vote on gambling per se, it works to the advantage of the opponents."

Francis told me how he had successfully changed the subject in a pair of Missouri votes on riverboat gambling. The Missouri legislature had passed a bill legalizing riverboat casinos in 1992, with a proviso that it must be approved by the voters—which it was. But opponents challenged the new law and won a ruling that it applied only to games of skill, like poker, and not to games of chance, like slot machines and roulette, which attract more dollars. In a special election in the spring of 1994, the gamblers tried to amend the law to make it clear it covered games of chance—but lost by a narrow margin.

Francis's firm was hired to manage a second-try initiative that fall, and they steered it to victory. The voter research Peter Hart had done gave them three important clues, Francis said. First, voters were initially skeptical about the claim that riverboat gambling would produce money for schools. They had heard the same thing about the state lottery, but it hadn't happened. To deal with that, the proponents obtained an official fiscal impact statement guaranteeing that "no less than $30 million would go to public schools."

The second clue was that the narrower the issue appeared to be, the better their chances of winning. If voters thought they were casting a third vote on riverboat gambling, the proponents might lose. So they framed it as correcting a technicality in the law "you [voters] already approved."

And finally, they learned that their strongest argument was the appeal "to keep Missouri dollars in Missouri," rather than let wagerers cross the river into Illinois or drive north into Iowa, which already had riverboat gambling. "So we closed with that," Francis said. The clinching ad showed a hand writing a check for $30 million, while the narration stated: "When Missourians go to other states to play slot machines and roulette, it's as if the people in Missouri were writing a check to those states, and it amounts to $30 million dollars every year. So those other states are getting Missouri's money and the jobs and economic growth that go with it. We can change this by voting yes on Amendment 6 to allow slot machines and roulette on Missouri's riverboats. [At this point, the picture showed hands ripping up the $30 million check.] A yes vote on Amendment 6 will keep Missouri dollars in Missouri. Vote yes on Amendment 6."

The triple repetition of "Amendment 6" in the ad's closing seconds illustrated another principle Francis taught me. "Very few people read the actual measure," he said. "What you try to do is have them make up their minds before they go into the polling place. At most they might read the ballot title; a few might read the summary. What you want them to know is Prop. 6—that's the riverboat gambling issue; that's the one I want to vote yes on."

As it turned out, Missouri, in 1998, gave Francis another chance to test his theories. Many of the gambling ships never set sail. They were built for and anchored in artificial basins next to the Mississippi River, making them easily accessible to the customers from St. Louis and other communities. But the Missouri Supreme Court took a narrow view of the issue—arguing that the gamblers were trying to redefine the river borders of the state—and insisted that a constitutional amendment would be needed to legalize "boats in moats."

This time the focus groups told Francis that the way to win was to make the issue "fairness." "We had thought going in that the main argument would be the jobs and revenues that had accrued to the state since gambling began," Francis said. "But it turned out they [the state officials] had done sort of a lousy job in the interim explaining the results, so the people weren't buying that. What they told us in the focus groups, and what we then used, was that it was a matter of fairness. These companies came in; they played by the rules that the gaming commission had established and complied with local zoning, and now the supreme court was changing the rules in the middle of the game, and that wasn't fair—even for a gaming corporation."

Francis rejected any slick or clever or funny approaches to the advertising campaign, in favor of a straight-on explanation from a credible source—in this case, the retired state supreme court justice John Bardgalt. Posed against a wall of law books, he intoned, "As you know, the people of Missouri have already approved riverboat casinos in statewide elections in 1992 and 1994. Because of these yes votes, hundreds of millions of dollars have gone to Missouri public schools and local communities. And, as many of you know, some of Missouri's riverboat casinos are docked in moats, set just back from the main river channel. Before they were built, these boats in moats received all necessary legal approvals from the Missouri General Assembly, the Missouri Gaming Commission, and from your local communities. But a recent lawsuit threatens to shut down these riverboats. That will mean lost investments, lost jobs, lost public revenue, a big loss to Missouri. That's why the issue is back on the ballot. We can clarify this law by voting yes on Prop. 9."

While Francis was saving "boats in moats" in 1998, his California partners were involved in a much bigger gambling initiative—to protect and expand casino gambling on Indian reservations. This was the late-starting initiative that had driven up the price of signatures to $1.50 a name in the spring of 1998, when I was interviewing the heads of the petition-qualification companies.

Francis was not formally involved in the campaign, because his clients in the Missouri riverboat fight included many of the same Las Vegas gambling interests who were opposing the Indian gambling measure in California. But he explained the strategy that his company used to win. "The positive value we found worked there was Indian self-reliance," Francis said. "I think there's a deep-seated feeling among Americans that Indians have been screwed over the years. And if this offered them a chance for some economic self-sufficiency and self-respect, even people who might have reservations about gambling or people who weren't gamblers themselves said,

'Look, why not let these folks do this?' Secondly, by making it Indians versus Nevada casinos, it put an exclamation point on the humanitarian argument."

The ads for the California measure referred to it as "the Indian self-reliance initiative." And they packed an emotional wallop. In one, a strikingly handsome Native American woman said, "Growing up on a reservation was lots of heartache, lots of poverty. No running water. No doctor. Until I was about thirteen years old, that was our life. Now we are breaking the cycle of poverty, and I'm seeing it in my own family with my own children [who came into the picture at this point]. I see a lot more things in their future than I did have access to. They're smiling a lot more than I used to. And that makes me happy. Makes me proud."

The Indian gaming initiative won 63 percent to 37 percent—an unusually wide margin for a gambling measure. The opposition campaign financed by Las Vegas casinos was run by Ben Goddard. He echoed Francis's analysis, saying, "Intuitively, people felt it was time to give back the Indians something, because they had been screwed so many times.... And they did a good job of making it a California versus Nevada outsiders issue."

Despite that experience, Goddard said he still thinks the advantage lies with the no side most of the time. "If you're on the yes side, you first have to convince people there is a problem to solve, and second, that you have found the solution. On the no side, you only have to show what's wrong with the solution."

Rarely, if ever, he said, does support for an initiative grow during a campaign. "Occasionally, on a bond issue in a special election situation, you can motivate and mobilize the backers of the bonds to turn out when no one else is bothering to vote, and you can get a bigger margin than you expected," he said. "But generally, if you have a chance to win, your ballot measure has to start out with support at least in the mid-sixties. Generally, all they know at that point is that they like the goal you say you have in mind. Later, the opposition starts raising all the questions about the solution you've proposed, and support drops away."

The questions I raised with each of the people—lawyers, signature gatherers, campaign consultants—who are part of the initiative industry were these: Is this a good way to make policy? Does it really put the voters in charge or does it make them dupes in a process manipulated by wealthy interests?

"These big swings do not show gullibility," Goddard insisted. "I think it shows people's ability to break issues down and look at them more carefully. As a small-*d* democrat, I think the initiative process is a valid tool. I think it's good to have it available, even if it is sometimes abused. The abuse is mainly forcing people to look at a lot of TV ads, and if these initiatives end up being defeated, there's no great harm done."

Barry Fadem acknowledged there may be other problems. "We have too many initiatives," he said. "I mean, it's ridiculous. How can you expect the voters of California to read through all this stuff? Some of these initiatives run to thirty pages of text." But he hastened to say that in every state with the initiative process, polling shows the public is strongly in favor of retaining it—and using it. "The public wants to vote on these issues."

The reason, he said, is that "the legislature's not doing its job. Just take the lottery, for example. For twenty years prior to 1984, when asked about a lottery for California, with the money earmarked for education, 70 to 75 percent of the people said yes. Every year, a bill would be introduced, and every year, the bill would be killed by the racetracks and the other folks who felt it would be competing for their dollar. Should that be the way it works?"

Fadem gave me a profile of his firm from the *Recorder,* a Bay Area legal newspaper. The story noted that Fadem and Bagatelos had collected a $92,000 fee from the principal sponsor of the lottery initiative, Scientific Games, an Atlanta, Georgia, company that prints lottery tickets. The article, published in 1994, also noted that Scientific Games had spent $2.25 million in support of the lottery initiative but had earned $108 million in state printing contracts for lottery tickets in the first ten years of the lottery's life. A pretty good return on its investment.

The conversation with Tom Hiltachk took a similar course. He began by readily conceding that wealth was a barrier to the initiative process. "When somebody walks in [with an initiative proposal], I always ask the million-dollar question, which is, 'Where's your million dollars?' It's very difficult to qualify something for less than a million dollars. The most popular initiative I've ever been associated with from start to finish was 'three strikes'"—a proviso that anyone convicted of three felonies must serve a life sentence. "We could not print petitions fast enough. We had people coming out of the woodwork, circulating petitions like I've never seen before. Even that initiative cost about a million dollars to qualify. And it would not have made it but for significant contributions by a handful of people."

Hiltachk made a further point—that broad-based public policy issues such as "three-strikes" normally are "much, much more difficult" to get on the ballot, because it's not obvious who has a large enough stake in their passage to justify the big investment. By contrast, he said, "if the insurance industry wants to qualify something like Prop. 213, the tort reform initiative on our ballot in 1996, that's easy. You make five phone calls and you can raise a million dollars. If you're trying to do criminal justice reform, just because maybe it's good policy, there's not necessarily financial backing to support that. And the legislature understands that. They don't react if they think an initiative doesn't have the resources to qualify."

Hiltachk highlighted "one other negative of the initiative process: There is no compromise along the way. If you're the proponent, you write it the way you want to write it. And to hell with the opponents or any of their concerns. That creates an environment that doesn't die on election day. If you are the teachers' union and you've been screwed by an initiative that passed, are you just going to walk away and take it? No. You're going to continue to fight, and the next place to fight is the courtroom."

Court fights, which are almost automatic for the losing side, mean more work for the lawyers, of course. But an increasingly popular tactic, as we will see in chapter 3, is to fight each initiative with a counterinitiative, making all of the people in the initiative industry even richer. The 1988 California ballot contained four competing insurance-reform initiatives and set what was a spending record for the time.

But even after conceding all these points, Hiltachk defended the initiative process. "Legislative enactments also end up in court if they are matters of similar import," he said. As for special interests exploiting the process, "very few of those I would call moneyed special-interest initiatives have passed," Hiltachk said. The reason: There is usually a well-financed opposition group, and the negative side has an advantage for all the reasons Goddard outlined for me.

Rick Arnold had a similar viewpoint. "I don't want to discount the fact that special interests can use this process," he said. "If the insurance companies want to put an issue on the California ballot, they can. But if it's merely an economic interest supporting it, identifying the sponsor will have a big effect." This is a view endorsed by some of the academics who have studied the initiative process, and I will discuss the reasons for my skepticism at greater length in chapter 5. For now, let me just note a contrary example Hiltachk had given me. When he was opposing an ambitious 1990 environmental initiative known as "Big Green," he said his clients decided it was better to identify themselves to voters than let it appear they were trying to remain camouflaged. "Our ads said something like, 'Major funding provided by Arco, Chevron, and Dow Chemical.' You'd have thought that would have been the death knell of our campaign, but the voters weren't offended. We did some focus groups, and what we learned was that voters understood that Arco, Chevron, and Dow Chemical had every right to explain why they ought to vote no on such a measure." And, in fact, the negative campaign, with its sponsorship disclosed, succeeded.

I pressed the liberals in the signature-gathering business for their reaction to the success their ideological opponents have had in recent years—imposing term limits on legislatures across the country, passing measures in California and Washington state to end affirmative action, curtailing benefits to the children of illegal aliens in California, setting mandatory minimum prison sentences in many states.

Ken Masterton conceded that some of these measures seemed simplistic to him, others "despicable and idiotic." But he said he took consolation from the fact that some provisions had been found unconstitutional. And, like others, he cited "the axiom that big money can defeat an initiative, but big money cannot pass one. You'd be hard pressed to think of one initiative that passed just because big money was behind it."

Angelo Paparella said, "Invariably you are going to have initiatives pass that you don't like. I certainly fall into that category. But you can't point to those propositions without also mentioning things like minimum-wage increases, the medical marijuana initiative—other progressive measures. It's not all on one side of the political spectrum."

Fred Kimball, who grew up in the business, not surprisingly defended it in classic populist terms. After he denounced the "ridiculous" way that "interest groups just go to war with each other and tie up the legislature in knots," I asked, "Is it more democratic to have these same groups fighting it out through the initiative process?"

"Absolutely," he replied. "Because we end up voting on it. It's taking it out of the hands of the lobbyists and the people up in Sacramento and letting the people decide. Instead of fighting a politician who's paid a couple of million dollars a year, let's say, by the tobacco industry, you get to see the ads on television, and then it's up to you to make up your mind. I very much believe in the initiative process."

Of all those I interviewed, Les Francis seemed to be the most ambivalent about initiatives. Perhaps, I speculated, because of the years he had spent working as a staff man in Congress and in the White House, he was less cynical about elected officials than some of the others. "The initiative process is more easily manipulated," he said. He had given me examples of successful manipulation by his own firm. When they were helping pass a Martin Luther King Jr. holiday initiative in Arizona, they discovered from voter research that the civil rights leader was still "a polarizing figure" in that conservative state. "So instead of making it about Martin Luther King, we made the campaign about the things King stood for: individual freedom and rights and dignity and all these grander themes. We didn't ignore him, but we didn't want a vote on Martin Luther King."

An even more striking example was an ad from a Massachusetts campaign, where Francis had worked for the opposition. This one did use humor. It shows a grocer who looked like Mr. Whipple, the character in the ads who admonished people, "Don't squeeze the Charmin," busily restocking the shelves of his store. A strand of red tape hangs from the ceiling, and as he works, he slowly twists himself into more and more of the red tape, until he looks like a mummy. The voice-over says, "They're at it again. Another attempt to find an answer with more government bureaucracy, more red tape. Question 3, the repackaging bill, would create three new state bureaucracies, twenty pages of red tape that would tie up Massachusetts store owners with regulation after regulation, forcing higher consumer costs. Question 3—the more you know about it, the less you'll like it."

The ad campaign worked, and Measure 3 was defeated, Francis said. And then he sprang his surprise. "There's an interesting example of framing," he said. "It was a recycling measure. Now everybody in Massachusetts is for recycling, but it would have required all these grocery manufacturers to put stuff in different types of packages. So by calling it 'repackaging,' as opposed to 'recycling,' we got people to think it was crazy."

When I asked Francis to reflect on the process, he said, "I think all of us in the firm would agree that initiatives are not the ideal way of making public policy. The cauldron of the legislative process, theoretically at least, produces better results. But what we're seeing now, with more and more ballot measures at the state and local levels, is one more example of the public frustration with the political system. Just as it was in the beginning of the century, with the Progressive movement, the public is taking issues into its own hands. If you have the resources, either money or people, you can get just about anything on the ballot."

Francis sees two negative effects. "It tends to let legislatures off the hook, and it can lead to the introduction of really contentious, polarizing issues, like immigration and affirmative action, that while they would certainly strike controversy, would be a little more containable if they were in the legislature."

But he concluded, "I guess I'm still a California Progressive at heart, and I have the belief that there are those occasions when, if the normal processes don't work and the public needs to have a way to express its will, the initiative is there. I still think it's good in principle. I think we just have to be careful about the abuses."

The practitioners made what I thought was a substantial case, even if one discounted for their self-interest in keeping a good thing going. But they expressed reservations—reservations that were strengthened for me by what I learned in a close examination of the biggest battle on the June 1998 California ballot—the fight over "paycheck protection."

Chapter 3

INITIATIVE WAR IN CLOSE-UP

"What you have," the former California assemblyman, now a Sacramento business lobbyist, told me, "is a lotta little lies fighting one big lie."

That was his thoroughly cynical description of the initiative battle on the June 1998 California primary ballot that exemplifies how the Progressives' great reform measure has been converted by competing interest groups into another arena of political warfare.

Proposition 226, the Paycheck Protection Act, would have required California unions to obtain annual written permission from each of their members for the use of dues for any political purpose. It also would have banned foreign contributions to political campaigns and applied the same restrictions to corporations and employees it imposed on unions and their members.

But the foreign-contributions provision was redundant; existing law already forbade them. And the application to business was window dressing; corporate PACs (political action committees) rely on voluntary contributions, even though there may be informal pressure on ambitious executives to help the company elect its friends to office.

For those who financed it, the real purpose of Prop. 226 was not, as the title claimed, to protect union members from being coerced into supporting causes and candidates they personally opposed or to protect their paychecks from the levies of the union bosses. It was to reduce the political clout of California unions—especially the California Teachers' Association (CTA)—which were a financial mainstay of Democratic candidates and a powerful barrier to conservative successes in the legislature and in initiative campaigns. Prop. 226 was important in itself, but it also was the linchpin of a national strategy to enact similar measures in the other forty-nine states and, ultimately, at the national level.

The unions recognized the stakes and mobilized nationally to defend the payroll checkoff they used to finance their lobbying and political work. For them, it was a life-or-death struggle in which money was no object and veracity no barrier.

Thus, the lobbyist's description: The one big lie—that this was a measure designed to protect individual union members' rights—was being countered by a welter of little lies about the causes and even the lives that might be sacrificed if Prop. 226 passed.

The motivations and the tactics had been a lot less complicated when the effort began with a handful of Orange County activists who were upset by the role teachers' unions were playing in local school board elections and disputes on education policy. Mark Bucher and his allies Frank Ury and Jim Righeimer were members of the Orange County Education

Alliance, a Christian conservative group with a deep-pockets patron in businessman Howard F. Ahmanson Jr. The Alliance championed school vouchers and supported changes in curriculum, including the teaching of creationism and sexual abstinence. They battled over school trustees' jobs, one of which Ury lost to a candidate backed by the CTA. Righeimer told California papers the teachers' union had spent $70,000 to defeat Ury, and asked, "How can you compete with people who can just pull money out of people's paychecks?"

Late in the campaign, after the battle had escalated far beyond Bucher's control, I went down to see him at the barebones space he had rented for his grassroots effort in a Tustin office park. He introduced me to two of the teachers who had joined him in helping launch the campaign. One of them, Roger Hughes, had taught history for thirty years at a high school in Fountain Valley and once headed the local chapter of the CTA. The other, Kim Jacobsma, had been on the faculty of a high school in Bellflower for eleven years and also had been active in the CTA.

Both of them had fallen out with the union leadership. For Hughes, the issue was bilingual education—a policy he was convinced was shortchanging students from immigrant families and denying them the opportunity to move into the mainstream of American life and its economic rewards. The union supported bilingual programs, he told me, mainly out of misguided political correctness and a need to protect the jobs of the teachers who had been hired for the separate bilingual classrooms.

Jacobsma said he objected to the CTA's endorsing and financing candidates in local school board races. "It was a power game for them [the union leaders]," he told me, "and I thought an improper use of our dues." His squawks were ignored and he was ostracized.

Unable to change the policies of their locals, both men did the only thing they could under existing law. They resigned their union memberships, while continuing to pay an "agency fee" for the representation the union provided in negotiating the terms of their employment contracts. But by quitting the union, they said, they had lost a great deal. Jacobsma gave me a copy of a letter he had received in 1996 from the president of the Bellflower Education Association, who addressed him mistakenly, "Dear Ms. Jacobsma." After acknowledging his request and promising it would be processed immediately, it said: "Please understand that as an agency-fee payer, you are not a member of the association. You will no longer be covered by the $1,000,000 liability insurance provided at no cost by CTA.... Should you be sued for child abuse, negligence, etc., you will not be covered under this policy as a fee payer. You will not have the right to vote in BEA/CTA/NEA elections. This means you will not be able to vote for officers, contract ratification, etc. You will no longer be eligible for any member services or discounts.... Also, should you become involved in a dispute between yourself and the district and request grievance or arbitration provisions of the BEA agreement be used on your behalf, you shall be responsible for paying...."

Both men insisted that, despite the claims of union leaders, internal democracy was nonexistent. "Not once in my thirty years did they poll the members to see what they should do politically, or even whether our dues should be used for politics," Hughes said. "I got fed up." Jacobsma said, "I've never been asked for my opinion" on any of the endorsements.

When I met them, both men said they were engaged in running battles over Prop. 226 at their schools. The CTA, which has contractual rights to communicate with its members at school sites, was showing in the teachers' lounge what Hughes called "propaganda films" against the initiative and putting anti-226 flyers in their school mailboxes.

But, Hughes said, when he tried to put pro-226 material in the same mailboxes, the union challenged him and the principal told him to stop. He was about to carry the issue to higher levels of the administration and ultimately to the school board—with little hope of success. Hughes said, "It just confirmed what I saw back in 1988 when I was the chapter president and went to a statewide (CTA) conference at Asilomar. The people running the union don't have any intention of getting out of politics. They want to exert their influence and they don't give a damn about us."

When later I asked about the dissident teachers' claims, John Hein, the political director of the CTA, offered a point-by-point rebuttal. Endorsements are made by vote of representatives chosen by and from the union membership. The funding of its political efforts comes from assessments approved by the members. Hein told me his organization collected $61 a year for its PAC and an additional $19 in a special assessment for fighting initiative battles that began when CTA defeated a vouchers initiative in 1993. Fewer than 1 percent of its 220,000 members had opted out of the assessment, he said, and statewide, only 2,828 teachers had followed the course of the Orange County pair and left the union, paying only an agency fee for representation services.

It was clear to me that however typical or atypical the teachers I interviewed were, or however one judged the merits of their complaints, they were voicing authentic reactions to their personal experiences as union members. Both of them insisted, "I am not antiunion." Jacobsma went on at some length about how much he thought teachers needed a union and how he had benefited from its advocacy on contract issues. "We just want to get them out of this political game," he said.

The volunteer efforts by Bucher and these dissident teachers were foundering when three very different big guys moved in and took over this modest storefront operation.

The first was J. Patrick Rooney, a multimillionaire Indianapolis insurance man and financier of conservative causes. Rooney was the head of Golden Rule Insurance Company and a man who, in his later years, devoted an increasing amount of time and resources to conservative causes, including school vouchers, medical savings accounts, and paycheck protection.

Despite his wealth Rooney likes to portray himself as a champion of populist causes. In almost every speech or news conference, he refers to his battle against Illinois insurance regulators he says were rigging the rules to deny insurance licenses to African Americans trying to get onto the next rung of the ladder to success.

It was his work in the minority community, Rooney told me, that alerted him to the "economic injustice" union members—especially those with low wages—face when dues are withheld from their paychecks to support movements that have little importance to them or that they may actually oppose. Now, it is also the case that Rooney was well aware the CTA had led and largely financed the effort in 1993 that defeated a school-choice initiative that was of great importance to him and other supporters of vouchers. And he also knew that unions were an important part of the liberal coalition supporting national health insurance legislation that would put Golden Rule and other private insurers out of business. That union-backed coalition also opposed medical savings accounts, which Rooney and Golden Rule promote and sell. Unlike standard health insurance policies, subsidized by employers, this scheme allows people to choose a policy that covers only catastrophic illness, rather than a full range of medical services, and to put the rest of what would otherwise be their premium payments into a savings account. They can pay ordinary medical expenses from that account, or if they can economize, convert it later to other uses.

Advocates like Rooney claim that medical savings accounts will encourage people to be more prudent in their medical spending. Critics say it will allow the healthier members of a group to opt out, benefiting themselves but raising premiums for those who remain. Golden Rule has made a specialty of selling catastrophic health insurance policies, so Rooney's advocacy on this issue was not entirely disinterested.

Rooney told me that he "happened to hear about" Bucher's fledgling effort while discussing a somewhat similar measure that had been enacted in 1992 in Washington state, as part of a larger campaign-finance-reform initiative. The Washington law had had significant effects on union political treasuries in that state—at least for a time. Trevor Neilsen, a spokesman for the Washington Education Association, the teachers' union, told me "it has had a dramatic negative impact on us." But the union soon found other ways to finance its work through a community-outreach fund.

Rooney got in touch with Bucher and quickly decided the Orange County group would never have the financial resources to qualify a paycheck-protection initiative for the ballot. He pledged $49,000 of his own, asked friends for more, and scheduled an appointment with Governor Pete Wilson to enlist Wilson's help.

Wilson had his own good reasons for taking on the unions. For most of his thirty-two years in elective office—as mayor of San Diego, California assemblyman, U.S. senator, and governor—he had been running against candidates supported by labor and had opposed the unions on issue after issue. Wilson liked to remind people he had once been a union member—the Laborers and Hod Carriers International—but that was a long time in the past. As mayor he had fought with unions of bus drivers and firefighters. As a losing candidate for the gubernatorial nomination in 1978, he backed an unsuccessful initiative barring strikes by public employees. Particularly during his years as governor, starting in 1991, he had been frustrated by the influence the unions—and especially the teachers—exerted in the Democratic-controlled legislature. CTA ads blaming him for a lengthy budget impasse in 1992 rankled the governor. And he fought the same union on legislation for charter schools, merit pay, and teacher standards.

During the budget crunch early in his tenure, Wilson froze pay for state employees and borrowed from their pension fund in order to limit the size of the tax increase that he was forced to seek—earning the enmity of their unions in the process. In an effort to make California more competitive in holding and attracting businesses, he reformed the workers' compensation laws, to the displeasure of industrial and building trades unions. But the biggest battles came over his efforts at school reform. "The CTA fought me every step of the way," Wilson complained to me, "even when I proposed reductions in class size that clearly were of benefit to its members. They had their own agenda, and they wouldn't let a mere governor interfere."

But Wilson was no "mere governor." He brought to his job as head of the nation's second-largest government the stubborn determination he had displayed during his service in the Marines. Deceptively bland in manner, with watery blue eyes and a voice thinned by maladroit throat surgery in 1995, Wilson was stubborn to a fault. When he set his jaw, as he did often, he could not be moved.

Entering his final year of term-limited office in 1998, he was determined to have one more go at education reform—either by legislation or, more likely, by initiative. Prop. 226 offered the prospect of crippling the CTA's ability to thwart him on the schools initiative he planned to place on the November 1998 ballot if the legislature, as expected, blocked his plans. That initiative would guarantee funding for smaller classrooms, toughen the policy against drugs in schools, and make it easier to close failing schools and fire inept teachers.

Prop. 226 was written to take effect immediately if passed. That meant the CTA and other unions would face the immense task of distributing and collecting authorization cards from all their members during the summer vacation months, before they could resume dues checkoffs that paid for the autumn political work. Thus, Prop. 226 constituted a powerful one-two punch against the unions: First force them to expend large sums and exhaust their treasuries in trying to defeat Prop. 226 on the June ballot; then delay and very possibly cripple their efforts to recoup in time to hurt Wilson, Republican candidates, and initiatives on the November ballot.

There was one other thing that appealed to Wilson. Striking a blow at union power could help him fulfill his ambition to win the Republican presidential nomination. That goal—a natural one for anyone in the corner office of the state capitol in Sacramento previously occupied by Ronald Reagan and Earl Warren—had been in Wilson's mind for a long time. In 1994, when seeking reelection as governor, his ambition for still-higher office was plain enough so that press questioning forced Wilson to make a public pledge to serve a full four years. Keeping that pledge became even more of a political imperative for Republicans who had helped Wilson, and the businessmen who had financed his reelection drive, because a pro-labor Democrat, Gray Davis, elected lieutenant governor in 1994, would succeed Wilson if the governor went to the White House. (In California, unlike most other states, the governor and lieutenant governor are not bracketed on the ballot, as the president and vice president are.) The prospect of giving

Democrats, who already controlled the legislature, full control of Sacramento by letting Davis succeed Wilson was anathema to the people who had put Wilson in office.

Nonetheless, Wilson stubbornly pursued his White House dream. In 1995 he joined the field of GOP aspirants and began cross-country excursions to Iowa and New Hampshire, where the reaction was tepid at best. Then came the throat surgery, designed to relieve a chronic hoarseness but instead leaving Wilson literally without a voice for critical autumn months when he should have been raising money and stumping the early caucus and primary states. Dispirited and discouraged, he pulled out of the race on September 29, 1995.

But even during this brief and futile effort, Wilson got a good taste of the ideological problems that would face him in seeking the nomination. The biggest of these was his position on abortion; like most California politicians of both parties (and like the majority of the state's electorate) Wilson favored abortion rights. That position helped him win election at home, but it hurt him with the religious conservatives who had written an antiabortion plank into every recent Republican platform and insisted that presidential and vice presidential nominees share that position.

There was little Wilson could do to ease that source of opposition. But there were other issues on which he could appeal to social conservatives. He had always had a strong anticrime record; three-strikes laws for mandatory life-imprisonment on the third felony conviction were an innovation of the Wilson years.

In 1994, trailing Kathleen Brown, the daughter and the sister respectively of former Democratic governors Pat Brown and Jerry Brown, in the early polls, Wilson threw the full weight of his office behind Proposition 187—a measure ending education, health, and other benefits for illegal aliens and their children. The measure passed and was immediately tied up in the courts. But it helped Wilson win a second term, and it gave him a national issue that appealed to nativist elements in the GOP, who resented the changing population mix of the country—and to a broader swath of voters alarmed by the costs of illegal immigration.

In 1996 Wilson joined Ward Connerly, an African American businessman he had appointed as a regent of the University of California, in pushing through the regents' board a policy change ending race-based affirmative action programs for admission of students and hiring of faculty. Against the opposition of university administrators, faculty bodies, and students, Wilson and Connerly asserted it was time for a color-blind policy. Connerly argued that he was simply helping fulfill Dr. Martin Luther King Jr.'s dream of an America where his children "will live in a nation where they will not be judged by the color of their skin, but by the content of their character." But his critics, who included King's widow, Coretta Scott King, and other leaders of the civil rights movement, said Connerly was trying to remove the ladder of opportunity while millions of women and minorities were still struggling for equality.

Wilson and Connerly prevailed in the university, and then in 1996 joined forces in supporting Prop. 209, which expanded the same policy to all of state government, effectively ending its affirmative action programs. After a bitter fight Proposition 209 carried by 54 percent to 46 percent.

Here were two deeply emotional issues—illegal immigration and racial preferences—on which Wilson had become the national champion of conservative causes, helping erase the moderate Republican label he had worn most of his California political life but found a curse in GOP presidential politics.

And now Pat Rooney was offering him yet a third link to the activist right, urging him to become honorary chairman of the paycheck-protection drive. It was an irresistible proposition: Payback to his political enemies and a boost to his year-2000 presidential ambitions, all in one package.

At the Republican state convention in Anaheim in October 1997, Wilson announced he was taking the leadership of the paycheck-protection-initiative drive, drawing a standing ovation with the declaration that "union members shouldn't be forced to have their pockets picked for candidates or causes they don't support."

The third player was a man virtually unknown to the general public, Grover Norquist, the head of an organization called Americans for Tax Reform. Norquist's power derived from his ability to make the conference room at ATR's headquarters, a Massachusetts Avenue town house not far from the White House, the communications center and campaign command post for the network of conservative organizations that sprang up in Washington during the Reagan-Bush years. Every Wednesday representatives of groups ranging from the National Rifle Association to the Christian Coalition, from the Libertarian Cato Institute to U.S. Term Limits, and from home-schoolers to property-rights advocates, would meet in Norquist's conference room to pool their intelligence on current battles in Congress and to plot future campaigns to advance their causes in the country.

Norquist, a bookish-looking fellow with round glasses on a round face and a neatly trimmed beard, had latched on to taxes as his chosen theme soon after graduating from Harvard in 1978. With his economics degree in hand, he became executive director of the National Taxpayers Union in time to assist in its support of Jarvis-Gann Prop. 13 and its clones in other states. Returning to Cambridge, he earned a master's degree from the Harvard business school. In the first year of the Reagan administration, he took over as director of the College

Republicans. (His first hire was Ralph Reed, later to be executive director of the Christian Coalition.) After a two-year stint as a speechwriter and economist for the Chamber of Commerce of the United States, he was asked by the White House, in 1985, to start Americans for Tax Reform to lobby for the big tax-simplification bill Reagan pushed through Congress, with bipartisan help from Dan Rostenkowski and Bill Bradley, the following year. His group distributed pledges to candidates at all levels, from the presidency down to city councils, committing them never to vote for or sign a bill raising taxes. ATR lobbied in favor of tax cuts and tax simplification. But as its financial backing and mailing lists grew and its staff expanded, it also jumped onto other hot issues, ready to mount an ad hoc campaign for almost anything that tingled the nerve endings and loosened the wallets of conservative activists around the country. Norquist became an unofficial adviser to Speaker Newt Gingrich, and in 1996 the Republican National Committee showed its confidence in his operating skills by sending him $4.6 million from its treasury for use in the presidential campaign.

What Elizabeth Drew wrote about Norquist in her 1996 book, *Whatever It Takes,* remains an accurate portrayal. "Norquist's mind is in a constant whir, making new connections between subjects, events, and people. There remains something of the graduate student in him—he comes across as the brilliant young man, not quite a grown-up, a boy-genius who lives within his own universe, spewing creativity."

For such a man, paycheck protection was a cause that offered many attractions—especially if Wilson and Rooney could give the struggling Bucher effort the mass and muscle needed for a successful initiative campaign in California. Knowing that time was growing short to obtain the needed signatures, Norquist put up $441,000 to pay for a mailing to

1.2 million Republicans, signed by Wilson and soliciting petition signatures. The mailing supplemented the traditional signature-gathering operation for which Wilson had employed American Petition Consultants, the firm run by Mike Arno and his brothers. The twin drives produced more than enough signatures. The battle was joined.

Long before Wilson and Rooney and Norquist became involved, labor smelled trouble. In the winter of 1997, shortly after the start of the legislative session, a Democratic staff aide found a copy of a private poll intended for Republican eyes that inadvertently had been left on a copying machine in the capitol. The poll surveyed a variety of conservative issues that might move onto the public agenda, and reported particularly strong support for a measure "to make sure all union political contributions are voluntary." The poll went to the Democratic leaders, who quickly shared it with their friends at the CTA.

Since no such measure had a chance in the Democratic legislature, as everyone knew, the threat lay in an initiative. By the spring of 1997, when the California Labor Federation and its affiliate unions met in San Diego to begin planning for the 1998 election, paycheck protection was very much on their minds.

But this was more than a California battle, and the mobilization had to reach beyond the borders of the state. Norquist had activated his network, and the results were beginning to show. On Capitol Hill, Speaker Newt Gingrich and Senate Majority Leader Trent Lott championed legislation that had been languishing under the sponsorship of junior Republicans. Both Gingrich and Lott announced that if the Democrats (and their handful of Republican allies) persisted in pushing broad campaign-finance-reform legislation, the GOP leaders would make paycheck protection part of the bill. Lott called it "the price of admission" to any comprehensive campaign reform, and twice forced the Senate into procedural votes on paycheck protection. Each time, the Democratic minority filibustered Lott's paycheck-protection provision, and each time, Lott failed to get the sixty votes needed to end the filibuster. On the second vote, he fell short of a simple majority. Stymied on Capitol Hill, Norquist started telling reporters that his allies in state legislatures would see to it that paycheck protection was introduced in forty-five states. "Where we have both Republican governors and legislatures," he said, "we expect it to be enacted this year or in the 1999 session. Where we have access to an initiative process, we will do it that way. It commands public support from 70 percent or more of the voters in every poll we've seen. We hope to win in California in June and be on the ballot in Nevada, Colorado, Arizona, Oregon, and perhaps Florida and South Dakota in November—and in many more states in 2000."

In the spring of 1998, at the Southern Republican Leadership Conference in Biloxi, Mississippi, Norquist told a group of conservatives paycheck protection had become "a national campaign." He said, "We will have the resources to assure it passes in California. We can raise $10 million dollars, and unless they raise three or four times as much, it will pass." (In an earlier interview, he had told me he would raise $10 million and allocate about one third of it to California.) Labor, he warned, "will fight it tooth and nail. We are arguing principle, but the other side is arguing survival." But, he said, "it will pass in all the initiative states, because their base is three to one against them. It's hard for them to argue you should not be able to decide how your political money should be spent. They have to make the Leninist argument: *Sit down and shut up. We know what's best for you.* And that has never worked in this country."

Thoroughly alarmed by such talk, the AFL-CIO held a press briefing in Washington on February 13, 1998. Associate counsel Larry Gold told reporters that labor was facing the gravest threat to its existence in a generation—"perhaps the most concerted legal attack on our right to exist since the New Deal." When Gold finished with the legal arguments, Steve Rosenthal, the labor federation's political director, said the unions were committed to throwing all their resources into the California battle and claimed—despite the polls—they actually had hopes of nipping the movement in the bud. (The stories from the Washington briefing did not sit well with California labor leaders, who complained to Rosenthal that the backers of Prop. 226 were making good use of the argument that "Washington labor bosses" would try to thwart the will of California voters.)

The first step in labor's campaign to defeat Prop. 226 was to strike at the heart of the opposition. Using a mixture of threat and blandishment, the unions set out to neutralize major California business. If business goes to war, they said, it better prepare to defend itself. The unions will not simply oppose 226; they will engage business and force it to defend its own prerogatives. The teachers' union hired Fred Kimball to collect signatures on a retaliatory initiative that would bar companies from using their funds for lobbying in Sacramento or engaging in initiative campaigns without stockholders' permission. They also passed word that they were considering a far more drastic threat: an initiative that would eliminate every provision in the California tax code that benefited corporations, unless that provision was specifically approved by a two-thirds majority in a subsequent initiative. To make the measure even more irresistible to taxpayers, the proposition would mandate that the billions of additional taxes corporations would pay would be redistributed, in amounts up to $1,000 a year, to individual taxpayers in California.

John Jacobs, the influential columnist of the *Sacramento Bee,* wrote in the summer of 1997 that the warring initiatives threatened "nuclear winter" in California—a struggle in which both labor and business would empty their treasuries in order to avoid crippling political setbacks. An article in the *California Journal* on the looming battle was headlined MUTUALLY ASSURED DESTRUCTION and also employed the analogy to nuclear war.

At the same time, John Hein, the top political operative of the CTA and member of the steering committee opposing 226, made an offer to his counterparts at the California Chamber of Commerce, the California Manufacturers Association, the California Realtors Association, and other business groups: *We will not file our initiative if you urge your members to stay out of the 226 fight and withhold their financial support from the Bucher-Wilson initiative.*

The offer of mutual disarmament faced all the obstacles similar negotiations do in international diplomacy. There was a long history of mutual antagonism and distrust between the parties. Business had fought the unions on the workers' compensation reforms Wilson had promoted and on minimum-wage legislation. The teachers' constant push for higher education-spending ran straight into the tax-cutting agendas of almost all the business groups.

But both sides had grown weary of the constant fighting and had begun reaching out to find common ground. The arena for these discussions was a little-known group called the California Governance Consensus Project, organized by

James W. Connor under the auspices of California State University, Sacramento. Their goal was to find ways to address "the anomalies of our tax and spending system," resulting from the initiatives that had put strict limits on state revenues, mandated some spending priorities, and then left it to the legislature to divvy up the rest of the money. For years the thirty-four groups around the table had spent their energies fighting one another—on behalf of their individual constituencies. Out of weariness and frustration, these organizations had begun meeting to see if they could agree on proposals that would meet the state's long-term revenue needs, improve the budget process, and clarify state and local government responsibilities in the interests of greater accountability.

Beyond the formal agenda, the meetings had begun to develop good personal chemistry, especially between Hein and the representatives of the business groups. When he approached them on Prop. 226, they had reason to believe he was serious.

They also had their own reasons to question the wisdom of 226. Many of the small businesses in the Chamber were nonunionized and had little interest in protecting the rights of dissident union members. The big companies with unionized workforces held an opposite perspective. They had a strong interest in labor peace and did not want to stir up trouble in their plants when they had matters of much larger moment—wages and work rules—to negotiate with their union leaders. As a lawyer-lobbyist in Sacramento with many business clients said to me, "We were asked to work on it [Prop. 226] and said no. This is a war nobody needed. We've basically had labor peace in this state, and once you start a war like this, it never ends. We tried to tell them [the proponents] this would galvanize labor, but they wouldn't listen."

With such advice reaching the business community, Hein's

neutrality talks went well. The only sticking point for much of business was the wish not to antagonize Wilson, who was pressuring his friends and allies to help him on the fight. But many of the key business people told the governor's friends they would continue to support his other political efforts (implicitly including his year-2000 presidential ambitions) but needed to take a pass on this one. The boards of the major business associations either agreed to stay neutral on 226 or postponed any action endorsing it, which had the same effect. The year-end financial report from Bucher and his committee showed few business contributions. By March, when the deadline for filing initiative signatures came, the CTA announced that, although it had gathered enough names to qualify, it would not file the initiative to curb business political activities.

The unions had just won the opening round of the battle. The initiative process—in the form of the threat of a counter-proposition—had been turned on the very people who had sought to use it for their own ends.

Labor realized that to defeat Prop. 226, it needed to mobilize all its resources and focus them into a single strategy. The question was who would run it. A coordinating committee was created, with the top political officials of each of the major unions aboard and Will Robinson, a veteran Washington consultant, representing the national AFL-CIO. After canvassing their own ranks, they decided in 1997 it would be better to hire an outside political operative—someone who had no long-term ties to any single union. They did not go very far from home, however. Gale Kaufman was a former aide to ex-assembly Speaker Willie Brown, the Sacramento power broker who was the main target of the term-limits initiative passed by

California voters. During those years, Kaufman coordinated finances and helped set strategy for many of the assembly elections in which Brown's Democratic allies ran. In that role, she worked closely with the union political directors, who almost always supported the same Democratic candidates. Having opened her own political consulting firm in 1987, Kaufman, a single mother with a young son, remained in Sacramento after Brown was forced out of his assembly post and won election as mayor of San Francisco. A short dark-haired woman brimming with energy, she was untested in a statewide race of any kind, but had the savvy and toughness the job would take.

The next key question was who would create the ads that would eat up most of the money and, the unions hoped, produce most of the votes. The top Democratic consultants in California wanted the lucrative business and so did many of the well-known Washington firms with long-term ties to the teachers or the AFL-CIO unions. But Kaufman, who interviewed the applicants, came away impressed by the pitch of one relatively unknown Washington operative, a woman named Dawn Laguens. A native of New Orleans, she first came to notice as the campaign director of the Coalition Against Racism and Nazism, an ad hoc group formed to fight David Duke's bids for governor in 1989 and senator in 1990. An ad Laguens made for that group won the top award from her peers in the political-consulting business and that was enough to launch her into her own consulting partnership in Washington, D.C.

After briefing Laguens on the background of each of the members of her Prop. 226 steering committee, Kaufman took her to meet the men who would pay the bills and, therefore, would decide who got the contract. "Dawn just blew them away," Kaufman told me. "I didn't want to make a pitch for her, and I didn't have to. All I said to them, when it was clear they were going to hire her, was, 'You realize, you have put two women in charge of this campaign.' And all those men looked at me and said, 'Well, what's wrong with that?'" And she laughed uproariously, thinking of the chauvinism that affects politics in California, as it does everywhere else.

Before the political consultants took over, the opposing lawyers engaged in the now-traditional fight over the ballot language that describes each initiative. When it was over, the proponents had gained essentially what they wanted. The description on the ballot and in the voters' guide said the initiative dealt with "political contributions by employees, union members, [and] foreign entities." And it emphasized that a vote for Prop. 226 would guarantee each individual control over the use of his or her money in political campaigns.

The voters' guide also gave each side a free page to make its argument—and rebut the other's claims—in a statement signed by any three people it chose to enlist. The proponents' message was signed by Wilson and two union members—one a teacher, the other an electrician. The parts that appeared in all-capital letters summarized their best arguments:

> BOSSES SHOULD NOT SPEND WORKERS MONEY WITHOUT CONSENT. IT IS MORALLY WRONG—DEAD WRONG—TO TAKE YOUR MONEY FROM YOUR PAYCHECK, WITHOUT YOUR CONSENT, AND SPEND IT TO SUPPORT A POLITICAL CANDIDATE OR ISSUE THAT YOU OPPOSE....IT'S LIKE LETTING UNION BOSSES GO INTO THE VOTING BOOTH TO MARK THE MEMBERS' BALLOT....FOR EXAMPLE, UNION MEMBERS SUPORTED AND VOTERS OVERWHELMINGLY APPOVED THE 'THREE STRIKES AND YOU'RE OUT' INITIATIVE FOR HABITUAL CRIMINALS. YET UNION LEADERS SPENT MEMBERS' MONEY TO OPPOSE THREE STRIKES....RANK-AND-FILE UNION MEMBERS DESERVE THE

SAME POLITICAL FREEDOM OF CHOICE AS EVERY OTHER CALIFORNIAN. GIVE THEM A FAIR SHAKE INSTEAD OF A SHAKEDOWN.

The opponents' ad was signed by the presidents of the CTA and the California Professional Firefighters and by Howard Owens, executive director of the Consumer Federation of California, a group which Kaufman said "polls very high in credibility with the public." The headlined arguments: PROPOSITION 226 IS NOT WHAT IT APPEARS TO BE. 226 WILL NOT REDUCE FOREIGN CONTRIBUTIONS. PROPOSITION 226 WAS PUT ON THE BALLOT BY OUT-OF-STATE INTERESTS. PROPOSITION 226 WILL COST TAXPAYERS MONEY.

While labor was getting organized, the proponents of 226 were already on the air. One advantage of having Norquist involved was that he could easily enlist help from other conservative groups that sent representatives to his meetings—and thus coordinate what appeared to be independent efforts on behalf of the initiative.

Knowing that the decision of California business to stay neutral would likely give labor a decisive financial advantage in the coming TV ad war, Norquist suggested that an "education" campaign, related to workers' rights, would help sustain support for 226, even if the ads never mentioned the proposition.

On April 1, California TV viewers began seeing ads sponsored by Citizens for a Sound Economy, a national organization that uses corporate and private contributions as a 501 (c) 4 tax-exempt education group to advance conservative causes. CSE had been a major force in the defeat of the Clinton health care reform in 1993 and 1994 and, capitalizing on that success, had raised funds and run ads in targeted congressional districts on tax cuts, balanced-budget plans, environmental deregulation, and a number of other key items on the agenda of the Republican Congress.

Its 30-second California ads said, "An important message for working men and women in California. Employers and labor unions may be taking money out of your paycheck and spending it on political causes without your permission. The United States Supreme Court has ruled this practice to be unlawful, and you may be entitled to a refund. It is wrong to take money out of someone's paycheck and to spend it on political causes without prior consent. Preserve your rights. Protect your paycheck."

The link to Prop. 226 was subtle almost to the point of obscurity. Some of the labor people thought the ads might actually be helping their cause by stressing that because of a Supreme Court decision, workers already had the right to demand a rebate on the portion of their dues allocated to politics. But the CSE people said they were satisfied the ads were helping raise public consciousness on an issue that, frankly, had been nowhere on the political agenda until Rooney and Wilson and Norquist decided, for their different reasons, to make it an issue.

The CSE ads ran for four weeks at a cost estimated at $1 million and immediately were followed by the first of a series of "informational" ads financed by the National Taxpayers Union, another of Norquist's allies. These were much more explicit but still stopped short of the direct advocacy that would have required disclosure under California campaign-finance laws.

The Taxpayers Union commercial showed what appeared to be a section of the ballot, while the narrator said, "On the June primary ballot, Proposition 226 changes California law on political contributions. Proposition 226 requires employees' or union members' permission to withhold wages or union dues for political contributions. Proposition 226 prohibits foreign contributions to state and local candidates. Be sure to read the official state guide to Proposition 226 coming to your mailbox soon or call 800-829-4258 for more information." That campaign also cost more than $1 million and included some print versions of the same message in leading newspapers.

By indirection the proponents had gotten in the first licks in the air war over Prop. 226. But the labor side was busy getting ready to take them on. Mark Mellman, a Washington pollster with longtime links to the teachers, had been polling the issue for months. And David Binder, a San Francisco political consultant, was running focus groups further testing what messages might be effective in peeling support away from 226.

Dawn Laguens had a theory about initiative campaigns, based on her previous experience in Maine, Ohio, and other states. "Initiatives never cry," she explained, meaning they have none of the human characteristics that define candidates for voters. "They are just a bunch of words on paper, usually backed by one set of interest groups and opposed by others. When you're on the negative side, you basically just try to create doubts." (Her colleague in this enterprise, Will Robinson, who represented the national AFL-CIO, liked to say that the no side was like the defense attorney in a criminal trial. "All you have to do is create a reasonable doubt.")

"The key is to make this abstraction real for voters," Laguens said. "That means you have to understand your audience and segment your message to reach each important part of it. Usually, the proponents will have described the objective of the measure in very positive, appealing terms. To get people off that and persuade them to vote no, you have to go after competing values—create conflict in their minds. You tell them the initiative is flawed. It will have unintended consequences.

The people behind it are bad. Anything that causes them to reconsider."

The polling and focus-group studies gave the opponents important clues. "We know the other side has the easier message to deliver," Gale Kaufman told me early in the campaign. "When you ask people if union members should have the right to direct political spending where they want it to go, they say yes. Same when you ask if all political contributions should be voluntary. But there are other issues that are more favorable to us. Not a lot of people think about unions and the way they are run. But most agree that if membership in the union is not compulsory, majority rule is fair. And, more important for our purposes, we found that most Californians don't dislike unions. They have a more favorable view of unions than of business. And when we ask about some of the issues the unions have supported, there is very wide support for them. So it's a two-step or three-step argument we have to make. I just hope we have the time and resources to make it."

Mark Mellman added two other significant findings from the early polling and focus groups. "Most people believe there should be a balance of power between business and labor," he said. "And when people are told the measure is being promoted by outside people with a very strong partisan agenda, they react very negatively." (Mellman also questioned the proponents' strategy of throwing in the ban on foreign contributions and thereby casting the whole proposition as "campaign reform." "That told me they didn't really have confidence in their own message. And in the end it helped us, because it confused people about what it was really about. The more complex you make a proposition, the more suspicion it arouses.")

The findings guided the ad strategy. If Prop. 226 could be redefined, not as an issue of internal union governance but as a referendum on the causes unions support, and if the motives of the backers could be made to look suspect, there might be a chance to win. At the very least, it offered the unions an opportunity to win back support of their own members and their families. Nothing was more disturbing to the labor leaders than the findings in the early polls that union households were in favor of Prop. 226.

Kaufman said the first step in the argument had to be, "This is not as simple as it appears to be. And then, second, we have to show these are bad guys behind it." She had hoped to be first on the air, but the "informational" campaigns by Citizens for a Sound Economy and the National Taxpayers Union beat her to the punch. "They got there first," she said, "but their ads were cognitive. We wanted ours to be emotive."

Emotive barely begins to describe it. The first ad began with a close-up of a man with a magnifying glass, examining the language of Prop. 226. The words dissolve into sinister pictures of Rooney and Norquist. The narrator says, "We've seen it before. Ballot measures that aren't what they appear to be. And when you take a closer look at Prop. 226, you'll see that a foreign lobbyist [Norquist, who had the Seychelles as a client], multinational corporations, and an out-of-state insurance tycoon [Rooney] are behind it. They're here to push the 226 agenda. Weaken patient protections against HMOs, privatize education, and export American jobs. That's why Prop. 226 has been called The Big Lie [the headline on a John Jacobs column in the *Bee*]. Take a close look. You'll vote no on 226."

Mark Mellman told me later, "The first step was to encourage people to read it. We knew the ballot language was confusing. The link between foreign contributions and union checkoffs was unclear. In the fiscal impact statement, it was not clear who paid the fees. The public is deeply suspicious and we believed that confusion was helping us."

Follow-up commercials expanded those two themes: the good things labor unions seek; the sinister designs of 226's backers. One ad, targeted directly on Rooney and Norquist, backfired. When it appeared, the agency buying airtime for the proponents of 226 called stations warning them they might have to give the two men free time to respond. Several stations pulled the ad, though Rooney and Norquist never made such a request. But Kaufman and Laguens quickly went to the next ads in their planned rotation.

One came on the screen with a quick montage of Wall Street, a sweatshop, the stock-exchange floor, and newspaper headlines: GIRLS NEARLY ENSLAVED FOR U.S. CLOTHING MARKET. VIRTUAL SLAVERY IN SWEATSHOPS. JEANS MAKER MOVING A LOT OF WORK SOUTH. All played off the contributions to Prop. 226 by owners of the Gap and Guess, sports clothes makers. The narration said, "Multinational corporations accused of sweatshop practices. Companies that have shipped American jobs overseas. These are the backers of Prop. 226. They're using 226 to advance their own agenda by weakening unions because unions fight against sweatshops and exporting jobs. Consumer advocate Ralph Nader says Prop. 226 would tip the scales against working people and put California jobs at risk. Prop. 226. It's not what it appears to be. Vote no on 226."

A more upbeat variation of the ad starts with pictures of a little girl eating a brownie, a child raising his hand in class, and another getting a checkup by a doctor. The narration: "Food, quality education, health care we can depend on—these important protections are guaranteed by California law. But now big business, a foreign lobbyist, and an out-of-state insurance tycoon are pushing Proposition 226 to take power away from ordinary citizens and advance the 226 agenda [the graphic showing the same sweatshop and job-exporting headlines]. They claim it protects union members, but Proposition

226 has been called The Big Lie. The League of Women Voters says it would shut working Californians out of the political process. Take a close look."

The mass-media campaign was aimed particularly at independents and "soft" Republicans. It talked about the cost to the state and private business of administering 226. The legislative analyst's office, an arm of the legislature staffed by supposedly nonpartisan professionals charged with the responsibility of assessing the fiscal impact of every piece of legislation and ballot measure, said in its statement for the official voters' guide that Prop. 226 would entail "unknown, but probably not major, net state enforcement costs. Annual costs of up to about $2 million and one-time costs of $2 million to $5 million to the state for administration of employee payroll deductions for political activities; costs offset by fees." And similarly for local governments.

But State Controller Kathleen Connell, a Democrat, had done her own estimates, and the unions used her figures. The ad said, "Prop. 226 isn't just unnecessary, it would cost taxpayers millions. The state controller says the paperwork could cost over $6 million for state workers alone. And the *San Francisco Examiner* says costs in the private sector could be millions more. Millions and millions of dollars for a proposition the *Sacramento Business Journal* calls 'nonsense' and the *San Jose Mercury News* says is 'unnecessary.'"

After a good deal of internal debate, the unionists decided not to include Wilson in their gallery of villains on statewide TV—for the very practical reason that they hoped to get some votes from "soft" Republicans and Republican-leaning independents who might have voted for the governor. But they went after Wilson hard in messages targeted to union families and to minority groups they knew had reason to regard him as an enemy. An ad on Univision, the Spanish-language TV network, linked 226 to two other Wilson-led initiatives that were resented by large majorities of Latinos. Wilson "attacked us with Proposition 187," the ban on social services to families of illegal aliens, and used Proposition 209, the anti-affirmative-action initiative, "to push our kids right out of the best colleges." Now, it said, he is trying to "silence our voices" by muzzling unions.

Wilson was also the target in mailings to union households. A supersize postcard sent out by the California Labor Federation, for example, showed a bald senior citizen with a target painted on his forehead. The text: "Pete Wilson, Newt Gingrich, and their allies have launched an all-out attack on public-worker pensions. To pay for tax cuts for the rich, they want to cut our pension benefits. But our unions have fought them all the way. So Pete Wilson, who has repeatedly pursued privatization of state jobs, launched Prop. 226 with Newt Gingrich to destroy the unions that are working to protect your pension." Another mailer, from the same source, said simply: "If Pete Wilson gets his way, California's working families lose their say."

The approach to union members was anything but subtle. A flyer distributed by the California Federation of Teachers claimed 226 "will cripple the ability of public-education supporters to advocate for more funding for schools and community colleges... greatly reduce your union's influence in local school and trustee elections... [and] silence your union's voice to speak out on your behalf in favor of higher salaries, benefits, and pensions.... It benefits antilabor, antieducation forces who want to cut your salary and benefits and raid your pension. It benefits extremists who want to take over local boards of trustees and privatize education." Another flyer from the same union was even blunter: "Prop. 226 imposes a whole new bureaucracy on unions. Your union will be hog-tied, hamstrung, and buried by new red tape and bureaucratic requirements. Prop. 226 forces workers to report their political activity to their bosses. Employers should not be allowed to violate workers' privacy by keeping records on your political activity."

The May–June issue of the magazine that goes to the 1.4 million members of the United Food and Commercial Workers, the largest private-sector union, said: "This is an all-points bulletin. Lock both hands around your wallet. Political con artists are running a nationwide scam on working people. They're slick... slicker than the proverbial wolf in sheep's clothing, slicker than wet on brick. And dangerous." It quoted a Buena Park union member, John Getz, as saying, "It always sounds good when someone says, 'Hey, we're going to protect you.' But these guys have never done anything to help working people. One day they're trying to eliminate job safety laws and the next they're going to guard my money? I don't think so."

Meanwhile, a focused effort was made to reach leadership elites—especially newspaper editorial boards. Experience has shown that when voters are unfamiliar with initiative issues, newspaper endorsements carry a much greater weight than they do in candidate elections. So the labor folks went after the editorial boards with a carefully chosen set of arguments and advocates.

For the visit to the *Los Angeles Times* editorial board, for example, Kaufman brought the presidents of the CTA, the Los Angeles Central Labor Council, and the Los Angeles League of Women Voters, along with a labor lawyer who walked the journalists through the complexities of the laws and court rulings governing union political activity and the rights of individual members to opt out of contributing. A last-minute addition to the group was an official of the Los Angeles Firefighters union, who reminded the editorial writers how his union had worked with them in support of a recent bond issue to finance improved fire and police services in their city. "Of course," he said, "if this passes, we wouldn't be able to do that."

Perhaps the key moment in the meeting came when Lois Tinson, the CTA president, said, "Just imagine what you would face if your readers were required to resubscribe to the *Times* every year. I'm sure most of them would want to do it, but think of the work you would have to do." Kaufman recalled one of the editorial writers saying, "I get it."

The *Times* came out against the initiative in an editorial saying, "There's no doubt that putting the responsibility on union members to sign up in order to allow political contributions will mean, out of indifference, inertia, or choice, that political fund-raising by unions will decline, possibly very substantially. And since money unhappily remains the mother's milk of politics, the political equation could be radically skewed. That does not serve the democratic process."

The same opposition was expressed by all but five of the papers in the state, the largest dissenters being the *San Diego Union-Tribune* and the *Orange County Register.* The anti-226 editorials furnished raw material for later union ads and flyers and—as much as the neutrality of major California business—sapped the vigor of the drive to pass the initiative. Indeed, the closing union ad consisted mainly of excerpts from no-on-226 editorials from the *Times,* the *San Jose Mercury News,* the *San Francisco Examiner,* the *Sacramento Bee,* and the *Riverside Press-Enterprise.*

That closing ad also got in one more lick at the hidden motives of the sponsors. But there was a significant difference from the opening ad, which, as Mellman said, was designed to get people to look more closely at the proposition. "After our campaign took off, we didn't want them to look that closely," he told me afterward. "So our final tag line was 'It's what you don't see that counts.'"

The participation of the League of Women Voters in the editorial board meetings was part of Kaufman's effort to expand the opposition coalition beyond her union clients. The League, which had been involved in many previous efforts at campaign reform, smelled a rat in Prop. 226. Its board decided the purpose was not to protect individual rights but to tilt the playing field toward conservative causes. "Everyone should play by the same rules, especially when it comes to elections that determine the future direction of our state and nation. This measure sets up two sets of rules"—one for unions and the other for everyone else—the board statement said. The League had moved early, and its opposition was featured in the opponents' statement in the voters' guide.

The coalition effort eventually produced a seven-page, double-column, single-spaced list of groups and prominent individuals who had signed on in opposition to 226. They included the Sierra Club and the League of Conservation Voters, the League of California Cities, and the California Nurses Association.

The coalition effort also spawned a truly bizarre sideshow involving the United Way of America (UWA) and demonstrating how far the networks of ideological allies on both sides of this fight were prepared to go in order to manipulate public opinion. It began when two lawyers in a Washington, D.C., firm were hired by OMB Watch to write a memo on the reach of Prop. 226. OMB Watch is a liberal group, set up during the Reagan administration to monitor actions by David Stockman and his successors at the federal Office of Management and Budget who were using their budget and regulatory powers to curtail programs and harass bureaucrats favored by the out-of-power Democrats.

The lawyers, Jane G. Gallagher and Robert A. Boisture, produced an eighteen-page brief, concluding conveniently that "while labor organizations appear to be the primary target of Proposition 226, the initiative is so broadly drafted that it will cause a variety of adverse consequences for state nonprofits.... Proposition 226 applies to all payroll deductions, including deductions for charitable giving." If any of the recipient organizations—or the groups to whom they passed on contributions, as United Way does—took a stand on an initiative or lobbied for their cause in the legislature, they might run afoul of 226, the lawyers said. "The many unanswered questions, and the substantial risk of liability that Proposition 226 imposes on employers, are likely to lead employers... to discontinue workplace-giving through charitable deductions," the legal memo said. "Voters should think carefully before they enact a measure that risks disrupting workplace fund-raising campaigns."

Late in April an employee in the legislative section of United Way of America headquarters in Alexandria, Virginia, sent out a "legislative alert" to its local affiliates, warning that 226 "is drafted so broadly that it would cause a variety of adverse consequences for nonprofits." Citing the legal opinion OMB Watch had obtained, the legislative alert said, "If you are concerned about Proposition 226's effect on your campaign, it is imperative that the California electorate hear your opposition." It provided web site directions to the groups opposing 226.

How the legislative alert came to be distributed is something of a mystery. Betty Beene, the president of United Way, told reporters it was the work of "a new member of our staff" who failed to obtain the necessary clearances from higher executives. Skeptical critics, noting that the United Way board has always had a certain number of union and management representatives and that an informal patronage system gives staff jobs to people from both constituencies, said they suspected a union sympathizer was at work.

In any case, the legislative alert stirred up a hornet's nest. When Governor Wilson's office learned of it, he went on the warpath. His first move was to call J. Michael Cook, the head of the giant accounting firm Deloitte and Touche and chairman of the board of United Way, to ask what was going on. He also contacted Elaine L. Chao, Beene's predecessor as president of United Way. Chao, who is married to Senator Mitch McConnell of Kentucky, the leading Republican opponent of federal campaign-finance-reform legislation, had taken a position as a fellow of the Heritage Foundation, which was issuing policy memoranda in support of 226. She promptly sent out a blistering two-page statement. "It is my strong belief that it is highly inappropriate for United Way... to interject itself into this highly political and controversial campaign. To do so compromises the integrity of the entire organization and runs the risk of alienating many corporate and individual contributors."

Betty Beene did not need a lawyer to explain the implications. On May 14 she issued a statement declaring "the United Way of America has not taken, and will not take, any position with regard to Proposition 226, nor does it participate or intend to participate in partisan politics." The legislative alert, the statement said, "that created confusion was released without review or authorization by the UWA board of governors and does not represent the views of the leadership of UWA. It should not be cited as evidence of UWA's opposition to Proposition 226."

But that was not the end of it. The legislative counsel's office in Sacramento issued a statement, in response to a request from a member of the assembly's Democratic majority, declaring that 226 "would apply to employee payroll deductions to a nonprofit organization" if that organization supported or opposed candidates or ballot measures. The California Association of Nonprofits, an umbrella organization of eighteen hundred groups, sent out a memo paralleling the United Way's legislative alert and refused to change it. Flo Green, its executive director, said that many of the organizations do lobby or take a stand on issues. "Many of them played critical roles on initiatives to clean up the beaches, limit smoking, ban guns, and so on.... We don't want to be placed in a position where we have to choose between payroll giving and our right to advocate on ballot measures." The California branches of the American Lung Association, the American Cancer Society, and the American Heart Association took the threat seriously enough to come out against Prop. 226, giving the unions yet more trusted, nonpartisan names to include in their final ads opposing the measure. Two dozen environmental groups, led by the Sierra Club, also weighed in against Prop. 226.

The charities issue gave labor a way of appealing to independents and to Republican women, Kaufman told me. "And at the micro level, it also freaked out business at a time when Wilson was hitting them up for contributions. I mailed a John Jacobs column [suggesting that the initiative was so loosely drawn it could well impact all payroll deductions] to every public-relations guy whose company belonged to the Chamber of Commerce."

Mellman told me later he had hoped to heighten the effect of the payroll deductions issue by claiming it could also affect checkoffs for health insurance, because Blue Cross and similar organizations often speak out on health issues. "But the lawyers said that was a doubtful claim, and in our polling people didn't believe it. The charities issue also didn't work very well when we first tested it. But when more organizations endorsed the idea, it began to work, and it became a cue to vote no for people who hadn't paid much attention to the other arguments."

Ron Nehring, who ran the Orange County end of the yes-on-226 campaign, told me in a primary day conversation that he feared the impact of the charities issue more than anything else. "From the beginning," he said, "they wanted to get the discussion away from workers' rights, because they can't win that argument. Our focus groups showed that no truthful argument could drive support below 50 percent. Even the 'outsider' argument didn't push it [the initiative] behind. But the charities argument soaked up a lot of public attention, especially when they got well-known groups like the Lung Association to buy into it. We were vindicated by the United Way statement, but it didn't stop other groups."

Labor's mobilization was not confined to California. In March both Vice President Gore and House Minority Leader Dick Gephardt (Democrat, Missouri) appeared before the AFL-CIO executive council in Las Vegas and pledged to help defeat Prop. 226. On May 4 President Clinton spoke at a Los Angeles fund-raiser for the no-on-226 committee and said the issue of coerced political contributions "is not a real problem." (It certainly was not a problem for most of the fifty people who attended a five-thousand-dollar-per-couple breakfast at the swanky Beverly Hills home of supermarket owner Ron Burkle.) Under existing law, union members can withhold contributions to labor PACs, he said, and retrieve the portion of their dues allocated to politics. "What this amendment seeks to do is to basically muffle the ability of the collective voices of working people to be heard, by putting on them a far, far greater administrative burden than corporations face when they spend their own money—they don't have to get their shareholders' permission every year... or other organizations like the Chamber of Commerce, the NFIB [National Federation of Independent Business], any other membership organization that spends money" on politics. "It's being done to alter the balance of power in the political debate."

Taking their cue from the president, others in his administration campaigned against 226. One of them, William Gould, the chairman of the National Labor Relations Board, got in trouble for his actions. The NLRB, a quasi-judicial agency ruling on labor-management disputes, is supposedly neutral—though administrations of both parties have satisfied their constituencies with appointments to the board. But when the NLRB posted a press release on its web site containing Gould's criticism of 226, a House committee called Gould in and reprimanded him.

Compared to labor's mobilization, the forces backing Proposition 226 were meager. The Orange County headquarters had a staff of seven, headed by Ron Nehring, who had worked on term-limits campaigns and then become executive director of the San Diego Republican Party. His operation was supposed to mobilize volunteers around the state to conduct the ground war against the massed forces of the unions. When Wilson came on board, he insisted that his own people would run the air war—raising and spending the larger sums of money involved in the television campaign. He took two young men from his own staff, Jeff Randle and Mitch Zak, and opened an office down the street from the capitol. And he brought in pollster Dick Dresner and media man Steve Powell to plot the message and make the ads.

Almost from the start the effort was plagued with internal problems. Rooney and his California-based public-relations man, K. B. Forbes, quarreled first with Bucher and the Orange

County people. They claimed that Nehring was alienating volunteers and was using the financial muscle of his San Diego friends to take complete control of the ground operation. Rooney cut off his financial support and announced he would stump for 226 on his own, a plan he abandoned when it became clear that the more visible his role, the more labor would attack the "out-of-state insurance tycoon."

It was not long before Rooney had a similar falling out with Wilson and his staff. Ostensibly the issue was Rooney's objection to the "antiunion" tone of Wilson's message. "He really regarded it as a civil rights issue," said Forbes, "and he had no interest in helping Wilson settle old scores with the unions." From the Wilson camp came leaks suggesting that Rooney wanted to control the campaign himself and "didn't understand that the governor is very hands-on" in any effort he launches. Wilson aides said the governor even rewrote the language for the voters' guide himself and laboriously counted words to be sure he had not exceeded the limit. In any case, Rooney refused repeated personal requests from Wilson for six-figure donations to the TV campaign.

All three groups began bad-mouthing one another to reporters, further weakening what was already a structurally divided campaign. In the end, Rooney took an undisclosed amount of money to the Claremont Institute—a conservative think tank run by Larry P. Arnn, a political scientist who had taken a lead role in passing the anti-affirmative-action Prop. 209—and paid for a rather strange ad that aired mainly on radio stations in the Los Angeles market. The ad began with barking dogs, who were likened to quarrelsome candidates. It then segued into a question-and-answer format in which an actress said, "Right now, your money can be taken from your pay, without your permission, for politics.... Proposition 226 means your employer must obtain your authorization before deducting your money for political campaign activities.... We're the nonpartisan Claremont Institute. Our responsibility is to educate about the issues....Your responsibility is to vote." The ad is notably silent on one key matter; the words *union* and *labor* are not heard, presumably in deference to Rooney's wish that this not be an antiunion campaign.

In Washington, Norquist's enthusiasm for the venture also seemed to wane, or at least struggle for attention, on an agenda that included many other issues. Once he had spoken of raising $10 million for the ballot drive. Later he said that was his goal for all of the paycheck-protection initiatives and legislative efforts around the country. Still later he said that he was predicting $10 million could be raised, not saying he would raise it himself. His allies in the Republican congressional leadership were not having much luck with the issue. When Lott offered it as a poison-pill amendment to the Senate campaign-finance bill he was trying to kill, opponents of paycheck protection had no difficulty blocking a cloture vote to cut off debate on the amendment. When Representative Bill Thomas of California made it a key part of an omnibus campaign-reform bill he sponsored in the House debate, it failed 74 to 337, with 140 Republicans joining a solid phalanx of Democrats in opposition. Paycheck protection no longer looked like the magic tool to remove labor's political sting and choke off the Democrats' main source of campaign funds.

Indeed, the National Right to Work Committee, a longtime antagonist of union power, quietly began passing the word that the California fight was a diversion—not a solution. Stefan Gleason of the committee's staff told me, "We are not opposed to this effort. We're happy people are trying to address the problem of compulsory unionism. However, we very much believe that while these efforts are well intentioned, they vastly overstate the impact these efforts will have on organized labor's coffers. They are trying for a regulatory scheme to mitigate the violation of employee rights, rather than removing the coercive power to force workers to support unionism in the first place. We have learned that fails."

But all the backers believed a victory in California was still in the cards and hoped that winning in the biggest state would reignite the movement nationally. No one was more determined to produce that result than Governor Wilson. In March he came to Washington to enlist the help of the major national business organizations. He spoke at a breakfast at the Chamber of Commerce of the United States, had lunch with the National Association of Manufacturers, and met with Norquist and others in the coalition of conservative organizations. Wilson dramatized the fight and its national implications. "California often has been a trendsetter for the nation," he told the Chamber of Commerce breakfast. "The state that gave America the Reagan Revolution" now leads the way with initiatives curbing benefits for illegal aliens, halting affirmative action and racial preferences, and next, Wilson promised, an initiative affirming workers' "fundamental right to choose for themselves if and how to spend their hard-earned money on politics."

Union members, he assured them, were ready to join the revolt against the "bosses" who had "sunk two-hundred-thousand dollars into a deeply flawed ballot initiative to legalize marijuana for 'medical' purposes" and had "taken members' money to defeat enactment of the three-strikes-and-you're-out initiative." If groups like the Chamber will help offset the heavy union spending against Prop. 226, Wilson said, "California will again strike a blow for fairness—a blow that will resonate all the way to this city as a growing chorus of Americans demand a return to... the principle of equal treatment and equal rights under the law. I hope you'll join this effort. This affects your workers, your businesses, your kids and their education."

He got results. The Chamber of Commerce formally endorsed Prop. 226—something the California Chamber had refused to do—and swung into action. (The Chamber does not have a federal structure; companies join the local, state, and national chambers of commerce separately, and the local and state chambers are not branch offices of the national organization.) R. Bruce Josten, the Chamber's top lobbyist, ticked off some of its efforts: "*Nation's Business,* our magazine, has a circulation of 860,000; it did an article in January, a lead editorial in May, and two more article updates. We also had an article in the separate publication we send to 400,000 activist members. Thomas J. Donahue, our president, did two op-eds, which we distributed to 520 regional newspapers. We prepared material on the issue and sent it out to all 687 local chambers in California. We did an action call on our WATS line to all our member companies in California, urging grassroots action." An April 28 memo from Josten to local chambers in California was headed DEFUNDING ORGANIZED LABOR BOSSES, a clear statement of the political objective. The memo said, "The union bosses' ability to freely spend other people's money for their own political purposes is the closest thing to unchecked political power that exists in California—or in America. It is power that no one else possesses."

Then, without a hint of irony, Josten appended a memo from a Washington campaign-finance lawyer, Jan Witold Baran, saying it is perfectly legal for "corporations and trade associations [to] disseminate information about Prop. 226, including materials provided by Yes on 226, to its members, employees, and shareholders," so long as the cost of such an effort was reported to Wilson's committee so it could be included in its filings with the state. Not a word about getting permission from members, employees, or shareholders.

Similar efforts were undertaken by other business groups such as the trade associations for wholesalers and distributors. They had begun working together as "the Coalition" in 1996 in a belated effort to counter the union television campaign targeting vulnerable members of the House Republican majority. Now they saw an opportunity to strike back at their labor antagonists.

Jack Faris, the head of the National Federation of Independent Business, said mailings and phone calls had urged its California members to turn out and vote for Prop. 226. The flyer NFIB sent out was like much of the union propaganda; it emphasized the causes on the union agenda more than the issue of internal union governance. The cover of the NFIB flyer read: "Your business is under siege. The union bosses demand: Minimum-wage increase; mandated health insurance; opposition to legal reform. You can fight back. Vote yes on Proposition 226 on June 2."

The National Association of Manufacturers alerted its members and—unlike its Coalition partners—also made a small ($9,000) contribution to the cause. NAM president Jerry J. Jasinowski and the Chamber's Tom Donahue signed a joint letter to business and association executives asking for contributions to the Coalition to support "a large, national education effort among our collective memberships in support of paycheck protection reforms nationwide. These efforts will increase employees' control over their own wages and keep the unions busy defending the indefensible while we take the offensive with our pro-growth, pro-business message." The conservative think tanks also got busy. In April both the Heritage Foundation and the National Center for Public Policy Research produced essay memos supporting Prop. 226.

While all this was going on, the opposing sides struggled—without much success—to interest political reporters in the fight. It was a frustrating experience for Mitch Zak, the public-relations man Wilson had assigned to the task, and for Kristy Khachigian—the daughter of veteran Nixon-and-Reagan-operative Ken Khachigian—who had the same responsibility at the Orange County headquarters. The California media were dealing with a hot three-way Democratic gubernatorial primary, a close two-way race for the Republican senatorial nomination, and a host of local contests. The public seemed turned off by politics, so space in the newspapers was limited and airtime on TV almost nonexistent. Among the ballot initiatives, priority went to Prop. 227, the measure that would end bilingual education in the state. Few reporters were deeply interested in the union money issue; like the public, they just didn't care that much about it.

Khachigian and Zak churned out press release after press release, only occasionally getting a response. When President Clinton spoke out against Prop. 226 in Beverly Hills, Khachigian got a paragraph from Wilson into most of the stories. The governor pointed out that 92 percent of the $48 million that labor PACs reported spending in 1996 went to Democrats and said Clinton's "administration has become a welcome mat for big labor bosses and their extremist agenda." But she had little success with a written statement from former President Gerald R. Ford endorsing Prop. 226.

The proponents believed that if they could keep the battle focused on their issue, they could win. "If people understand it, or just read it, they will vote yes," Mitch Zak told me in our first conversation in the spring of 1998. "The fairness issue wins." That was the theme of the slick brochure they produced—a handsome mailing piece with a portrait of Thomas Jefferson on the front and a quotation from the author of the Declaration of Independence: "To compel a man to furnish contributions of money for the propagation of opinions which he disbelieves is sinful and tyrannical."

Still, it was almost the middle of May before Wilson's committee ran its first commercial. It was defensive in tone. Opening with a shot of the *San Diego Union-Tribune* editorial headline THE ART OF DECEPTION in the labor ads, and following with headlines from other papers about the TV stations' pulling the ads attacking Norquist and Rooney, the TV spot had this narration: "Big labor's ads saying Proposition 226 is about HMOs, education, and the kitchen sink are scare tactics, not to be believed. Newspapers call them 'outrageous, wild exaggerations and deception.' Proposition 226 simply amends the Political Reform Act to ban foreign contributions to politicians and prohibit employers and unions from withholding money from your paycheck for politics without your permission. Read it yourself, then vote yes on 226."

The purpose was in part to refocus on the core question on the ballot but even more to inoculate voters against the more numerous labor ads. But it had limited impact. "It slowed our slide, but it didn't stop it," Mitch Zak told me. "It was a relatively small buy, and we felt we had to do it to set up our second ad. And we were encouraged that when we asked in our tracking how many agreed 'the labor ads are just not to be believed,' the number shot up." But when the labor people tested this ad against their own ads in focus groups of undecided voters, the union message prevailed. "When we're talking about sweatshops and they're talking about deception, we win," Steve Rosenthal told me. "And when people tell us after watching both that their view is a little muddy, that's not bad for us." Historically, he knew, voters confused about an initiative either skip it or vote no.

A week later, and just ten days before the vote, Wilson finally aired the ad that drove home his essential message. It opened with a headline from an April *Los Angeles Times* poll, saying, 58 PERCENT OF UNION MEMBERS SUPPORT PROP. 226, then cut quickly to the faces of four diverse union members saying, in sequence, "It's unfair and morally wrong... to take money from our paychecks... and use it for politics... without our permission."

Then the scene shifts to what the printed script describes this way: "Grainy black-and-white footage of [actors playing] overweight, cigar-smoking union bosses laughing and pushing large sums of money across the table. The seal of the AFL-CIO is evident on the wall behind them." The narration is: "Prop. 226 eliminates the big union bosses' political slush fund taken from workers' paychecks without their permission. Big labor uses this money to buy favors from politicians."

Next is a brief reprise of the newspaper editorials from the first ad, while the narration continues: "Their desperate campaign against 226 has been called 'the El Niño of Big Lies, deceptive and outrageous.' Two-twenty-six is campaign reform that protects your paycheck and bans foreign political contributions." The ad closes with a shot of the four real union members saying in unison, "Vote yes on 226."

Both Gale Kaufman and Dawn Laguens conceded it was a "terrific" ad and rejoiced privately that their opponents had only gotten around to it in the closing days of the campaign. Mellman told me, "Most of their ads were 'flat-liners'; they didn't move the numbers at all. But the last ad was the right message for them." The union consultants had anticipated the approach; in fact, Laguens had made her own version of the ad and had tested it on focus groups. She knew that it would work, so she did the only thing she could. She made her own workers' ad, with an equally gender-and-racially balanced set of union members giving the standard reasons for opposing 226, and put it on the air as soon as the opposition ad appeared. But now it was labor on the defensive—for the first time since the issue had been joined.

When I talked to Randle and Zak on the Friday before the primary, they were cautiously optimistic that their closing blitz would pull out a victory. They marveled at the intensity of the labor campaign—with Zak saying twice that Kaufman had "run it as if it were an assembly race," something she was very familiar with from her Willie Brown days—trying to reach every likely voter several times with several different messages. "They just pushed every button they could think of," Zak said. "They changed their message often, hoping to create the shadow of doubt in people's minds."

In contrast to the virtually unlimited resources on labor's side, Randle said "our media campaign was back-loaded. We bought from primary day backwards, as the money came in." And then he added, in what I took to be a significant sign of apprehension, "I wish we had another week."

Wilson hit the road to make a personal counterattack on the labor ads. Traveling with dissident union members, the governor denounced the unions' "scare tactics" and accused them of waging "arguably the most negative, dishonest, and deceptive campaign in political history."

Particularly galling to Wilson, who had for a long time cultivated a reputation as a crime fighter and who prided himself on his support from law-enforcement people, was a campaign against Prop. 226 launched by the California Organization of Police and Sheriffs (COPS). In press interviews and formal statements, COPS president Don Brown said Prop. 226 would endanger police by requiring them to put their names and addresses on forms for withholding union dues, which then would become a matter of public record. The *San Diego Union-Tribune* quoted Brown as saying, "Violent criminals will be allowed easier access to seek revenge against peace officers and their families. This is a matter of life and death for every peace officer in the state."

Wilson and his committee did their best to knock down the unsubstantiated claim. He pointed out that several sections of the California public-records act, unaffected by Prop. 226, prevented disclosure of that kind of personal information about police officers. He got letters and affidavits from the heads of several other law enforcement groups, backing up his assertion and denouncing the COPS statement.

Nonetheless, the same charges became the central message of a telephone campaign mainly from union phone banks outside of California. One phoner, questioned by the woman whose number she had dialed, said she was calling from Tallahassee, Florida. The Orange County committee also identified other union phone banks operating in Oklahoma, West Virginia, and Nebraska. At the end of the campaign, Kaufman and Laguens told me they had tested the message early and "knew it was powerful." But they chose to use it in mailings and phone calls targeted to women Republicans, independents, and older Democrats—people sensitive to the law-and-order issue—rather than put it on television, where the press was more likely to scrutinize and criticize the message. And they had COPS deliver the charge, rather than issuing it directly from their own headquarters.

To respond, Wilson's people put the governor on tape for a final weekend of phone blitzes. In the space of seventy-two hours, they completed an estimated 633,000 calls, Randle and Zak told me on primary day, aimed at "high-propensity

Republican women voters," plus all the Republican households in San Diego and Orange Counties, "where the governor remains very popular." When someone picked up the phone in one of those homes, she heard Wilson's voice say, "This is Governor Wilson urging you to vote yes Tuesday on Prop. 226. Don't believe big labor's lies. The California District Attorneys' Association says Prop. 226 will not endanger any policeman's life and the United Way says it will not hurt charities." The labor folks thought that was smart. "We had targeted Republican women," Mellman said, "because they were responding more like independents than like male Republicans. And many of them were really undecided right up to the end. The Wilson people had some success with their phone calls. It probably saved them two or three points."

When Wilson's people used the same theme in their final TV ad, however, Dawn Laguens rejoiced. That ad showed Michael P. Bradbury, the district attorney of Ventura County—not a widely known figure but a credible television presence—forcefully rebutting the charges that Prop. 226 would endanger charities and, especially, endanger police officers. Like the phone campaign, it was designed to reach moderate Republicans, particularly women. At the time, Randle and Zak told me, "We're doing great with independents and libertarian-minded Republicans, but we're weaker than we should be with Republican women and moderates." Early on, Laguens had told me that in her experience, the "target voters" at the end of initiative campaigns "almost always turn out to be middle-aged and younger women." Now the Wilson forces had made the same discovery.

But Laguens insisted the ad was a mistake, "a classic case of using the wrong medium. They went on TV, publicizing a charge no one had seen. I couldn't believe they'd do it." Mellman made the same point: "They spent vast amounts of time and money rebutting arguments we weren't making on TV."

While this ad was running on the final weekend, labor's closing message featured the editorials opposing Prop. 226. Once again the volume was greater for the opponents than for the backers of paycheck protection.

The mismatch between the two sides was even bigger when it came to the ground war—the direct contacts leading up to a voter turnout mobilization on June 2. On primary day Gale Kaufman said, "The backers of 226 assumed we could not organize the ground troops in June the way we do in November. That's why they wanted it on the primary ballot. But we knew we had to get union members excited, because that would give us a base that the other side could not begin to match. So we went after them."

In March two key organizers moved out from AFL-CIO headquarters in Washington to coordinate precinct work done by staff members of the affiliated unions. Both Arlene Holt, the executive director of AFSCME (the American Federation of State, County, and Municipal Employees) and Amy Chapman—who went to work for Steve Rosenthal after managing successful Democratic campaigns in Oregon and Michigan—knew grassroots politics. When I went to see them at their second-floor command post in San Francisco a couple weeks before the voting, the wall chart listed fifty-six paid area coordinators and field directors who were supervising what they said were "hundreds" of union staff members. They also described a mail and phone-bank operation designed to reach every union household and everyone who had voted regularly in past Democratic primaries five to eight times before June 2. Of the 1.6 million union households, 900,000 were considered likely voters, Chapman told me. "In the past, union members have turned out at about 41 percent. We're trying to boost that to 50 percent or more."

On the final weekend, Steve Rosenthal said, there were "at least three thousand people" walking precincts on both Saturday and Sunday—among them Art Pulaski, the head of the California Labor Federation. Pulaski was part of a new breed of union leaders, just eighteen months in the job. He saw Prop. 226 as a threat not only to his political clout but also to his mission. "It would turn us into a bunch of bureaucrats, running around getting authorization forms signed every year, instead of representing and advocating for our members." Imbued with the spirit of the community organizer, he told me, "When union members talk to other members, it has a dramatic impact. When I walk precincts, I'm just a union volunteer talking to a fellow union member. My goal as president is activating members by talking about what is significant in their lives. We're using this issue as an opportunity. There's nothing new about this. Saul Alinsky did it in Chicago two generations ago. Kirk West [the recently retired head of the California Chamber of Commerce] told me when this issue came up, 'If I were you guys, I'd use this as an organizing tool,' and that's exactly what we're doing."

Pulaski had nothing but scorn for Wilson and his professed motives. "When I hear him talking about workers' rights, I just laugh," he told me. "When was the last time Pete Wilson advocated for workers? He fought us on the minimum wage, on overtime pay, on damn-near every issue we've had in Sacramento. If Pete Wilson wants to tell us how to operate, he should join a union." A couple days later, when I quoted Pulaski's comment to the governor in an interview, Wilson was equally biting: "Poor little unions being picked on by me," he said. "Give me a break."

John Hein, the CTA political director, told me that in the

final days, his organization was manning phone banks in its eighty offices around the state, utilizing staff members and teachers working after-school shifts to reach its 220,000 members and their families. Their campaign had been organized since January; by April a video decrying Prop. 226 had been distributed throughout the state. Eventually it was shown in teachers' lounges in three quarters of the schools, Hein said. "Once the teachers realized who was behind this—the same people we had fought in the vouchers campaign—the argument was over."

By contrast, Ron Nehring had a paid staff of seven at the Orange County yes-on-226 headquarters and relied on volunteers to help mail material to a list of 4,700 supporters around the state.

The results showed on primary election day. Prop. 226 was defeated by a 53 percent to 47 percent margin. The *Los Angeles Times* exit poll found that one of every three voters was from a union household, and two thirds of them opposed Prop. 226. That was an exceptionally high union turnout. Mervin Field and Mark DiCamillo, who run the Field Poll, had told me they had expected union households to provide only 15 percent of the primary electorate. But the turnout was no surprise to Steve Rosenthal. In a pilot project in two counties, unionists found that they could significantly boost opposition to Prop. 226 by one phone call to a union household, and drive the opposition score to 83 percent with a personal visit at the workplace or at home. And such calls and visits also motivated people to vote.

All of this cost money—big money. The final total of reported spending, according to the secretary of state's office, was over $29.6 million—$6,052,614 by supporters of paycheck protection and $23,595,874 by those who opposed it. At its Las Vegas meeting in early winter, the AFL-CIO executive committee had voted a special assessment of $1 per member to raise $13 million to fight the measure in California and other states—a decision that Mark Bucher said amounted to "raising union dues in order to deny members their rights." The national AFL-CIO put slightly over $3 million into the fight, and individual unions much more. The teachers' groups also spent heavily. The California Teachers Association reported almost $6.5 million, and the parent National Education Association, an additional $2.7 million.

Money was not so easily come by on the proponents' side, especially after Rooney went his own way and Norquist failed to deliver on his promises. In the end, Wilson was left holding the bag. In the final weeks before the vote, he transferred $1.25 million from the Governor Pete Wilson Committee, his personal PAC, to the Californians for Paycheck Protection Committee, which was running his part of the campaign for Prop. 226. On May 15 Wilson sent out a three-page letter on stationery bearing the seal of his office, asking for help. The letter was all about Prop. 226, concluding with an appeal to "send your campaign contribution today to help me launch our advertising campaign against the union bosses' attacks." But the letter directed that checks be made payable to the Governor Pete Wilson Committee. California Common Cause and the California Nurses Association both filed complaints alleging that Wilson was laundering money through his personal PAC in order to avoid timely disclosure of the sources of money going into the fight for Prop. 226. More likely, he was putting the heat on California business, which was reluctant to be identified directly with the 226 battle.

When I asked Wilson about the transfers, he said, "It was not my choice to do it that way. It was the donors'. I told people I was backing a variety of efforts, on paycheck protection, on education, and on criminal justice, and some people said they'd rather I decide how the money be used. Except for those who expressed a particular interest, I said I'd use my best judgment."

When I asked if some businesses and their owners might not want to be identified directly with Prop. 226, the governor said, "I didn't ask or question their motives. But there's no question there's been an effort to intimidate business, and some people presume they are vulnerable."

Nonetheless, the California Restaurant Association, which had fought the unions on minimum wage and other issues over the years, contributed $250,000, and companies like Federal Express, Bristol-Myers Squibb, and CSX Corporation provided $25,000 to $50,000 apiece. Richard Mellon Scaife, the Pittsburgh millionaire who has financed many conservative causes, gave $100,000 for the TV side of the campaign. Bucher was the biggest individual contributor to his own end of the effort, listed at $161,000, but his ally in many education battles, Howard F. Ahmanson Jr., routed $223,000 into the campaign through various corporations and individuals.

Although national Republican campaign committees contributed $205,000 to the cause, Wilson readily admitted in our interview ten days before the primary that he had hoped for more money from both inside and outside the state. But he said he knew his side would be outspent and just hoped "we'd keep the ratio fairly reasonable." At the time, he was still optimistic. "I think we will win," he said, "because people are resentful when they've been lied to and manipulated. That's a dangerous tactic."

Both public and private polls tracked a steady decline in public support for Prop. 226. The Field Poll, carried by many California newspapers, showed the margins dropping from 71 percent to 22 percent favorable in February to 60 to 29 in March and to 55 to 34 in April and to 45 to 47 in late May. As a measure of the effectiveness of the unions' attacks, the Field Poll found that among those in union households, opinion shifted from 67-to-30 favorable to Prop. 226 in February to 68-to-27 opposed in May—a complete reversal. Along the way, the issue became much more partisan, reflecting in part Wilson's prominence and the opposition from Clinton and other leading Democrats. In February Republicans had been slightly more supportive of Prop. 226, but Democrats favored it by more than two to one. At the end of May the Republican margin had declined to the two-to-one level and Democrats were opposed two to one. A similar trend was charted in the *Los Angeles Times* poll, although it never showed Prop. 226 actually losing.

Private polls for both sides painted quite a different picture. Gale Kaufman told me early on that one reason Dawn Laguens believed that the fight could be won was that their polling never showed Prop. 226 enjoying "more than the high fifties in support, and even then, there were some arguments we could make that knocked it down below fifty." Mark Mellman's polls showed support for the principle of requiring union members' permission fluctuating between 53 percent and 58 percent from mid-1997 through January of 1998. Fewer than 20 percent of those polled opposed the principle, leaving one third of the voters uncertain.

As soon as the measure qualified and actual ballot language was available, Mellman—unlike the public pollsters—began using that exact language in his poll. The first time he tried it, in April, he found—to his employers' joy—that Prop. 226 enjoyed only an eight-point lead. (Field, at roughly the same point, had it up twenty-one points, using a paraphrase of the ballot language.)

In early May the lines crossed on Mellman's polls, with 40 percent opposed and 31 percent supporting. This was the time when labor was buying heavily for its first and second rounds of ads, and only the National Taxpayers Union informational ads were providing any counterweight. The margin widened very slightly over the next two weeks, as labor ads vied with the first of Wilson's messages. By the third week in May, Kaufman said, "I'm not sure we're out of the woods, but it feels a lot better." The margin in Mellman's final poll was thirteen points, but as he later told me, "We knew they would close it up at the end and that turnout was tricky to gauge." Encouraging to the union side was a separate Mellman finding that when voters were given just the number and title of Prop. 226, they were opposed to it by even wider margins.

That meant two things: One was the traditional reluctance of California voters to say yes to any initiative whose meaning they did not understand. And second, the unions had succeeded with their ad campaign stigmatizing Prop. 226 as a sinister threat. Among these less-informed voters, reacting solely to the number and title, the margin of opposition grew from 36-to-22 against in early May to 45-to-25 against at the end of the month.

The proponents' polls, from what I was able to learn, were slightly different, but not flatly contradictory. They also measured a steady decline in support during the time the labor ads were essentially unanswered. But when the second yes ad—the one with the actual union members and stereotyped union bosses—went on, the picture changed. That ad began running on May 19, and Dresner's tracking ticked upward on May 21. Just before that, Randle said, they were down 10 points in a three-day rolling average of daily tracking results. By May 24-25-26, the tracking showed them down 2, 3, or 4 points a day, "but clearly we were back in the game." (Dresner, like Mellman, was using the actual ballot language in his surveys.) In that late polling, fewer than one fourth of the sample agreed with labor's argument that Prop. 226 was an effort by big business to hurt working people, while half or more thought it was about workers' rights. But by a four-to-three margin, they believed Prop. 226 might hurt charities or endanger cops—"so we had to go back on that in our final ad," rather than make the basic argument for Prop. 226.

Each player tried to put his best gloss on the results. On the morning after the primary, Governor Wilson said that when he took up the fight, "we fully expected that we would be outspent by as much as we were and perhaps even more. We knew that was going to happen, and we knew that they wouldn't tell the truth....The thing is, the more they rip off people's paychecks, the more money they have in their war chest...and they will be just as arrogant and high-handed as they can get away with."

As for the effect on his presidential ambitions, Wilson was philosophical. "You know, you pick your fights because you think it's the right thing to do. And sometimes you pick fights that you know are going to be very tough or you know the odds are very long against you. You do it because it's the right thing to do." (In 1999, shortly after leaving office, Wilson announced he would not run for president in 2000.)

Such high-mindedness did not spread very far. On June 3 Pat Rooney's spokesman, K. B. Forbes, issued a statement that made no mention of Wilson or the Orange County group but claimed Rooney "has succeeded in making paycheck protection a national issue....Proposition 226 is the first battle of a long war....Pat Rooney is determined to continue his fight to protect the civil rights of working Americans."

The next day came another statement from Forbes, implicitly pointing the finger of blame at Wilson for losing the battle.

Describing Rooney as "the public-policy visionary who had spearheaded" the fight for paycheck protection, it quoted from an article by Doug Sword in that morning's *Indianapolis Star.* According to Sword, "Three months ago, Rooney warned that Proposition 226... would pass only if supporters presented it as a matter of fairness. If Republicans stooped to union-bashing and presented it as a fight between the political right and left, it would fail, Rooney predicted. That's apparently what happened."

Grover Norquist's statement said, "Paycheck protection is a winning reform, despite the results in California on June 2.... The union bosses have done everything in their power to confuse the issue.... In spite of all their efforts, Proposition 226 did not lose badly. In fact, given the spending disparity between the two sides, the relatively close result attests to the enduring popularity of the concepts behind paycheck protection.... Paycheck protection is a national issue, active in thirty-four states, with more to come in 1999. A setback in California may steal some wind from our sails, but it does not jeopardize the national effort." Later Ron Nehring did a report for Norquist's Americans for Tax Reform, asserting that "Americans in general and Californians in particular remain supportive of protecting a worker's right to decide where his or her political contributions go," and blaming the defeat of Prop. 226 on disproportionately high Democratic turnout, "lopsided funding" for the opposition, and the readiness of "union leaders to lie to maintain their stranglehold on workers' paychecks." He concluded, "Proposition 226 was defeated, not paycheck protection."

On the winning side, they could barely contain their braggadocio. Art Pulaski, the head of the California Labor Federation, said, "California voters as a whole saw this initiative for what it was: a thinly veiled attack on working families and their unions,...a partisan attempt to silence the only voice that speaks out for fair wages, safe pensions, and healthy workplaces. We emerge from this campaign stronger than ever."

Bob Chase, president of the National Education Association, said, "Proposition 226 was a transparent attempt to take advocates for public education out of the political arena. The public saw it for what it was—an attempt by proponents of private school tuition vouchers to limit the effectiveness of public education advocates."

And in Washington a jubilant John J. Sweeney, president of the AFL-CIO, told a news conference that California had dealt a deathblow to "Grover Norquist's fantasy of a 'national sweep' on the artfully named and deceptive issue of 'paycheck protection.'...The defeat of Prop. 226 sends a clear message about the prospects of other such worker-bashing initiatives in other states, and the message is, simply put: Pounding working families is a losing proposition."

An overnight poll, taken for the unions by Peter Hart, found 71 percent of those from union families voted against Prop. 226, and almost half of them cited a contact from their union as the main influence on their vote. Gerald McEntee, the president of AFSCME and overseer of the labor federation's political operations, claimed that unionists had made 650,000 phone calls, delivered 500,000 pieces of mail, and walked 5,000 precincts to deliver the anti-226 message. This "newly energized union movement" will make itself felt "in the November elections and beyond," McEntee promised.

The consequences were widespread. California was to have been the launching pad for taking paycheck protection national. In fact, Republican leaders in Congress postponed voting on federal campaign-finance legislation beyond June 2 in hopes a California victory would build momentum for similar legislation at the national level. In the aftermath the steam went out of the effort on Capitol Hill.

The California defeat impacted directly on Nevada, where the Republican Party's conservative leadership was gathering signatures for a similar initiative. When I visited that state early in May, I found the GOP and the business community even more divided on the wisdom of pressing the issue than was the case in California. Businessman and educator Kenny Guinn, who was leading in the polls for the Republican gubernatorial nomination and was the early favorite for election, was outspokenly opposed to the initiative. (Guinn was elected in November.) "I don't want to spend my time arguing about six cents a day in somebody's paycheck," he told me. "This issue won't make me a better governor."

His attitude reflected the antipathy of the gaming industry, Nevada's largest employer. Steve Wynn, owner of Las Vegas hotel-casinos and a leader in that industry, said, "This is a waste of time and a waste of energy. None of us in the gaming industry sees a reason to pick a fight with a union that has been very reasonable with us," referring to the 45,000-member Las Vegas local of the Culinary Workers, an affiliate of the Hotel Employees and Restaurant Employees International.

Nonetheless, Sheldon Adelson, a dissident casino-operator with many union problems, pumped money into the signature-gathering campaign, as he did in support of Prop. 226, and Newt Gingrich gave the effort a boost in a Las Vegas appearance. The unions prepared their own countermeasure, as they had done in California, and also filed a court challenge saying that the "workers'-rights initiative," as Nevada sponsors called it, violated unions' First Amendment rights and conflicted with federal law. A state judge agreed, and after the California vote, the initiative backers sat down with labor and negotiated a truce. They would not appeal the ruling if labor would not file its countermeasure. So the issue disappeared from the Nevada ballot.

Colorado was the next state on Norquist's list to abandon a paycheck-protection initiative planned for November 1998. Officially, sponsors said they had run out of time and wanted to delay the battle until 2000. Unofficially, reports were that senior Republicans were worried that a vote on the initiative would mobilize so much labor opposition it might cost them a Senate seat and hurt their chances to reclaim the governorship, which had been in Democratic hands for twenty years. In November Republicans won both races.

That left Oregon. There, the antilabor initiative was targeted at the public-employee unions—including the teachers—and it took the form of a prohibition on use of state funds to subsidize political activity by any group. It was aimed at barring payroll deductions for any organization engaging in partisan politics. The measure was sponsored by Bill Sizemore, the veteran conservative activist who had captured the Republican nomination for governor against popular Democratic incumbent John Kitzhaber. Sizemore was a leader of Oregon Taxpayers United, which had success with earlier initiatives capping property taxes and limiting state employee pensions. He also headed a company that was paid $154,675 for collecting signatures to get the Oregon version of Prop. 226 on the ballot.

But Norquist contributed only $15,000 to the Oregon effort, and money was hard to come by from conservative donors in the state. When I saw Sizemore in October, he complained, "The loss in California was a real setback to everyone's morale. The money has really dried up."

Money was no problem on the union side. Roger Gray, the former Oregon Education Association executive who was running the opposition campaign, said he would have $4 million—"and more if we need it." The unions were handed a golden issue when the official summary of Sizemore's Measure 59 included the information that, if passed, it would jeopardize an Oregon institution: the voters' pamphlet sent to every household with a registered voter. In addition to neutral information on candidates and measures, the pamphlet is stuffed with three-hundred-dollar ads from individuals and groups arguing their merits. Because the nominal ad charge does not meet the cost of printing and mailing the pamphlet, it involves a public subsidy of partisan candidates or groups. The secretary of state ruled—and the state supreme court agreed—that the description of Measure 59 should include the statement that its passage would mean "eliminating candidates' statements and measure arguments" from future pamphlets.

Even with all these advantages, the opponents ran an inept campaign. Their first ads pictured Norquist and Sizemore in caricature. The script reads: "Visual: Cut-out heads of Bill Sizemore and Grover Norquist, against appropriate background. Heads bounce, jiggle, revolve around one another, etc., in response to various copy points. Mood is creepy, sneaky, evil. Music: Background melody is appropriately angular, disjointed, discordant, sort of 'Twilight Zonish.' Narration: Meet the backers of Measure 59. Bill Sizemore, who wrote it. And Grover Norquist, who bankrolls him. Norquist is a registered foreign lobbyist, a close advisor to Newt Gingrich, and he heads up an extremist agenda to limit the voice of working people in America.... Let's just call Measure 59 what it really is—the Norquist Agenda, spearheaded by Bill Sizemore. Vote no on Sizemore-Norquist 59."

A pollster who tested the ad in a focus group said, "It created a backlash. Oregonians don't like negative ads, and this was one of the five worst ads I've ever seen."

Even so, money talked, and Measure 59 lost by a narrow 52 to 48 percent margin. A union-backed counterinitiative, which purported to be a multipurpose campaign-finance reform measure, passed by a two-to-one margin. Buried in it was a provision embedding in the state constitution the right to a dues checkoff for public employees. But it was immediately challenged in court and a year later was still in legal limbo.

In California, Prop. 226 turned out to be an organizing tool for labor. Amy Chapman, who came out to California from AFL-CIO headquarters as a coordinator of the ground campaign, said, "We are the other side's worst nightmare. They thought all they had to do was put this on the ballot and it would win. But we have had more contact with our members over this than we've had in years. And you'll see the effects for a long time." The labor effort clearly helped Lieutenant Governor Gray Davis, the union-endorsed candidate, win the Democratic gubernatorial primary over two wealthy, self-financed rivals, who had led in the early polling. "Prop. 226 is my secret weapon," Davis said.

As Chapman forecast, the mobilization effort carried over into the November general election. Davis won by twenty points over his Republican opponent, Attorney General Dan Lungren, giving the Democrats control of the governor's office for the first time in sixteen years. Democrats increased their margins in both houses of the legislature and captured all but two of the statewide offices, making California the site of the worst Republican setback of the year.

Before he left office, Wilson tried to pass yet another initiative in November and once again was thwarted by the teachers' unions. This one was a pastiche of proposals he had tried to push through the legislature, without any success. Among other things it would mandate a permanent maximum twenty-to-one student-teacher ratio in kindergarten through the third grade and earmark revenues to guarantee it. It would require expulsion of every student found with illegal drugs, not just those caught selling. It would require current and future teachers to pass a competency test in their subjects and give principals free rein to fire any teacher not performing well. And it would create a new office of chief state school inspector, whose staff would publish quality ratings on each of California's eight thousand schools. Wilson argued that it made no sense to put more money into the schools "until there is accountability for results and an atmosphere in the classroom conducive to teaching and learning."

There was something in his hodgepodge of proposals for everyone to hate. Rival claimants for state funds objected to earmarking more money for smaller classrooms. The CTA—"educrats," in Wilson's vocabulary—opposed the teacher testing and discretionary firing provisions. The school boards' association disagreed with another provision, creating at each school site councils that would share the budgetary power now exercised by the boards. And conservative groups, alarmed by analysts' estimates that the new inspector general's office would cost "up to $60 million"—mostly diverted from other education programs—and force local school districts to spend "in the high tens of millions annually," also joined the opposition. Wilson found himself fighting not just the CTA but the Howard Jarvis Taxpayers Association, the Christian Coalition, and the state Young Republican Federation. Once again he was heavily outspent by the teachers, and this initiative went down by a 62 percent to 38 percent margin in November.

What can we conclude from the saga of Prop. 226? That the lobbyist's cynical comment I quoted at the beginning of this chapter was essentially correct: A lot of little lies narrowly defeated one big lie.

I think the evidence shows that the original sponsors of Prop. 226—Mark Bucher and his Orange County friends—were sincere in what they set out to do. Whatever one thinks of their agenda for education in America—and it is plenty controversial—they had a genuine belief, based on their personal experience, that the teachers' unions and their allies in organized labor were exploiting the financial power of their members' dues to damage the best interests of students and parents in California.

But, as they readily acknowledged, they lacked the resources to wage that campaign on their own terms. They did not even have the money to come close to qualifying the initiative for the ballot. So they turned, as modern initiative campaigns almost always do, to deep pockets, powerful individuals and groups, who basically took control of the effort and used it for their own purposes.

Pat Rooney may well have a philosophical agreement with Thomas Jefferson about the immorality of coerced opinion. But he is also a man with a public-policy agenda of his own, which often has been thwarted by unions' political muscle. His self-interest makes him a strong advocate of medical savings accounts—and his insurance company has a lucrative business in selling policies to that market. Unions and their Democratic allies have fought against them.

Grover Norquist is a conservative power-broker with an explicit antiunion view. Gale Kaufman's press releases loved to quote from a February 1997 interview the head of Americans for Tax Reform gave to *Reason* magazine, a libertarian journal, in which he hailed the Beck decision—the Supreme Court ruling that, though rarely applied, allows workers in unionized facilities to withhold all of their dues except the portion used to negotiate and enforce their own contract. Norquist said that ruling "will help us break the unions." Enforcing it, he gloated, "would crush labor unions as a political entity," a consummation he devoutly wished.

It was Norquist's enthusiasm that helped spur Trent Lott and Newt Gingrich to see paycheck protection as a way to retaliate against the unions, which had spent millions in 1996 trying to dislodge Republicans from their newly acquired control of Congress.

As for Governor Pete Wilson, his battles with the unions were long and bitter, and his intent finally to break their power before he left Sacramento, undisguised. That success in this effort might also help his presidential ambitions was an added bonus. For Wilson it was essentially payback time for all the times his bills and his initiatives had been opposed or defeated by the teachers' unions and others in the labor movement.

The camouflage for this coalition of power brokers was the argument that they were defending workers' rights. And while they lost the vote, they sold the California public their version of their own motivation. The managers of Wilson's campaign gave me the results of one question the polling firm Wirthlin Worldwide had asked in daily tracking polls on Prop. 226 during the third week in May. Asked "which of the following statements most accurately describes your opinion regarding Proposition 226," only 23 percent said it "is an attempt by big business and special interests to silence the voice of average workers," while 64 percent chose, "It is unfair and morally wrong to take money from workers' paychecks and use it for politics without their permission. Proposition 226 will end this practice."

True, the wording of the question tilted the response in that direction, but even the labor people admitted that if the issue was defined as one of workers' right to control the use of their dues, the unions would lose.

So they did everything in their power—and did it well—to create other issues. The whole campaign was an effort to sow confusion about what Prop. 226 really was, who was behind it, and what its consequences would be. "We don't mind confusion," Dawn Laguens told me in a moment of candor.

Never once in all their ads and all their mailings did the opponents of Prop. 226 engage the basic question of the use of union dues. True, they argued that their internal polls showed most members supported the legislative causes backed by the unions and they claimed that the Beck decision provided dissident workers everything they needed if they wanted a portion of their dues money back—without, however, acknowledging the extent to which they made it very difficult in practice.

But basically they threw up a lot of dust, creating bogus scares about the people behind Prop. 226 and the consequences of its passage. Kristy Khachigian, the press secretary for the undermanned Orange County yes-on-Prop. 226 headquarters, exhausted herself putting out what she called Truth Memos for the media, rebutting all the union bogeymen.

To a charge that Prop. 226 would weaken the unions' ability to lobby for strong health-and-safety measures, she replied, "Prop. 226 does not limit in any way a union's ability to lobby or participate in issue advocacy.... Under California law, 'political expenditures' are only funds given to or against a political candidate or ballot initiative."

Another claim was that workers would have to inform their bosses of every single political donation they authorized. Their privacy would be invaded, and they would leave themselves open to retaliation. Not so, Khachigian said. One authorization form per year, with no specifics about where the money was going.

By the end of the campaign, she was up to a dozen "false claims" per press release and reduced to quoting some of the hyper-rhetoric of the union side in hopes reporters would be as offended as she was. Among other claims she quoted were statements that Prop. 226 was "antichildren"; "would make it almost impossible for us [nurses] to preserve our working conditions and protect our patients"; would mean that "the state's public-sector employees, who are primarily women... could no longer help elect their own bosses"; and would make it "impossible for unions to collect money to spend on November elections."

All of these claims, exaggerated though they might be, eroded support for Prop. 226. As Dawn Laguens said, "We didn't have a magic bullet, but we had a lot of magic beebees." But the initiative probably would not have lost if most Californians thought it addressed a real problem that mattered to them. The reality was that this was an imported issue, fostered by national conservative groups and a governor with a clear political agenda of his own. As the reaction of the vast majority of California businesses showed, it was a solution in search of a problem.

Revealing evidence on this point came from the polls. In April, when the *Los Angeles Times* polled voters, it found that 76 percent said they knew little or nothing about Prop. 226. When the initiative was explained to them in terms similar to the ballot language, they backed it 65 to 24 percent. But on a separate survey question, 57 percent said labor had too little or about the right amount of influence in California politics, while only 30 percent said it was too powerful.

In an early May survey by Mark Baldassare for the nonpartisan Public Policy Institute of California, Prop. 226 led 59 to

33 percent among likely voters. But the poll also asked separate questions on approval or disapproval of "placing restrictions on the ability of labor unions or business corporations to contribute to political candidates and ballot initiatives." Restricting unions had a narrow 50 to 44 percent lead; restricting corporations was favored by 59 percent, with only 33 percent opposed.

That is probably as true a reflection of public attitudes on this aspect of campaign-finance reform as one is likely to get—a belief that if any further controls were to be imposed, more voters would apply them to business than to labor. Baldassare's poll suggests labor might have had success if it had gone for the "nuclear winter" strategy of placing a countermeasure on the ballot to cut off corporate donations to candidates and initiative campaigns. Instead it negotiated for passivity by major California business groups on Prop. 226 and then raised millions to defeat the measure. As *Washington Post* columnist E. J. Dionne Jr. wrote, "Voters have many real worries. Fear of a dangerously powerful labor movement is apparently not one of them."

Mark Mellman polled likely voters at the end of the campaign about the probable consequences if Prop. 226 passed. Six out of ten said it would end compulsory union dues for politics. But four out of ten said it would cost the taxpayers money to run the program, and a similar proportion said it would give big business an unfair advantage. Most significant, Mellman said, "they [the proponents] never got 50 percent of the people saying it would protect workers' paychecks, and we had it almost that high saying it would cost the taxpayers money." On the basic pocketbook level, the proponents never made their case.

After the primary, Harold Meyerson wrote in *LA Weekly,* "Proposition 226 neither arose from nor was rooted in a public clamor to do something about a social problem. To the contrary, it arose from a very select clamor: that of Republican leaders and strategists, who were shaken by the scope and effectiveness of the union effort during the '96 campaign.... What this meant, however, was that 226 was rooted in nothing more than a strategic conceit, as the dearth of volunteers working on its behalf made abundantly clear. Arrayed against it was a constituency that felt its very life was on the line; that without the ability to engage in politics, the American labor movement would shrivel and die. In the campaign just completed, labor had both the resources and the passion on its side, a combination that in politics is almost always unbeatable."

A large question is how well the voters understood what they were doing. When the *Los Angeles Times* polled voters two weeks before the primary, 48 percent of all voters, and 38 percent of the likely voters, answered, "Don't know," when asked how they felt about Prop. 226 on union dues. Mark Mellman found that on May 29, just three days before the primary, 30 percent of those who vote regularly in primaries said they knew little or nothing about Prop. 226, with 70 percent claiming they knew some or a lot about the issue. In the week before the primary, I did some interviewing of my own to gauge how clearly defined the issue was.

I went to the university town of Davis and to the Sacramento airport, places where I believed I would find many well-informed voters. The first voter I met made me reconsider that assumption. In a coffee shop across the street from the Avid Reader bookstore in Davis, I met David Busse, a psychology student at the university. From the seventeen names on the primary ballot for governor, he had isolated Gray Davis as his choice. But when I asked about Prop. 226, he said, "I'm not sure what it's all about." He paused to search his memory of the TV ads he'd seen. "As it is now," he ventured, "unions have to get permission to donate money to candidates. Under this, they wouldn't. I'm not sure that's a good idea."

He was a thoughtful voter—but he had it backward. And he was far from alone. Three others among the two dozen voters interviewed seemed just as confused. Ramsey Dowell, a federal auditor in Sacramento, said, "I'm against it. If I want my money to go to a particular candidate, I should decide, not the union leaders. They should ask my permission." Roger Matson, a retiree from Stockton, said, "I'll vote no. The money belongs to the people who work for it. The union shouldn't be able to use it for its own purposes."

And others were quite uncertain. Janet Das, a Gold River housewife, said, "I don't think it's fair for them to use anyone's dues for political contributions without permission. I'll vote that way. I'm not sure if that is yes or no. I'll have to look carefully how it's phrased."

When I reported these conversations to Mervin Field, he said he was not surprised. Confusion is rampant because there had been a heavy cascade of ads asking for no votes on four substantively different but similarly numbered propositions: Prop. 223 dealt with education funding; Prop. 224, with contracting out state services; Prop. 226, with union dues; and Prop. 227, with bilingual education. "When you're dealing with three digits and four initiatives are getting heavy play," Field said, "you get confusion."

The narrowness of the final loss and the momentum the victory gave to labor and the Democrats made it a bitter defeat for those backing Prop. 226. Their mood was not improved by a postelection poll conducted by Republican consultant Frank Luntz. Even though the reported votes in the six-hundred-person sample mirrored the actual results—with a five-point margin for the opposition—68 percent of those surveyed said they agreed with the basic principle of Prop. 226, that "unions should be required to get a member's written permission before using part of his or her dues for political causes." More than 50 percent of the sample said they felt "strongly" about that view. But Luntz also found that each of the negative arguments the unions had advertised were accepted by 30 to 40 percent of the sample, and cumulatively, they sank Prop. 226.

He also found that almost half the people in his sample recalled receiving a phone call or a letter or both from a union urging them to vote no, during the last two weeks before the primary—a measure of the intensity of the opposition campaign. And when Luntz asked "if you were sure that charities would still be able to raise money freely and that the privacy of all individuals was protected," 65 percent said they would vote for requiring individual permission for political use of union dues.

The sponsors could only gnash their teeth in frustration at all the evidence that the initiative results reversed public sentiment on the underlying principle of making union members' political contributions voluntary. But the larger lesson of Prop. 226 is that the voters were not the source of the initiative campaign; they were its targets. They were not agents of political change; they were closer to being pawns in this interest-group struggle. And the same thing was true in many of the other initiative battles of 1998.

Chapter 4

THE MONEY GAME

Money does not always prevail in initiative fights, but it is almost always a major—even dominant—factor. Like so much else in American politics, the costs of these ballot battles have escalated enormously in the past decade. To a large extent, it is only those individuals and interest groups with access to big dollars who can play in the arena the Populists and Progressives created in order to balance the scales against the big-bucks operators.

Just as in presidential campaigns, the first test for any contender is the ability to raise the needed money. In the autumn of 1997 more than two hundred petitions were circulating for initiatives the sponsors hoped to place on the ballot the following year. The vast majority of them did not make it. Some lacked the necessary support. But the hurdle that eliminated most of them was the ready cash needed to hire the people who wage initiative campaigns.

In the 1997–98 cycle, total spending for and against statewide initiatives reached $257,053,852, according to figures collected from the secretary of state offices in the initiative states. That number does not include the costs incurred by sponsors of measures who either failed to collect the number of signatures required or—as in the case of the countermeasure California unions threatened to file but then withdrew—were completed but not filed. Nor does it include spending on the hundreds of local initiatives. Even so, the reported quarter-billion-dollar-plus total is one third of the $740 million reported by the Federal Election Commission as being spent in 1998 by candidates for the House and Senate.

Nor was this unusual. In 1996 in California alone, initiative spending totaled $141,274,345, according to Secretary of State Bill Jones. That is 33 percent more than the candidates for the California legislature spent getting elected. Several hundred candidates ran for eighty assembly and twenty state senate seats and spent $105.7 million in the process. In fact, the initiative campaigns in this one state cost just a shade less than the $153 million the taxpayers gave President Clinton and rivals Robert J. Dole and Ross Perot for that year's presidential campaigns.

In 1998 the most expensive initiative campaign, by far, was the battle between the California Indian tribes and the Las Vegas casinos described in an earlier chapter. The tribes spent $66,257,088 to win, and it cost the rival Nevada interests $25,756,828 to lose. The $92 million total set a new record for California initiatives. This battle was solely about money—who would profit from the seemingly insatiable lust of Californians to hit the jackpot and enjoy the good life they see their wealthier fellow citizens so conspicuously embracing. In 1997 California Indian tribes grossed $1.36 billion from their gambling, and Las Vegas did not want them siphoning off even more.

As often happens, the fight was not over when the votes had been counted. The losers—the Las Vegas operators and the union representing casino workers—went to court. They said the initiative was in conflict with the provision of the state constitution that voters had approved in 1984 when they authorized a state lottery and simultaneously banned Nevada-style casinos in California. The legislative counsel had issued an opinion to that effect during the summer of 1998, but the voters ignored it as 63 percent of them approved the Indian gambling initiative. But in August of 1999, the California Supreme Court ruled by a six-to-one margin that the 1998 initiative did violate that part of the state constitution. Some of the tribes struck a deal with Governor Gray Davis. Others threatened that they would be back in 2000 with an initiative amending the state constitution to permit all the games they wanted to introduce into their casinos. "We've come too far at this point to throw in the towel," said Mark Macarro, chairman of one of the gambling tribes. His words were music to the ears of all the consultants who had cashed in on the 1998 fight—and would do so again in a rerun.

At the other end of the spectrum were a number of initiatives that might be considered humanitarian or altruistic—ones where the intended benefit would be widely shared by society, whether human or animal. In 1998 the Humane Society of the United States, the leading national organization on animal rights, turned in another impressive performance at the polls. Animal-rights forces banned cockfighting in Arizona and Missouri, and in California outlawed the slaughter of horses and the use of steel-jawed leg traps on fur-bearing animals. The antitrapping campaign had its Hollywood touches.

It enlisted film stars Alicia Silverstone and Martin Sheen, and a three-legged dog named Dillon came to news conferences. The coalition supporting the measure was called ProPAW. Despite opposition from farmers and ranchers and a small group of trappers who hire out to rid growers' irrigation canals of beavers and muskrats, it passed by 57 percent to 43 percent.

In the same category is the initiative, sponsored by an organization called Oregon Trout, that set aside a fraction of state lottery receipts each year to expand parks and protect streams and natural habitats. On the other hand, Ohio voters rejected protection of mourning doves from hunters, and Alaska voters turned down a ban on snaring wolves. Perhaps because the animal-rights forces have been so successful throughout the 1990s, Utah sportsmen succeeded in passing a 1998 constitutional amendment initiative requiring that any future wildlife protection measure would need a two-thirds majority for approval.

Some commentators would also assign to this group of disinterested or unselfish initiatives the Clean Elections measures approved by voters in Massachusetts and Arizona in 1998. A response to public frustration with the "money chase" in politics and the repeated failures of Congress to pass any legislation to remove the taint of special-interest money from federal campaigns, these initiatives provided qualified candidates access to public funds. In Massachusetts the money would have to be appropriated by the legislature from general revenues. Arizona tapped special sources—a registration fee on state lobbyists, and an override on criminal and civil fines assessed in Arizona courts.

Ironically, these Clean Elections campaigns were financed not by small contributions but by a few big givers. The Arizonans for Clean Elections Committee, for example, reported that only $547 of its $891,718 contributions came in amounts of $25 or less. In Massachusetts the pattern was similar. Passing the initiative cost $1,066,770 and almost three fourths of the contributions came in amounts of $10,000 or more. Businessman Arnold Hiatt personally contributed $145,000. In both states there was a huge mismatch in the financial resources. The opponents in Massachusetts spent only $60,957; in Arizona, $53,002.

Like their self-interested counterparts, many of these "public-interest" initiatives got onto the ballot not through some mass movement but because a handful of highly motivated people were prepared to pay for signatures to qualify the measures and persuade the voters that they were worth supporting. The Oregon Trout initiative, for example, benefited from a large gift from Phil Knight, the chairman and CEO of Nike.

What was striking to me as I traveled the initiative states was the discovery that so many of the measures had been designed by a handful of people and were being sold with their dollars. Whether their motivations were financial or ideological, they had mounted this Populist warhorse and were riding it hell-for-leather to achieve their own purposes.

I found one striking, if isolated, example of this in Oregon. Helen Hill of Nehalem, a forty-two-year-old teacher and adoptee, was frustrated in her pursuit of the identity of her natural parents. Oregon once kept open birth records, but a law passed in 1957 had closed them. Hill herself had lobbied in Salem to get the law reversed, arguing that sealing birth certificates "only engenders shame" among adoptees like herself. "People have tried dozens of times" to change the policy, she told me, "and the bills never even make it out of committee." Adoption agencies, the Catholic church, and other groups opposed to the open-records policy always prevailed.

So Hill took $89,500 out of her bank account—virtually all her savings—hired a Portland signature-gathering firm, and got her initiative on the ballot. "I thank God we have this initiative process," she said. When Hill was criticized for her use of paid signature-gatherers, she wrote a letter to the editor of the *Oregonian,* saying she was "proud of our choice.... I feel our choice to use them was an honest, principled one."

She went on to argue that on an issue like hers, "it would be impossible and perhaps even wrong to ask our limited volunteer force to do the bulk of the petitioning, to essentially wear their hearts on their sleeves and confront the public en masse with an issue that is deeply personal and, in many cases, unresolved. Once a man said to me while I was petitioning, 'Your mother got rid of you for a good reason. That's all you need to know.'" Hill called the experience "devastating," and asserted that both professional signature-gatherers and those who hire them deserve public gratitude, not condemnation. "Far from decrying a group of citizens' concerted efforts to put an issue before a vote of the people by any lawful means necessary, I believe we should support this kind of active participation, for citizen participation is the true essence of democracy."

I found her example compelling, and she was not the only citizen who showed that the initiative process could be a way to advance a strongly held view about what public policy should be. On the same June ballot where Proposition 226 was fought out, a fundamental question of California education policy was settled—thanks to the persistence and the bankroll of one individual, Ron Unz, a Silicon Valley millionaire who had challenged Pete Wilson unsuccessfully in the 1994 Republican gubernatorial primary. Unz is a character—a welfare whiz kid with an IQ of 214, the winner at seventeen of the Westinghouse Science Talent Search, a software entrepreneur who struck it rich in his early thirties, a bachelor who grabbed his meals at Burger King and who became hooked on the intellectual conservative movement. In the course of fighting Wilson's Prop. 187—the measure denying social benefits to the families of illegal aliens—he became convinced that thousands of Latino immigrant students were being shortchanged when they were sequestered in public school bilingual programs. The issue was not new, but with one of every four students in California schools being unfamiliar with English, it had gained greater importance. For years one group of educators had argued that the best way to handle students for whom English was a second language, not spoken in their homes, was to give them lessons in English while teaching other core subjects in their native language. That view was challenged by critics—both inside and outside the teaching profession—who believed that isolating these newcomers in special classes, with a separate set of instructors and a different curriculum, would inevitably deny them a chance to enter the mainstream of this society.

Unz and others had tried to lobby the legislature in Sacramento to reform bilingual education. But the Democrats who controlled the assembly and state senate responded to two pressures—leaders of the Latino community, who predominantly favored bilingual classes as a way of preserving their distinctive culture, and the teachers' unions, which wanted to protect the jobs of the 47,000 members hired to run the bilingual classrooms.

Frustrated by what he regarded as the legislature's political obduracy, Unz put up the money to place on the June ballot an initiative that would end the bilingual programs and substitute a one-year total-immersion program of intensive English instruction for these students—and then place them in classrooms where all the teaching would be in English.

Once it was clear that the issue would come to a vote, things began happening in Sacramento. The state board of education announced a policy—the board claimed it was merely reaffirming a policy it had long ignored—of local discretion as to the best method for educating the children who were part of the recent wave of immigration. And less than a month before the election, a bilingual "reform" bill suddenly moved through the legislature to the desk of Governor Wilson—who promptly vetoed it as both "too little and much too late" and a patently obvious attempt to undercut Unz's Prop. 227, which Wilson had endorsed. The bill sent to Wilson would have allowed local districts to choose from several options for non-English-speaking students. Wilson's veto message said, "Although I firmly believe in local control in carrying out education standards, it is the state that has the responsibility to set those standards."

In the end, Unz put up $650,000 of the $976,632 spent on Prop. 227. He scored a big victory on June 2, when Prop. 227 was approved with a 61 percent majority, mandating a significant shift in the education received by about 1.4 million students. But the measure was far more popular with the Anglo majority than with the Latino minority most affected. Exit polls showed less than 40 percent of Latino voters supported 227. Ambrosio Rodriguez, an attorney for the Mexican American Legal Defense and Education Fund, complained, "This strips away all the flexibility that parents and school districts now have to decide what kind of program is right for these students." But after a brief legal challenge, Prop. 227 became the law in California.

Matthew Miller, in a 1999 *New Republic* profile of Unz, suggested that he might represent a third stage in the evolution of initiative politics. Writing of Unz's success with Prop. 227 and his plans for a 2000 initiative on campaign-finance reform,

Miller said, "In California, Unz is bringing the initiative movement full circle, from grassroots movement at century's dawn to special-interest takeover of a process meant to curb them to a rich man's way of empowering voters. On bilingual education, and now perhaps on campaign finance, Unz is an unlikely new brand of populist, a lowly born aristocrat of talent teeing up fixes for the masses out of a sense of nerd oblige." It may be a new model, but Unz is not nearly as unique as Miller suggests. Plenty of other millionaires have also found the initiative handy for "empowering" voters to endorse the initiatives' sponsors' agendas.

Perhaps the most striking example of "empowerment" occurred in Washington state in 1997. Paul Allen, one of the cofounders of Microsoft and a billionaire from its profits, had bought the Seattle Seahawks football team. He wanted a new football stadium for his team, and he wanted the taxpayers to foot some of the estimated $425 million cost. So he spent $6,321,832 securing the signatures for a ballot referendum on its construction and campaigning for its passage. He even paid the $3,998,284 cost of running the special election at which voters across Washington approved the expenditure. It passed with 51 percent of the votes, in June of 1997, and a court challenge, based on his paying for the election, failed.

Reed Hastings is another Silicon Valley tycoon who figured out how to use the initiative process to impose his education agenda on California—and, in his case without ever having the measure approved by the voters. Hastings is a former teacher, who made his fortune in the software business, A Peace Corps veteran, looking for ways to improve society after selling his company for three quarters of a billion dollars at age thirty-seven, Hastings adopted charter schools as his vehicle for reform. Charter schools are usually part of the public school system, supported by taxpayer funds. But they follow innovative models, devised by teachers or community leaders or business people. Once chartered by the authorities, these schools are usually allowed to waive many of the rules and regulations applied to conventional schools.

Because the charter school movement developed considerable momentum in the 1980s and some of the early examples showed signs of being significant successes, Governor Wilson was able to get the Democratic legislature to authorize one hundred charter schools in 1992. When Hastings went to Sacramento to urge that the number be increased to five hundred—or, even better, be left open-ended—he was brushed aside. Once again the teachers' union was resisting, fearing that all of the job protections built into standard teacher contracts might not be guaranteed in charter schools.

So Hastings, like Unz, decided to sponsor an initiative. With backing from other Silicon Valley CEOs, who were understandably concerned about the shortage of skilled workers coming out of California schools, Hastings went first-class on his first venture into initiative politics. He hired a lawyer from Steve Merksamer's Sacramento firm to do the drafting. He signed up Rick Claussen to direct strategy and create advertising for the campaign. And he chose Angelo Paparella and Progressive Campaigns to collect the 1.2 million signatures needed to assure enough valid names to place a constitutional amendment on the ballot. With sponsors paying one dollar a name—they got in before the Indian gaming initiative exploded the market—Paparella had no trouble delivering.

Seeing what was coming, the teachers' union decided to cut a deal. And in short order the legislature approved a bill that authorized an additional 250 charter schools in 1999 and raised the cap by 100 schools each year thereafter. The same measure made it easier for parents to start such schools, limited the authority of school boards to reject their applications, and made it easier for charter schools to take over unused school facilities. Governor Wilson happily signed the measure. Hastings won without the expense and effort of a popular vote.

Another California businessman also scored a notable success in 1998—but in Washington state, which is no mean feat. As mentioned in the previous chapter, Ward Connerly, the head of a consulting firm that advises cities on housing development, was a political ally of Governor Wilson. As a Wilson appointee to the University of California board of regents, Connerly led the successful fight to end race-based or gender-based affirmative action employment and admission policies in the multicampus university system. But the battle at the board of regents was simply a prelude to a larger effort, led by Connerly and endorsed by Wilson, to ban such affirmative action programs throughout state government. The vehicle for this sweeping change in state policy was Proposition 209, which appeared on the California ballot in 1996 and prevailed by a margin of 55 percent to 45 percent. As with Proposition 13, the California model soon inspired talk of similar efforts in other states.

In 1998 Connerly turned his attention to Washington state, where a policeman-turned-state-representative named Scott Smith claimed that as a white male, he had been a victim of reverse discrimination when he applied for the King County (Seattle) force. Smith tried in successive sessions to pass a bill paralleling Prop. 209 but was unable to get it out of committee in the Republican-controlled legislature, and so he turned to the initiative process.

Smith's effort was foundering, with only 17,000 of the needed 179,248 signatures in hand, when Connerly came to the rescue. Through his California-based American Civil Rights Institute, he supplied $170,000 for the lagging signature drive. Later, Americans for Hope, Growth and Opportunity, a political committee controlled by Republican presidential challenger Steve Forbes, donated mailings and other in-kind support valued at $35,000.

Connerly also recruited John Carlson, the host of a popular Seattle radio talk show, to take over the leadership of the initiative drive. Carlson had worked on a Republican congressional staff and had previously promoted two successful anticrime initiatives. This fight, however, was more controversial, and when protesters marched by Carlson's station, denouncing his role in the Connerly initiative, Carlson was fired. He took his talk show to the Internet, and at least some of his audience followed him there.

The woman Connerly and Carlson hired to run the signature drive is one of the great characters of the initiative industry, a onetime freelance photographer in Tacoma named Sherry Bockwinkle. A frizzy-haired free spirit and political activist of hard-to-define views, she won a degree of national fame by challenging then–House Speaker Thomas S. Foley, a Spokane Democrat, on the issue of term limits. Bockwinkle, a self-proclaimed liberal Democrat in those days, was frustrated by the political invulnerability of her congressman, Representative Norman Dicks, a Democrat who was liberal on social issues but a strong advocate of defense spending. Unable to beat him, she threw her efforts into a term-limits initiative, which would have applied retroactively, forcing Foley, Dicks, and other longtime incumbents to leave office at the end of their current terms. Foley made the issue a personal crusade—arguing that Washington would be disadvantaged, compared to other states, by discarding people whose seniority had put them in powerful positions. In 1991 Bockwinkle took him on. The initiative lost by a margin of 54 percent to 46 percent, but the battle had major consequences. The Supreme Court later ruled that states may not constitutionally impose term limits on federal officials. In 1994 Foley was defeated by Republican George Nethercutt, becoming the first Speaker in history to lose at the polls. During the campaign, Nethercutt condemned the Democrat for "suing his own constituents" to block term limits, and promised to step down voluntarily after six years. In 1999 Nethercutt reversed himself and announced for reelection to a fourth term, explaining that he had learned how advantageous seniority could be.

Parlaying the renown she had won in the term-limits fight, Bockwinkle set up a business called Washington Initiatives Now (WIN) and took up a wide variety of causes. Now calling herself a libertarian, she worked on gay-rights initiatives and on an environmentalist measure to ban gill-net fishing. When Carlson launched his anticrime measures, Bockwinkle gathered signatures for him. And she hired out again to collect the signatures for what became Initiative 200. Bockwinkle told me that with a twenty-cent-a-signature override, she can make about $25,000 per campaign—a good deal better than she was doing as a photographer.

The first time I interviewed Carlson, two months before election day, he maintained that he would be heavily outspent but would prevail. By that time the state Republican Party, controlled by conservatives, had endorsed 200, but Carlson said, "The issue frightens Republican officeholders. They know how they feel, but don't want to roll up their sleeves and confront the issue." Republicans in the legislature, caught between grassroots activists who backed the measure, and the Republicans' main contributors, who opposed it, decided their safest course was to keep the legislation from coming to a vote.

The opponents had more big names, more dollars, and more visible clout. Governor Gary Locke, the Democratic incumbent and probably the most popular politician in the state, was adamantly against 200. He is the son of Chinese immigrants, and the first Chinese American to be elected as governor in the continental United States, and he told me, "I benefited from affirmative action" when admitted to Yale Law School. Joining him in opposition were the Democratic Party and almost all its elected officials, the state AFL-CIO, the Washington Council of Churches, and the Washington State Catholic Conference. Two of the state's most prominent Republicans added a bipartisan blessing—longtime Secretary of State Ralph Munro and Dan Evans, the former governor and former senator whose prestige was so great that the University of Washington named its public-policy school for him. The president of the university, Richard McCormick, in his commencement address that summer, defended the affirmative action programs that he said had "opened the doors" to many African Americans, Native Americans, and Latinos. "These figures are one way of measuring the new nature of opportunity in America," he said of the enrollment statistics. "They are another hallmark of our society, something for which we will be remembered hundreds of years from now."

"Who wants to turn his or her back on this record of American achievement?" McCormick asked. "Who wants to return to a time when only advantaged white men could obtain the most prestigious university degrees or advance to the most respected and lucrative positions in our society? Who wants to live in a country where opportunity depends on your gender or your race? Not I—and I hope not you."

But it was on the business side that the imbalance was most striking. Carlson said he was getting help from the Association of General Contractors, whose largely white male membership argued that they lost out in bidding to women- and minority-owned firms. But lined up against 200 were an array of the biggest names in the Washington economy: Microsoft Corporation; the Boeing Company; Starbucks Coffee Company; U.S. Bank; Eddie Bauer, Inc.; Weyerhaeuser Corporation; Hewlett Packard Corporation; and Costco Wholesale. All of them had made five-figure contributions and more was coming in. The press establishment was also lined up in opposition. Virtually every major paper in the state opposed 200, and in the case of the *Seattle Times,* the editorial page condemnations of the measure were reinforced by full-page ads paid for by the Blethen Corporation, majority owner of the newspaper. Publisher Frank Blethen decided the issue was so important that he would risk some readers' criticizing him for overkill.

While Connerly and Carlson represented the affirmative side in public debates and on innumerable talk-show interviews, the opponents brought in dozens of big-name critics to reinforce their message. Vice President Al Gore; the Reverend Jesse L. Jackson Jr.; NAACP president Julian Bond; Arthur Fletcher, the former chairman of the federal Civil Rights Commission and the man widely credited with "inventing" affirmative action in the Nixon administration—all of them visited Seattle to raise money and rally the opposition. Retired General Colin L. Powell, the former chairman of the Joint Chiefs of Staff, said, "The language [of 200] is simple and elegant, but the results are diabolical. Affirmative action has a goal of helping to remove a contamination from this country. Three hundred years of white male preference are slowly being eroded away. My fear is that Initiative 200 would stop that progress."

Despite the formidable character of the opposition, both Connerly and Carlson told me they thought the California victory would be repeated—and that it would inspire similar legislation or initiatives across the country. "This is Gettysburg for them [the opponents]," Carlson said in our first interview. Connerly told me, "Victory here will reignite the movement and make this the national issue it should be."

Clearly Connerly had a lot of his own ego—as well as his organization's money—invested in 200. "This will end up being to a large extent a litmus test on Connerly," he told the *Seattle Times.* Michelle Ackermann, who ran the opposition campaign, complained to me that "Mr. Connerly basically came in here and bought the signatures to advance his personal political agenda." But when I talked to Connerly, he made it clear he was thinking in bigger terms than Washington state. "The Republican Party nationally has been very skittish on this issue," he said. "They are frightened of losing the minority vote—especially Hispanics. The Hispanic leaders tell them, 'The blacks had their turn [with affirmative action] and now it's our turn.' Republicans get scared, but if we win here, we will put a little spine in them." And he spoke scornfully of big-business opposition. "They are the real scaredy-cats," he said. "They're just deathly afraid that if they are accused of being against affirmative action, Jesse Jackson and the NAACP will put them on their hit list. But we're going to win without them."

One reason for the proponents' optimism was that they had won an important skirmish in the courts over the official ballot description of the initiative. Connerly wanted to use the exact words that had prevailed in California: "Shall government be prohibited from discriminating or granting preferential treatment based on race, sex, color, ethnicity, or national origin in public employment, education, and contracting?" Polls on both sides had shown that, phrased that way, most voters would say yes to a ban on preferences or any other form of discrimination. But the same polls showed substantial public support for affirmative action—which, to many people, meant no more than going beyond the "good old boy" network in filling jobs, handing out contracts, or putting together the freshman class. A *Seattle Times* survey in July showed the Connerly-Carlson language prevailing by a 64 percent to 25 percent margin. But when those same voters were told it would "effectively end affirmative action for women and minorities in state and local government, public education, and college admissions," the results were 49 percent yes and 35 percent no. The margin dropped from 39 points to 14. So the opponents sued to force the words *affirmative action* into the title—and lost.

Thus it was not a complete surprise to me when I made a return visit to Washington two weeks before the election and found high anxiety had infected the no-on-200 headquarters. Their first ad, using their strongest spokesman, Governor Locke, warning that 200 "is misleading and full of hidden consequences" and "will abolish affirmative action and hurt real people," had been running for ten days but private polls continued to show the initiative was likely to pass. Sue Tupper, the consultant for the opposition, conceded, "This is an uphill struggle for us."

In a state where 86 percent of the population is white, Michelle Ackermann said, it upset her that Connerly and Carlson "just want to talk about race. The fact is that the biggest beneficiaries of affirmative action in this state are white women." Connerly and Carlson were, in fact, playing good-cop-bad-cop with the race issue. In soft-focus, beautifully photographed "educational ads" paid for by Connerly's tax-exempt foundation, a black youngster was shown playing with a white friend. The white child asks, "Does it matter what color someone is? Should it matter?" Initiative 200, the narrator says, is about "bringing us together." Meantime, Carlson's committee, in its first ad, focused on the controversial case of Katuria Smith, a white woman who had fought her way out of poverty and a broken home to become the first member of her family to earn a college degree. Though she was an honors graduate of the University of Washington, she was refused admission to its law school. She said it was a case of reverse discrimination; the law school adamantly denied it, saying she had omitted pertinent information about her background on the application form. But the ad cut through all the controversies and asserted, "The UW law school rejected her. Why? She was white. Ninety percent of the blacks who enrolled had lower qualifications."

The opponents were desperately trying to rally women by making 200 a gender issue. At the end of the campaign, they did a mass mailing of a slick-paper flyer and put on a television ad aimed directly at women. Both electronic and print messages used Liz Pierini, the president of the state League of Women Voters, to claim that "I-200 will roll back the progress Washington state women have made towards pay equity. Women still make only 75 cents to every dollar that men make for the same work. By blindly abolishing all affirmative action in our state, I-200 will eliminate programs that have been successful in allowing women to gain the skills and knowledge to compete fairly in the workplace. I-200 would turn the clock back."

Carlson said that exaggerated claim was "a lie." "I-200 has no effect on private employers," he said, "and it explicitly bans governmental discrimination based on race or gender. Making claims like this shows just how desperate the opposition is."

When the results came in, Connerly's cause had triumphed by a 58 percent to 42 percent margin. On a day when Democrats were scoring electoral gains up and down the ballot, the initiative opposed by Governor Locke and his entire party leadership—to say nothing of the business establishment—prevailed in every county but one: Seattle's King County. Exit polls found that almost two thirds of the men supported 200, and—despite opponents' efforts to make it a gender issue—so did half the women who voted.

As always, there were disputes about how well the outcome of the up-or-down vote reflected the nuances of public opinion. A poll taken for the *Seattle Times* on the eve of the voting indicated that most voters understood the choices—at least in broad terms. The survey found that only 7 percent of those supporting 200 said they wanted affirmative action endorsed, and only 10 percent of the opponents of 200 said affirmative action should be eliminated. Pollster Stuart Elway said, "A plurality of both supporters and opponents favored reforming affirmative action. It became a question of how to achieve reform, and most voters felt that a vote for Initiative 200 was the way to do it."

But earlier in the year, four months before the voting, the same newspaper had conducted a poll that gave voters more precise choices. That survey found only 36 percent supported the state setting hiring quotas for minorities and women. But 44 percent supported set-asides of government contracts for companies owned by minorities and women. And 56 percent favored requiring recruitment of women and minorities for apprenticeship programs in skilled trades. Fully 62 percent endorsed programs for recruiting qualified women and minorities to increase diversity in public colleges. These distinctions were, of course, wiped away in the simple up-or-down vote.

Official figures showed that opponents had raised and spent $1,680,752, while Carlson's committee reported spending only $505,491. Frank Blethen's independent ad campaign in the *Seattle Times* was valued at $162,000—a figure not included in the opponents' total. On the yes side, Connerly's PAC, the American Civil Rights Coalition, was the biggest donor, with $264,000. But press reports said Connerly's tax-exempt American Civil Rights Institute spent an additional half-million dollars on its "educational ads." The state Public Disclosure Commission, deeming them political expenditures, demanded that Connerly identify the donors of that money, but he refused. A year later the dispute was still unresolved.

Another emotional issue was fought out in Michigan—the question of physician-assisted suicide. This too was a cause championed by a handful of people, not one that resulted from a great populist protest. Michigan, of course, is the home state of Dr. Jack Kevorkian, known to the tabloids as Dr. Death because he had made a career of escorting patients into the next world when they came to him seeking escape from painful or terminal illnesses. One such patient was Merian Frederick, an Ann Arbor civic activist and patron of the arts, who in 1989 contracted Lou Gehrig's disease, the progressive loss of nerve and muscle control, for which there is no known cure. Four years after the diagnosis, when she could no longer speak and could write only a few lines at a time, she persuaded close friends to take her to Kevorkian and his "death machine." He was acquitted of killing her at a trial in 1996, and that same year, a group of her Ann Arbor associates formed Merian's Friends, seeking to pass a voter initiative that would make it legal for patients with incurable illnesses to avail themselves of such help without putting their doctors or their families in jeopardy.

It took them a year to get the proposal written, and when the lawyers were finished, they had concocted a twelve-thousand-word behemoth, which revised many different sections of the

Michigan civil and criminal code. During that year, the Michigan legislature moved in exactly the opposite direction, enacting a criminal statute that closed the legal loopholes that had allowed Kevorkian to escape punishment in all three of the assisted-suicide cases on which he had been tried.

A month before the election, when I visited Michigan to report on the controversy, Merian's Friends knew they were in trouble. Edward C. Pierce, a retired physician and former state senator, who led the group, told me that their polling "shows support dropping significantly." They were out of money, having gone into debt in the process of qualifying the measure for the ballot. Although they had set out to collect through volunteers the quarter-million signatures they needed, they realized, Pierce said, that "we're too old. We couldn't do it." So they hired professionals, but as the deadline for filing the petitions came closer, the company kept boosting the price, eventually asking $1.50 per name. Pierce and others in their circle of academics and clergymen came up with $180,000 in personal loans to keep the effort going, and after surviving a challenge to the use of out-of-state circulators, they made the ballot.

But then the opposition swamped them. Organized as the Citizens for Compassionate Care, the coalition drew on the Michigan Catholic Conference; major Baptist, Lutheran, Christian Reformed, and Assembly of God churches; the Michigan State Medical Society, hospice groups, advocacy organizations for the elderly and the disabled, Right to Life of Michigan, the state Republican Party and its leader, Governor John Engler.

The proponents gained endorsements from former Republican Governor William Milliken and his wife, Helen, former United Auto Workers president Douglas Fraser, and several Democratic officials. But the campaign was one-sided. Final reports showed that Merian's Friends raised and spent $1,155,376, much of it just getting on the ballot, while the

Citizens for Compassionate Care had a budget of $5,299,603. The opposition's TV ads began right after Labor Day and were never answered. The ads left the moral and religious arguments to be made by priests and ministers in their churches and used the classic tactic of highlighting the most dramatic flaws in the complex initiative. One ad focused on the new state agency that would supervise the administration of lethal prescriptions, warning that a "costly new bureaucracy" would be created. Another targeted the provision requiring that the underlying disease—not the prescribed drugs—be listed as the cause of death. This proposal, the ad said, "would force doctors to lie." But the biggest opening was created by a provision specifying that physician-assisted suicide would be available not just to Michigan residents but to their close relatives in other states. With creepy organ music in the background, the ad opened with the theological question, "Where do we go when we die?" It ended with a photograph of a cemetery where all the headstones were engraved with the word *Michigan.* John Pirich, the Lansing election-law specialist who served as spokesman for the opposition campaign, told me, with just the slightest hint of irony, "Northwest will sell a lot of one-way tickets to Detroit if this passes."

It did not even come close, going down by a 70 percent to 30 percent margin. Pierce and his allies mustered only the puniest of efforts. They sent out mailings urging voters to "repeal the state's ban on letting patients control their last days. Show the dictators of pain and suffering in the legislature that you won't allow them to take these rights away from you." Kevorkian was an unspoken issue. The proponents' literature said that "Merian's Friends is not connected with Dr. Kevorkian and does not approve of his methods." Kevorkian, in fact, wanted no regulation by the state and would have chafed under the restrictions included in the initiative. But Pierce conceded, "A lot of the public thinks we are connected to him, even though we never have been." A year after the initiative failed, Kevorkian was tried again, under the statute the legislature had passed in 1998, and this time he went to jail.

At the height of the Populist movement, no one loomed larger than William Jennings Bryan of Nebraska, so it is no surprise that the initiative process is deeply embedded in the political culture of his old state. But a 1998 battle gave dramatic evidence of how the very groups who were the targets of Populist protest—bankers and big business—can attempt to use the mechanism for their own purposes.

Walter Scott Jr., is chairman emeritus of Peter Kiewit Sons, Inc., the Omaha-based construction giant whose worldwide projects produced annual revenues of more than $3 billion. When he calls a meeting, people who matter show up. Early in 1998 Scott called, and four dozen other CEOs of major banks and businesses responded to discuss what to do about the spending habits of the unicameral legislature sitting in Lincoln. While Nebraska enjoys a conservative reputation nationally and the sitting governor, Democrat Ben Nelson, was someone who described himself as "tight with a dollar," the business leaders saw things differently. They believed that the unicameral, nominally nonpartisan but controlled by Republicans, had been on a spending spree and Nelson had done nothing to stop it.

Bob Ball, a veteran of thirty-seven years of Navy service, who ran the Omaha Chamber of Commerce, soon brought it into line supporting the Scott group. Ball told me, "Our population has been absolutely stable at 1.6 million, but our state budget has been doubling every ten years. That is not sustainable. Businesses look at our budgets and taxes and decide to go elsewhere." The budget had in fact been growing at a compounded rate of almost 10 percent a year, jumping 12 percent in the most recent biennium. But state budget officials said the increase was the result of a bipartisan decision to shift part of the school financing burden from local property taxes to the more rapidly expanding state income and sales tax base.

In Nebraska, as elsewhere, education is by far the biggest item in the budget. In the previous decade, the state share of education spending rose from 24 percent to almost 50 percent. But property taxes, even after adjusting for inflation, still rose slightly. The result was that Nebraska ranked in the middle of the nation on its per capita tax burdens but slightly higher than some of its neighboring states. In 1997, with the economy flourishing, the legislature voted $110 million of increased aid to local governments for property tax relief and also approved a temporary half-cent cut in the 5 percent sales tax. It reduced the top income tax rate slightly to 6.99 percent. But none of these measures was enough to stem the tax revolt.

Over the years, the spending pattern had produced a genuinely populist protest through a grassroots organization called the Nebraska Taxpayers Association. Its leader was Ed Jaksha, a retired telephone company worker who, for almost half his eighty-three years, had been waging war on the politicians and lobbyists in Lincoln he blamed for raiding the voters' wallets. I met him at his favorite hangout, a fast-food restaurant on the western edge of Omaha. He recounted his long battle—marked by far more defeats than victories—and then marveled at how things had changed in this year. "I kept harassing Walter Scott and Bill Henry at First National Bank to put a stop to all this spending," he said. And when they decided enough was enough, "I'd have to say they have really taken the leadership. They loaned me the attorney to draft the petition" to put

Measure 413, an antitax initiative, on the ballot, "and of course they've raised the money for the campaign."

Indeed they did. The final financial report showed Kiewit-related companies and individuals had put up $724,000 of the record $4,726,562 spent by the Citizens for Nebraska's Future, the sponsor of Measure 413. Scott put in $80,000 of his own money. First National Bank contributed $230,000 and lent another $301,000. Conagra, the agribusiness giant, put in $235,000. Jaksha was named cochairman of the Citizens group, but instead of occupying the cheap storefront headquarters he had rented for his previous antitax campaigns, this campaign was run out of the Omaha Chamber of Commerce's downtown headquarters building, with the full panoply of campaign consultants and media advisers befitting a top-dollar operation. Jaksha told reporters, "All I can say is I'm grateful to these people for giving. They're risking their wealth—they didn't have to do it—and they're doing it because of principle."

The lawyers came up with a 3,525-word constitutional amendment that would limit annual state spending increases to the inflation rate multiplied by the growth in population or, for school districts, enrollment. It allowed the unicameral to suspend the limits for emergencies and to adjust spending upward for unfunded federal mandates. The measure said the limits could be overturned by popular referendum or, after a five-year moratorium, by a three-quarters vote of the legislature. Otherwise, any revenue accruing to the state beyond those spending limits would have to be returned to taxpayers in the following year by reducing sales and income tax rates.

Bob Ball told me that, though Ed Jaksha had failed often, this year would be different. "Ed never had the money to take on the biggest business in the state—the government. This year we've got it." The signature-gathering drive cost $1 million, a record for the state. Walter Scott wrote the other CEOs in his Business Leaders' Summit, asking them to follow his example and invite the paid petition-passers into their workplaces. No one questioned whether there might be unspoken pressure on the employees to help the boss's project.

The opposition was slow in organizing and never entirely overcame suspicions among its members. The Farm Bureau and the teachers' union, perhaps the two strongest lobbies in Lincoln, had often been at swords' points about the priority of school funding versus property tax relief. But eventually organizations representing farmers, teachers, senior citizens, and union members came together, arguing that Measure 413 would hurt the schools, weaken prospects for property tax relief, and funnel millions into the hands of its big-business backers. Chuck Hassebrook, program director of the Center for Rural Affairs, said at the news conference launching the opposition coalition, "This initiative is a brazen attempt by a small cadre of Nebraska's richest citizens to rig the constitution and democratic process to enable them to capture any tax relief resulting from economic growth."

Craig Christiansen, executive director of the Nebraska Education Association, became the coordinator of Nebraskans for a Good Life, as the opposition to 413 called itself, and used office space in his organization's Lincoln headquarters to house the effort. The cochairmen included Senator Bob Kerrey, a Democrat; Representative Bill Barrett, a Republican; Helen Boosalis, the former mayor of Lincoln and national chairwoman of the American Association of Retired Persons (AARP); and the heads of the Nebraska Farm Bureau Federation and the Nebraska Independent Bankers Association.

But the backers of 413 portrayed the opposition as an altogether different group. In a flyer sent to homes across the state by Citizens for Nebraska's Future, voters were invited to "look who's opposed to Amendment 413. Special Interests, lobbyists, and bureaucrats. Tax spenders, not taxpayers.... 413 is opposed by most of the 400 registered lobbyists who spend every day in the state capitol rotunda trying to convince the legislature to spend more money on their programs. None of these lobbyists represent Nebraska taxpayers."

Barrett's role in the opposition coalition was particularly significant. He had a solid conservative reputation as the congressman from the big western district, which was home to most of Nebraska's farmers. When he joined the opposition group, he told reporters, "I'm not opposed to tax relief and cutting spending, but it appears to me Measure 413 is going to end property tax relief"—an issue especially important to farmers.

Barrett's stance made life difficult for Mike Johanns, the mayor of Lincoln and the Republican nominee for governor. During a competitive, three-way Republican primary in the spring, Johanns joined his rivals in endorsing 413, then still in the signature-gathering stage. When he won the nomination, he wavered publicly but signed the petition on the final day it was on the streets. Less than a week later, he reversed himself and announced he would vote against it. His opponent, Democrat Bill Hoppner, had opposed the measure from the start and accused Johanns of calculating his position from the polls, which showed his candidacy needed shoring up in rural areas. Johanns replied, rather weakly, that it was not until the primary was out of the way that he had time really to study the measure. And, he said, he realized belatedly, "it has the potential for tearing this state apart."

The campaign on 413 was notable for its ferocity. The opponents were slow getting started, but when they hit, they hit hard. The education community, from the University of Nebraska down to local school boards and PTAs, denounced the measure as a threat to students. Nebraska University's president, L. Dennis Smith, activated its huge alumni network with warnings that the impact on their alma mater would be "devastating," that it would force big increases in tuition, and even threaten a shutdown of one of its four campuses.

The sponsors responded with an ad in which Kathleen McCallister, president of the elected state board of education, assured voters that "it won't hurt schools." But the polls showed support eroding. In the final round of ads, both sides resorted to graphic oversimplifications. The backers staged a scene with a giant red balloon inflating on the steps of the state capitol, symbolizing the expansion of state budgets. The narrator intoned, "For the last twenty years, lobbyists and politicians have been on a spending spree. And you're paying for it." In the final frames, the balloon explodes, sending shards across the landscape.

But that was nothing compared to the opposition ad. Christiansen had told me that "the issue is so complex and the promise of tax relief is so appealing that we need a powerful icon to combat it." They found one. In the closing ad, Measure 413 was depicted as a bottle of poison, complete with skull and crossbones. Swallow it and schools will shrivel, family farms be consumed by runaway property taxes, the message said. "It's not a tax lid. It's poison for Nebraska."

Ten days before the election, the *Omaha World-Herald,* the state's largest paper, ran a page-one story pointing out an apparent drafting error that could have the effect of holding down state aid to schools and local governments to a smaller percentage than overall state spending would be allowed to rise. On election day, the measure failed by a 36 percent to 64 percent margin. The Omaha business leaders dropped $4,726,562 in their losing effort. The opposition groups spent $1,013,769.

Of all the millionaire ventures into initiative politics in 1998, the most successful was engineered by a handful of wealthy men who set out to change the drug laws of five states. Operating as Californians for Medical Rights, they had come together first in 1996 when they financed a successful initiative that legalized the possession and use of marijuana for people who had a physician's prescription. Operating out of the same Santa Monica headquarters, but now expanding their target and calling themselves Americans for Medical Rights, they placed parallel initiatives on the ballots of five states—Alaska, Colorado, Nevada, Oregon, and Washington. An independent group submitted the same kind of initiative in the District of Columbia, and many of the same sponsors financed a much broader assault on the drug laws of Arizona.

I first came across the medical-marijuana folks in Oregon. Rick Bayer, a physician from Lake Oswego, said he had seen too many of his patients suffering from the effects of cancer, AIDS, or multiple sclerosis (MS), and from the debilitating nausea many of them experienced from the chemotherapy and medication that kept them alive. At the Veterans' Administration hospital where he had served his residency, he had witnessed how the experimental use of marijuana—sanctioned in government test programs—had relieved pain and nausea in similar patients. He and his wife, a cancer specialist, knew that some of their private patients had found illegal ways of obtaining—or growing—marijuana to cope with their own symptoms. But he said, "I share their indignation at being called criminals for using a God-given, natural herb."

Dr. Bayer had enlisted a compelling spokeswoman in his cause. Stormy Ray was a forty-three-year-old computer artist and MS patient, who had been using illegally grown marijuana to cope with her disease. Maintaining that she would be bedridden were it not for the drug, she said, "I don't think patients should have to be exposed to the underworld to get their medicine."

I quickly learned this was no amateur venture but part of a well-coordinated and richly financed effort organized by three men who had convinced themselves that the national "war on drugs" was a dreadful mistake in policy. The best-known of the trio was New York financier George Soros, who had made a fortune in currency trading and whose charitable projects included the revival of democratic institutions and a free press in the central European states of the former Soviet Union and the promotion of campaign-finance reform in the United States. His partners were Peter B. Lewis, head of the Cleveland-based Progressive Corporation, one of the country's largest auto insurers, and Phoenix entrepreneur John Sperling. Dave Fratello, the spokesman for Americans for Medical Rights, told me, "The goal is to change national policy, but we know we will have to win more battles in the states in 1998, 1999, and 2000 before that happens."

The Arizona project was different from—and broader than—the initiatives in the five other states and the District of Columbia. The leader there was John Sperling, president of the Apollo Group, Inc., which owns, among other businesses, the for-profit University of Phoenix, with twenty-three campuses in thirteen states and 61,000 students. With support from Soros and Lewis, he launched the Drug Medicalization, Prevention, and Control initiative, which Arizona voters approved by a margin of 65 percent to 35 percent in 1996. The three men personally contributed more than 75 percent of the

$1,575,017 spent on the initiative, with most of the rest coming from foundations in which they had influence. That measure, in addition to legalizing marijuana prescriptions, provided that instead of jail, the first two convictions for drug possession would result in probation and participation in a drug treatment or education program.

When I met with Sperling and his allies in 1998, he told me he believed the federal "war on drugs" was fatally flawed, that it was ineffective and biased—with sanctions being enforced against poor people and racial minorities. "You might as well call it class war," he said. Sperling enlisted significant bipartisan support. Marvin S. Cohen, the chairman of the Civil Aeronautics Board during the Carter administration, and John Norton, a deputy secretary of agriculture in the Reagan years, endorsed and raised money for the initiative. But the most important endorsement came from former Senator Dennis DeConcini, who had served three terms and was one of the best-known politicians in the state. Sperling told me that he had assembled ten years' worth of clippings in a thick scrapbook and given it to Dino DeConcini, the former senator's brother, with a request that he pass it along. Sperling then met with Dennis DeConcini for half a day to argue through all the issues that had made DeConcini a hawk on the drug issue during his Senate career. He achieved a complete conversion. In a TV commercial, DeConcini told voters, "As a former prosecutor and U.S. senator, I've spent my life fighting against drugs, and I can tell you that the Drug Medicalization Act will strengthen our drug policy."

The ads in the 1996 initiative campaign stressed a provision requiring those convicted of violent crimes while under the influence of drugs to serve their full sentences, without any possibility of parole. The ads also argued that clearing prisons of people convicted of simple possession would save money and make space for hardened criminals, who ought to be behind bars.

What was not revealed either in the ads or in the news coverage of the initiative was that it applied to 116 other "Schedule I" drugs, including LSD, heroin, and PCP. That was not a mistake in drafting. When I interviewed Sperling in 1998, he said, "We want to medicalize all of them—and not be namby-pamby." The opposition campaign, led by local law-enforcement officials, raised little money and never got on television, though they did obtain a letter signed by former Presidents George Bush, Jimmy Carter, and Gerald Ford opposing the initiative. But, as Senator Jon (CQ) Kyl, the Republican who succeeded DeConcini when he retired in 1994, told me, the opposition never really mobilized, because no one took charge. "When it's everybody's responsibility, it's nobody's responsibility."

When the full import of the initiative was discovered after the 1996 election, the political reaction was swift. State Representative Mike Gardner, the Republican chairman of the House Judiciary Committee, met with his Senate counterpart and they quickly drafted and passed two bills. One ordered jail time for anyone convicted of possession who refused treatment. The other suspended medical use of any of the 117 drugs—including marijuana—until it was approved by Congress or the Food and Drug Administration—neither of which was likely to happen.

Sperling and his allies struck back. Renaming themselves The People Have Spoken coalition, they quickly collected the signatures to force Gardner's two bills to referendum in November 1998. Their campaign bypassed the underlying drug issue and cast the choice as "the people versus the politicians." One of their ads asserted that the 1996 initiative "received approval of 65 percent of Arizonans. But that didn't stop the politicians from gutting it. They had the nerve to say that voters were ignorant." Voting against the repeal measures in the upcoming referendum "will let the politicians know that we're smarter than they think."

Once again it was a spending mismatch. The People Have Spoken coalition reported spending $1,618,640, while their opponents spent only $67,322. In 1996 retired General Barry R. McCaffrey, director of the White House Office of National Drug Control, had stumped against the initiatives passed in California and Arizona. But in 1998 he stayed in Washington, D.C., because he had been persuaded that there had been a backlash against White House interference in the first round of voting. His aides distributed talking points to community anti-drug coalitions and urged newspapers in the six states with drug measures on the ballot to editorialize against them. The position papers they sent out argued that other, legal drugs can meet the medical needs of cancer and AIDS patients, and urged that marijuana not be legalized, at least until the Food and Drug Administration and the Institute of Medicine completed ongoing studies of its safety and effectiveness. But McCaffrey's efforts had little impact.

Then the Arizona battle escalated beyond the drug issue. Angry at the legislature's meddling with his first initiative, Sperling and his allies filed a second initiative for the 1998 ballot—a constitutional amendment called the Voter Protection Act, barring future legislatures from making anything more than technical changes in voter-approved measures, and requiring a three-fourths majority even for those. The legislature replied with a countermeasure that would sunset all initiatives after five years and permit substantive amendments by a two-thirds vote.

The result was a rout by Sperling and Co. The Voter Protection Act passed by a 52 percent to 48 percent margin. The countermeasure offered by the legislature failed by 45 percent to 55 percent. And the referendum on the bill repealing their 1996 initiative failed by 43 percent to 57 percent. Three for three for the millionaires.

The narrower medical marijuana measures also passed in four other states. The majorities for approval ranged from 59 percent in Alaska, Nevada, and Washington to 55 percent in Oregon. The Colorado initiative carried by a narrow 51 percent majority, but a judge ruled belatedly that it should not have been on the ballot because insufficient signatures had been collected. The prospect that it had also passed in Washington, D.C., led conservatives in Congress to add an amendment to the appropriations bill for the District of Columbia, barring the use of any funds for counting the initiative ballots—a response that the proponents condemned. It was not until September of 1999 that the courts ruled Congress had overstepped its bounds, and ordered the ballots counted. To no one's surprise, the initiative had passed by a margin of 69 percent to 31 percent.

In almost every state, Americans for Medical Rights found a local version of Stormy Ray—someone who could tell a compelling story of the humane benefits of medical marijuana. A flyer in Nevada, for example, featured Ginny Kochan. The text read: "Ginny Kochan is a nurse. Having raised her children in the 1970s, she has always been opposed to drugs. But when her husband was dying of cancer earlier this year, she watched helplessly as he suffered, unable to gain relief from a litany of painkillers. Then, at age 74, out of desperation, he tried medical marijuana—and it worked. Now Ginny has studied Ballot Question 9 and she wants Nevadans to understand one more thing: It's only for patients. If you're not suffering from a debilitating illness such as cancer, AIDS, or glaucoma, then you cannot use medical marijuana."

In the aftermath, Representative Gardner complained to me, "The initiative was part of our constitution when we became a state, because it was supposed to offer people a way of overriding special-interest groups. But it's turned one-hundred-eighty degrees and now the special-interest groups use the initiative process for their own purposes." Referring to Soros, who with a $50,000 gift was the largest individual contributor to the Arizona Clean Election initiative, in addition to helping Sperling on the drug referendum, Gardner asked, "Why should a New York millionaire be writing the laws in Arizona?"

When I relayed this question to Soros in a phone interview, he replied, "I live in one place, but I consider myself a citizen of the world. I have foundations in thirty countries, and I believe certain universal principles apply everywhere—including Arizona."

Chapter 5

LAWS WITHOUT GOVERNMENT

The spectacle of three millionaires rewriting the laws of five states—including Oregon—is a far cry from what William U'Ren had in mind when he imported the initiative process from Switzerland and installed it in Oregon a century ago. The question that remains to be discussed in this chapter is whether the initiative process as it actually operates today serves the public interest or subverts it.

I found a fierce debate on that issue flourishing in Oregon—in part because no other state has used the initiative process more frequently than Oregon in the last two decades. Its voters found a total of ninety-seven initiatives on the ballots between 1978 and 1998—an average of almost nine per election cycle. In the last three cycles, the average jumped to fourteen.

Proponents of the initiative process told me that it is under perpetual threat from its enemies in the legislature and the business-political establishment. The Oregon Coalition for Initiative Rights includes in its leadership two men from opposite political poles. Lloyd Marbet is a bearded, self-described hippie who has spent his adult years fighting public utilities and power companies over nuclear plants and rate issues. His greatest victory came when he and his allies forced the shutdown of the Trojan nuclear power plant. To his mind, "business interests control the legislature, lock, stock, and barrel." Lon Mabon, his partner in the proinitiative coalition, is a conservative Christian activist who heads the Oregon Citizens Alliance (OCA). During the 1990s, his group has promoted initiatives to ban abortion and block ordinances guaranteeing rights for homosexuals.

When I interviewed them in 1998, both men were feeling particularly embattled. Mabon had failed to qualify either an antiabortion measure or one writing the definition of the traditional family into the state constitution and had even spoken, briefly, of disbanding his organization. He blamed part of the problem on an aggressive campaign by the Oregon Employment Division to force firms that use paid signature gatherers to treat them as employees, not independent contractors. Requiring the firms to pay the minimum wage and unemployment insurance and workers' compensation taxes for the people with clipboards made it markedly more expensive to get the signatures. Marbet and Mabon claimed the measure was a form of harassment by the state, and Marbet said it was having "a real chilling effect."

1998 also saw the state supreme court invalidate a voter-approved anticrime initiative and set forth an extension of the single-subject rule that would make it much harder to amend the Oregon constitution. The court said the anticrime initiative amended two separate sections of the Oregon constitution and should have been split before being presented to the voters. Kevin Mannix of Salem, the principal sponsor of the overturned initiative, pointed out that this was the fifth time in just three years that the state's highest court had found reason to upset a voter-approved initiative. But he vowed to keep fighting. With help from Loren Parks, a millionaire businessman, who put up $85,000 to collect the signatures, Mannix tried to place an initiative on the November 1998 ballot to increase sentences for property crimes, but failed. The number of signatures he filed was "on the cusp" of meeting the minimum requirement, but by the time the courts and the secretary of state's office had agreed on a ruling, it was too late to qualify. Mannix, whose four-term legislative career was short of notable achievements and who failed to win nomination for attorney general, told me he was a fervent advocate of the process he used so often. "If you have a heartfelt issue that can engender a lot of public support, it can't be hacked to death by special interests the way it can in the legislature," he said. Parks, who in 1996 put more than three quarters of a million dollars into signature-gathering drives, told the *Oregonian* that the initiative process "is the only thing we have to protect ourselves from the abuses of big government. I hate to see people taken advantage of by shyster lawyers, crooks, and smooth-talking, conniving politicians."

Petition passers for a wide range of Oregon issues were also involved in a long series of court cases, pitting them against chain-store owners and shopping-center managers who tried to keep the signature gatherers off their property. Those actions, along with the dozens of bills regulating or restricting the initiative process that had been introduced in the legislature, angered the initiative-rights folks. Mabon told me the critics of initiatives were as relentless as they were misguided. They don't realize, he said, the initiative process "is a safety valve" that helps preserve the other governing institutions. "Powerful groups have great influence in our legislature," he said. "'Good old boy' clubs develop and the average citizen feels left out. With the initiative, if you've got a gripe, you can get access. You don't have to take up arms."

That view was flatly contradicted by others I interviewed. "The more you substitute a plebiscite for the checks and balances of the legislative process, the more you run afoul of the fundamental idea of our Constitution," University of Oregon president David Frohnmayer told me. "In three terms in the legislature, I never saw a vote change hands for money. But the gambling interests came in here, spent $184,000, and bought themselves a lottery off which they've made millions."

Frohnmayer, a former Republican state attorney general, lamented that "initiative battles totally overshadow legislative elections." He argued that initiatives that limit taxes without cutting spending or that mandate spending without providing revenue "usurp the role of the legislature and governor in managing the ledger of state government. It especially diminishes the role of the legislature as the central instrument of government. And that is bad for democracy." Frohnmayer said the initiative, as originally conceived, may have had virtues, but when the courts upheld the use of paid signature gatherers, "that was the beginning of the end. It's no longer citizens fighting the oligopoly. Now it's the oligopoly paying people to act as citizens." As if that were not enough, he said, "Initiative campaigns enhance the new tribalism in our politics. It's an up-or-down choice between extremes, all-or-nothing, take-no-prisoners deal. I have no idea how we're supposed to live together in a civil society with a system like that. It plagues us."

Inevitably, much of the debate comes down to a struggle between legislatures and citizens. It was not an accident that the most popular initiative issue in the last two decades has been term limits. Voters used the initiative to limit the tenure of their representatives in eighteen of the twenty-four initiative states. And it is equally no accident that Colorado, the first state to pass term limits, also has produced more legislation aimed at limiting the use of the initiative than any other. The anger of veteran legislators at having their tenure cut short spawned bill after bill—including the law invalidated by the Supreme Court in 1998 which would have required signature gatherers to wear name tags and be registered voters. Mike Arno, head of one of the major California signature-gathering firms, told me that the year after the term-limits initiative passed in his state, "there were forty-four bills put in the legislature to severely alter or completely destroy the initiative process." None, however, passed.

In an amicus brief filed with the Supreme Court in the Colorado case, the Initiative and Referendum Institute documented the charge that "state legislators regularly restrict, rather than facilitate, the people's right, in their respective states, to exercise the initiative and referendum process. Indeed, not a single example of truly facilitating legislation has ever been enacted by state legislatures." In 1998 the U.S. Term Limits Foundation showed the wide sweep of the battleground in a report titled, "The Empire Strikes Back: A History of Political and Judicial Attacks on Term Limits." The author, Marta Hummel, wrote that "officials at every level and branch of the government have actively sought to prevent term-limits measures from being voted upon, sued the initiatives after becoming law, and attempted to alter term-limits laws in the backrooms of state capitols.... Through lawsuits and legislative sleight of hand, the governing elite has demonstrated that the perpetuation of its own power is more important than addressing the people's repeated calls for reform." Between 1990 and 1998, she said, thirty-seven lawsuits were filed in twenty states seeking to block or invalidate term-limits measures.

Nonetheless, she concluded, "eighteen state legislatures, thirty-nine governors, and nearly three thousand local officials now serve under term limits."

Not everyone is as enthusiastic about that result as Hummel and her allies in the term-limits movement. Some think it has crippled the legislatures. As Hans Linde, a former Oregon Supreme Court justice, said, "When legislators are relatively anonymous and term-limited, they cannot display any leadership profile of their own. In states like ours, the major policy changes are now made by initiative. The only thing left for the legislature are the marginal adjustments that are of more interest to the lobbyists than to the citizens."

Alan Rosenthal, professor of political science at the Eagleton Institute of Politics at Rutgers University and probably the leading academic scholar of state legislatures, wrote in the August 1999 issue of *State Legislatures* magazine that continuity is an important ingredient in the successful functioning of those institutions. "Some continuity of membership and staff not only provides for greater knowledge and skill on the parts of lawmakers, but it promotes institutional values," he wrote. "Continuity does not require extremely low turnover of membership, but only that some members serve for a decent period of time. By requiring that everyone turn over with relatively brief regularity and by discouraging legislators from identifying with an institution they are passing through, term limits run counter to institutional continuity. The eighteen states that currently limit terms are at a disadvantage when it comes to having a good legislature."

In that same issue, Rich James, a staff member of the National Conference of State Legislatures, said it is likely that "those states that currently have an active initiative process, such as California, Oregon, and Colorado, will use the Internet to promote direct democracy. It is also likely that this form of cyberdemocracy will be used in these states to limit legislative powers by adopting limits on spending and taxing, directives to spend money on certain activities or changes in the legislative process. These actions may influence other states to try more forms of direct democracy and to use them to limit legislative powers."

When I talked to leaders of the legislatures in states with the initiative process, some seemed sanguine with that prospect—while others clearly viewed it with alarm.

John Donso, the Republican minority leader in the North Dakota house, strongly supported the initiative process, saying it had "made the legislature more responsive," without weakening its legitimacy in the eyes of the public. The main impact in his state, he said, has been to restrain the lawmakers from raising taxes, except on gasoline, since 1989.

Initiative petitions are still circulated by volunteers, Donzo said, and expenditures are modest. When national term-limits groups moved in to try to pass an initiative, the legislature responded with a counterinitiative extending the terms of house members from two years to four. "Not only did we clobber the term limits, we actually passed our own," Donso said. "People in North Dakota trust the legislature."

California state senator Jim Costa, a veteran of eighteen years in the assembly and state senate, drew quite a different picture. After praising the populist origins of the initiative process, Costa, a Democrat, said, "In the last twenty years, it has run amok. It has become a multimillion-dollar cottage industry. It's been used by special-interest groups to raise money for their organizations and expand their membership bases. Several of my colleagues have used it to attach their careers to the rising popularity of the initiative process. Tom Hayden tried to do that with the Big Green environmental initiative. Tom Campbell pushed the blanket-ballot initiative because he couldn't get past the right wing in a Republican Senate primary, so he wanted the independents to be able to vote in the primary. I view it as a form of blackmail—pass my bill or I'll take it to initiative."

Ken Gordon, the Democratic minority leader of the Colorado house, offered a more nuanced view. Gordon, blocked four years in a row on his efforts to get campaign-finance legislation through the legislature, joined the League of Women Voters in sponsoring an initiative that received 66 percent of the vote. He sees it as a way to bypass the roadblocks that are erected when incumbents bring their own special interests to bear on a piece of legislation, as they did with campaign-finance legislation.

But Gordon is anything but an enthusiast for the initiative. He supported the bill requiring signature gatherers to wear name tags—the restriction the Supreme Court found unconstitutional in 1999. He said the initiative is appropriate for "simple issues" but not for writing tax law or other complex legislation. "In the legislative process," he said, "you learn a lot as you go along. It's a deliberative process. You can amend and improve a bill. You can't do that with an initiative."

Some advocates of the initiative process have a direct financial interest in protecting it. The busiest practitioner in Oregon in recent years has been Bill Sizemore. As head of Oregon Taxpayers United (OTU), he and his group passed a series of tax-limitation measures in the 1990s. Eyebrows were raised when, in 1998, official disclosure forms showed that a company created by Sizemore, called I & R Petition Services, Inc., had been paid $154,675 by OTU for work on qualifying the initiative ending the state checkoff of political dues for public-employee unions. The report said Sizemore's company paid out about two thirds of the money to a firm that actually collected the signatures and retained $51,707 for his own services in promoting the initiative.

I found no current officeholder in either party in Oregon—or, for that matter, any of the other states I covered in 1998—who argued for abolishing the initiative. Governor John Kitzhaber said, "The process is a blessing, but the way it's being used is a curse. With paid signature gatherers, it means anyone can buy access to the ballot." Kitzhaber said that the lack of legal review by the attorney general, the legislature, or the courts before initiatives go on the ballot "means there are often unintended consequences. It's extraordinarily easy to amend the constitution, and the way that is being used is very detrimental. It reduces complex issues to sound bites and the question of who has the most money."

Phil Keisling, until recently the Oregon secretary of state, who administers elections and deals directly with initiative promoters, is ambivalent about the process but says it has more pluses than minuses. "I'd rather live in a state with the process than without," he said. "I think, over the years, it's probably done more good than harm." But he has reservations. The 1996 Oregon ballot, which included sixteen voter-sponsored initiatives, six others referred by the legislature, and one referendum, was too much of a good thing, he said. "The initiative process is like 190-proof alcohol," he said. "A little goes a long way." The voters' pamphlet, containing explanations of all these measures and paid advertisements from backers and opponents, ran 248 pages. "It was almost as long as *War and Peace,*" Keisling remarked at the time, "but with less of a discernible plot." Ralph Nader replied, with not the slightest trace of humor, that "one would think that a day or two a year reading the ballot booklet, asking some questions, and then going and voting is not too much of a burden for people who count among their midst millions of Americans who spend twenty-five hours a week watching television."

As secretary of state, Keisling sponsored legislation to raise the number of signatures required for initiatives that would amend the state constitution—but it went nowhere. He also railed against what he called "the bounty system" of paying petition-passers on a per-signature basis, claiming the practice led to fraud. But that effort, too, was thwarted. "We've had many bills to change the process," Keisling told me, "but none has passed. The legislators know what low regard the voters have for them, and a vote that can be characterized as anti-initiative would hurt them in the next election." Because he was stymied in the legislature, Keisling used the authority of his office to organize an ad hoc committee of former law-school deans, who analyze the legal and constitutional implications of ballot measures. Their views—a prescreening device without force of law—are included as paid ads in the ballot pamphlet.

In every state where polling numbers are available, the initiative process is enormously popular with the voters. In mid-1999, Rasmussen Research surveyed a five-hundred-person sample of Washington state voters and found the initiative favored by 84 percent, while only 8 percent wanted it eliminated. The Field Institute did a comprehensive survey in California in 1997, and those results reflect broader currents of opinion. By a margin of 74 percent to 7 percent, voters said ballot propositions were a good thing, not a bad thing. That was down slightly from a similar question in 1979—the year after Prop. 13 was approved—when the margin of approval was 83 percent to 4 percent. But it is still an overwhelming endorsement. A follow-up question found that 59 percent of those surveyed said the initiatives "reflect the concerns of organized special-interest groups" and only 19 percent said they reflect the concerns of the average voter. Only two out of five said they know what interest groups are supporting or opposing initiatives most or all of the time. More than three quarters of the voters favored spending limits on initiative campaigns, and nearly as many would require sponsors to submit initiatives to the secretary of state for review and comment on their clarity and conformity to present law, before the signature gathering begins. But they overwhelmingly opposed letting the legislature amend initiatives after they have been passed. A survey taken in the same year by another firm, Charlton Research, found that 51 percent of California voters cited initiatives as the main reason for voting in 1996, compared to 36 percent who said the presidential contest was the principal motivator.

There is no shortage of ideas on how to improve the system. In 1996 the City Club of Portland prepared an extensive report on the process, which noted that the increasing number of ballot initiatives—particularly constitutional amendments—was a matter of concern, and so was the increasing role of money. Measured in constant 1988 dollars, it said, the cost per ballot measure jumped from $50,000 in 1970 to $900,000 per measure in 1990. There was a lack of deliberation in the process, the report said, and too much oversimplified sloganeering. It cited specifics.

"In 1990," it said, "Ballot Measure 5, a proposal to limit property taxes, affected hundreds of thousands of homeowners, created a new demand upon state revenue of more than a billion dollars annually by 1995–96, and substantially affected the funding of local government and public schools. It went on the ballot lacking a fiscal impact statement."

"Ballot Measure 11 in 1994," the report continued, "contained a series of mandatory sentences to prison for certain offenses, exceeding sentencing guidelines approved by the 1989 and 1991 legislatures. The measure had the effect of doubling the number of prison beds required by 2001, with an estimated fiscal impact of $461,800,000 for construction and annual increased operating costs of $101,000,000 by 2001, and an estimated requirement of an additional 3,000 beds between 2001 and 2005, for which no further cost estimate was provided."

The Oregon voters' pamphlet is regarded as the most reliable source of information on initiatives, but the report pointed out that anyone can buy an ad in the pamphlet for $300 and "there are no procedures for screening purchased arguments for accuracy. A totally false statement of fact... can be published with no opportunity for rebuttal in the pages of the pamphlet."

The City Club recommended several changes: Initiative amendments to the Oregon constitution should relate only to the structure and organization of government and not be used to limit or dedicate revenue or impose other fiscal policy. Those initiative amendments should go first to the legislature for consideration and only then be submitted to the people. And when submitted, they should require a three-fifths supermajority for passage. Similar restrictions on statutory initiatives were also recommended, but as yet none has been passed. In 1996 the Oregon League of Women Voters framed a somewhat similar set of recommendations but went further in one respect by saying that, in its view, the state constitution should not be amendable by initiative.

In California—the biggest state with the initiative process—the bipartisan, private Commission on Campaign Financing published a comprehensive report in 1992 on the use and abuse of the initiative. Its main recommendations were designed to make the initiative process subject to more of the checks and balances of normal legislation and to help voters understand what they were being asked to decide.

The commission would have required the Fair Political Practices Commission, a state agency, to hold a public hearing on the merits of any initiative that had gathered a quarter of the signatures needed to qualify; required the legislature to hold a public hearing on each initiative within ten days of its qualifying; allowed proponents to amend the initiative after the legislative hearing; created a forty-five-day "cooling-off" period in which the initiative sponsors and the legislature could negotiate compromise legislation; allowed the legislature to enact the initiative during those forty-five days and the sponsor to remove it from the ballot; and required the legislature to vote on any initiative reaching the ballot, and the secretary of state to publicize in the voters' pamphlet each legislator's vote. It also would have required amendments to the state constitution to receive a 60 percent supermajority or a majority vote in two successive elections, and it would have permitted the legislature to amend statutory initiatives with a similar 60 percent majority vote.

To help the voters, it would have limited the length of initiatives; improved financial reporting, including disclosure of principal sponsors in the ads; and made the voters' pamphlet more reader friendly. As things stand, the report said, too many initiatives smack of "drunken drafting," and baffle the voters. And the exclusion of the legislature from any meaningful part in the initiative process makes "many initiative proponents view the legislature as irrelevant or hostile and ignore it altogether." The Commission report is a catalog of the system's shortcomings: "Qualification by signature petition is too easy with money and too difficult without.... One-sided and deceptive media campaigns distort election outcomes.... High spending dominates the elections." It documented the domination of money more thoroughly than any other report I read. In 1990 exactly two thirds of the total contributions to initiative campaigns came in amounts of $100,000 or more. And a nearly identical percentage came from business.

Notwithstanding all of that, the report said the governmental shortcomings that gave birth to the initiative "still exist," with elected officials subject to pressure from their contributors and "reluctant to develop bold new policy initiatives" that might upset the status quo.

Nothing came of these recommendations. So it was not surprising that a twenty-three-member California constitutional revision commission, created in 1993 by Governor Pete Wilson and the legislature and urged to be "bold and creative" in its thinking, came back in 1996 with an exceedingly modest set of proposed changes in the initiative process: First, except in rare circumstances, proposed constitutional amendments should appear on the November ballot—not in primaries or special elections. Second, it proposed that after six years, the legislature be allowed to amend statutory initiatives. Finally, it urged that after an initiative has qualified for the ballot, the legislature would have an opportunity to hold hearings on it and propose technical or clarifying amendments to it. The sponsors could, if they wished, incorporate those changes in the version submitted to the voters. Modest though they were, none of these suggestions was adopted.

It is not just academics and blue-ribbon citizens' panels who recommend reforms in the initiative system. I found that many of the practitioners had their own agendas for changes. Fred Kimball, the current-generation dean of California-initiative-petition signature collectors, finds it frustrating to "go through all of the work of qualifying an initiative for the ballot and getting it passed," only to see it thrown out by the courts. "I'd like to see some form of judicial or constitutional review before it gets on the ballot." Angelo Paparella of Progressive Campaigns said he wanted the requirement that petition circulators be registered voters removed. It "doesn't make any sense," he said, "to have a voter's signature invalidated just because the person who handed you the board happens not to be a registered voter." The tedious process of validating signatures, not only by name but by address, also needs reexamination, he said. "If your signature matches what's on file with the voter registration folks, that signature ought to count. You shouldn't be disempowered because you moved and forgot to put down the old address. It makes no sense to me." Ken Masterton, another California signature gatherer, said he favored a requirement that TV commercials on initiatives "have to disclose who the big financial backers are. If the voters know it's from the trial lawyers or the timber industry or the Sierra Club, it's a real important piece of information."

Thomas Hiltachk, the Sacramento initiative lawyer, said he would like to be able to edit the often lengthy documents between the time they are circulated and the date they go on the ballot. "If somebody points out something that you hadn't noticed before, everyone would be better served if you could fix that along the way." Hiltachk also favors tightening the single-subject rule, which applies in California and many other states but is open to interpretation. Often, he said, the backers "try to put too much in there. If they were more focused, you'd get a better product and the voters would have a better sense of what they're voting on."

A modest set of changes was proposed by T. Anthony Quinn, a political scientist and a successful campaign consultant in Sacramento. In a report for the California Chamber of Commerce, Quinn suggested that business ought to look for ways to reduce the cost and frequency of initiative campaigns. He pointed out that California businesses had spent more than $119 million between 1990 and 1996 to defeat a dozen initiatives sponsored by environmentalists, trial lawyers, health care advocates, and other liberal groups. Quinn said business should support higher signature thresholds for qualifying initiatives, raising the state fee for filing initiatives, introducing attorney general opinions on the constitutionality of proposed initiatives, and allowing time for constitutional review and possible action by the legislature before the voters pass judgment.

The Supreme Court, in a series of cases, has made it virtually impossible to limit spending on, or contributions to, initiative campaigns, and, as we have seen, it has upheld the use of paid signature gatherers. Nonetheless, these ideas and others continue to draw support in public-opinion polls. A 1995 Oregon survey found 95 percent approval of tougher, faster financial disclosure; 78 percent support for requiring the attorney general to review each measure and provide an opinion on its constitutionality; 68 percent support for increasing the number of signatures required to place a constitutional amendment on the ballot; and 62 percent support for banning paid signature gatherers. On the other hand, 59 percent opposed letting the legislature decide which issues get on the ballot. And when it came to an actual vote in Oregon on a measure that would have made it more difficult to qualify ballot measures by requiring that a proportional number of signatures be obtained in each of the five congressional districts, Marbet and Mabon and their allies were able to defeat it by an eight-point margin.

Oregon provided the most passionate arguments for and against the initiative process I found anywhere. Gregory Kafoury, a lawyer who worked with Marbet and the Coalition for Initiative

Rights, gave me a speech he had delivered in February 1998 at an initiative symposium at Willamette University Law School. "In our nation," he said, "we see the Congress, the presidency, the state legislatures, largely bought and paid for.... Does anyone think in a hundred years that the Oregon legislature would have taken on the Trojan nuclear plant?... Whereas we need people who can rip and tear and fight, we are getting a bunch of very polite cowards in the next generation. Worthless.... So what the hell is the liberal answer to this? Well, we will destroy the initiative process.... A good liberal solution. That is what this conference is all about."

After speaking scornfully of legislative efforts to make it more cumbersome and expensive to qualify initiatives, Kafoury demanded, "What kind of future do we want? Do we want a future where guys like Lloyd Marbet can make a difference? Can be players? Can have their cause and their blunt pencil and change the world? Or do we want those blue suits in a big room, everybody on a payroll, to decide what our fate will be? The human fate. You tell me. What side are you on?"

An equally passionate reply came from Hans A. Linde, a retired justice of the Oregon Supreme Court now teaching at Willamette Law School. His tone was more scholarly, but the bite was equally strong. Decrying what he called "lawmaking without government," the liberal jurist said the time has come "to reexamine the rhetorical premise on which the Populists and Progressives built lawmaking by plebiscite."

"Unlike legislators," he said, "individual voters are under no obligation to vote on any particular ballot measure, or to vote at all.... An act of 'the people' is always the act of some changing fraction of the people, often a small fraction.... Representative lawmakers, too, are elected by changing fractions of all eligible voters. But there is a crucial difference. The self-selected lawmakers who vote on initiatives do not and cannot claim to represent anyone but themselves. They are entitled, and they are likely, to vote for or against a measure because they have a personal interest in it. In contrast... once elected, no matter by how many votes, legislators are bound to represent all the inhabitants of their districts, and collectively of the whole state, voters and nonvoters, supporters and opponents, old, young, even the yet unborn. Legislators publicly proclaim those dual responsibilities and accept the obligation to explain their acts, whatever local or special interests they in fact favor, as good public policy for the state."

Linde argued that the initiative process, far from promoting the public interest, was inherently tailored to private, personal interests. "There is a difference between deciding to reduce taxes on one's constituents and deciding to reduce taxes on oneself," he said. "In lawmaking by plebiscite, no retired homeowner is obliged to weigh the needs of, or to represent, the children who live in the next block; no urban weekend camper needs to consider the jobs of loggers; no logger, those of fishermen. Indeed, the arguments made to the voters, especially on fiscal ballot measures, explicitly urge them to weigh their personal costs and benefits, complete with charts of taxes saved or services reduced.... No lobbyist's testimony could appeal to the personal (as distinct from the electoral) self-interest of legislative committee members in the crass and simplistic terms routinely addressed to the voter as personal lawmaker."

And the jurist-professor said there was a third difference that reflected adversely on the initiative process. "Votes on ballot measures are cast in isolation, in carefully guarded privacy, and without obligation to hear anyone else or explain one's vote to anyone—in short, in a carefully constructed antithesis to the public process of making collective public decisions in the public interest, and in antithesis, also, to the New

England town meetings that are falsely held up as models for modern plebiscites."

Linde concluded that "these criticisms strike at the central theory of direct lawmaking.... If self-selected and secret voting on ballot measures is self-regarding and nonrepresentative in principle... this would seem to invalidate all such participation in lawmaking." But even he was not willing to go that far. So he conceded that "initiatives can survive for most purposes, if a state's citizens so wish," but argued that they should not be used as casually as they are for amending state constitutions. He argued, but so far to no avail, that the Supreme Court decision refusing to find that state initiatives were incompatible with the clause of the Constitution guaranteeing each state the republican form of government should not inhibit state courts from examining that issue for themselves. Especially, he said, the use of the initiative to insert fiscal rules in state constitutions beyond review or alteration by the legislatures cries out for scrutiny by the courts.

When it comes to evaluating the initiative process, I believe there are two different sets of criteria to apply. The first asks: Are there particular causes, ideologies, or interests that are advanced or impeded by this process? And if so, how well do they represent the public interest? The second set of issues goes to the structure of our system of government. Is the increasing use of the initiative a boon or a curse for the American democracy?

On the first set of questions, the evidence seems to me to make it hazardous to offer sweeping judgments. As previous chapters have shown, the initiative has been used by groups of the political left and right—and of no fixed ideology—to advance their agendas, often when those agendas have been stymied in the political tug-of-war of the legislative process. A woman in Oregon who wanted to know her birth parents; a millionaire in California who thought he knew a better way to teach immigrants English; unions in Washington that wanted to boost the minimum wage; reformers in Massachusetts who favored public financing of campaigns; animal-rights supporters; tax cutters; yes, and opponents of racial preferences and people eager to curb the flow of immigration—all of them have found it a useful tool.

A volume published in 1998 by the Ohio State University Press, entitled *Citizens as Legislators: Direct Democracy in the United States,* provided a forum for political scientists to wrestle with these questions. Their verdict on the first question—how well does it reflect the public interest—is generally positive, though not uncritical. In one of the essays, Todd Donovan, Shaun Bowler, David McCuan, and Ken Fernandez write: "Despite the escalating costs of direct democracy, we find that organized groups with modest resources—groups who represent fairly broad, diffuse constituencies—continue to place measures on the ballot that do pass. . . . A respectable proportion of these measures pass in spite of the fact that they threaten well-organized, wealthy interests who wage expensive opposition campaigns. . . . Although state-level direct democracy does not resemble grassroots populism, those policies that do come out of the process typically serve a broad constituency."

But the argument cannot be pushed very far—even by authors generally sympathetic to the initiative. Elisabeth R. Gerber, in another chapter of that volume, points out that many initiatives are promoted, not in the expectation they will pass but in hopes they will put pressure on the legislature to move in the direction of the group promoting that ballot measure. These tactics "do not provide a means for otherwise underrepresented groups to influence policy outcomes. Rather, they provide yet another way for politically important groups to promote their political interests."

That observation is reinforced in yet another chapter, written by Donovan and Bowler. It cites evidence that the tax limitation measures (like Prop. 13) that pass so readily when presented to the voters often have the perverse effect of reducing expenditures on popular public services—like parks and libraries—below what the public wants, the very point that Peter Schrag argued in *Paradise Lost,* his book on the effects of Prop. 13 and its successors in California. They also found that initiative states have less progressive tax systems, so "the poor bear a greater share of the burden of funding public services" in those states. "If responsiveness to the actual spending priority of voters is something that is desired, direct democracy in the American states might need to be reformed in some way that links decisions over tax cuts and tax rule changes to decisions about spending."

More disturbing are the indications that in a pluralistic society, a majoritarian instrument like the initiative can often be wielded to the disadvantage of minority groups. In the 1980s, for example, California, Colorado, and Florida all approved initiatives designating English as the "official language" of their governments, a not-very-subtle message to the immigrants within their borders that they better conform—or be excluded. In California in the 1990s, an electorate that is still predominantly white and Anglo, aware that demographic trends will soon make them the new minority group, passed the initiatives heavily promoted by the ambitious Governor Wilson, denying education and nonemergency health and social service benefits to illegal aliens and ending race-based affirmative action programs in the universities and government agencies. Exit polls showed a clear polarization. On Proposition 187, the anti-illegal-immigration measure, whites supported it by two to one, while Latinos were more than three-to-one opposed. In 1994 alone, ballot measures opposing protections for homosexuals appeared in eight states. Even where they failed to pass, studies indicated that they heightened antagonism toward gays. Donovan and Bowler argue that the threat to civil liberties is much greater in local initiatives, but instances of minorities losing rights as a result of state initiatives are rare.

If that is true, it is largely because the courts usually have been vigilant about protecting individual and minority rights from being jeopardized by successful initiatives. California's Prop. 187 was blocked by a federal judge from being implemented during the whole of Governor Wilson's remaining tenure. His Democratic successor, Governor Gray Davis, declined to appeal the district court decision and opted instead for a process of mediation which left virtually all of the proposed restrictions in abeyance.

But that did not happen to the anti-affirmative-action initiatives passed by voters in California and Washington, so the courts are not certain protectors of minorities.

Many of the academics who have written on initiatives have concluded that the influence of money and of economic interest groups is exaggerated—at least when it comes to getting ballot measures passed. For example, Elisabeth R. Gerber, in *The Populist Paradox,* rejects "the allegation that economic interest groups buy policy outcomes through the direct legislation process.... The measures that economic groups support pass at a lower rate than those supported by citizen groups.... Even though economic interest groups spend a lot of money in the direct legislation process, this does not serve as proof that they now dominate the process that was intended to circumvent their power."

That conclusion does not jibe with what I observed—or with what I was told by the practitioners in the initiative industry. It is undoubtedly the case, for all the reasons they cited, that the negative side has the easier time in almost any initiative campaign. That explains why, over the decades, fewer than half the initiatives that reached the ballot have been approved. But it ignores the fact that the campaigns that defeated them were usually very expensive efforts—as was the case with Prop. 226, the paycheck protection battle.

Where economic interests have been able to significantly outspend the opponents—as in the 1998 California battle between the Indian tribes and the Las Vegas casinos—they have carried the day. And when the opposition cannot muster significant money, as was the situation in the Missouri "boats in moats" fight, the result is an easy victory for the folks with the dough. Recall how the millionaires were able to rewrite education policy in California and drug policy in all of the states where they put marijuana initiatives on the ballot.

Those who would argue that money is not a major factor in today's initiative politics have not heard Tom Hiltachk ask "the million-dollar question," testing how deep are the pockets of anyone who walks into his law office with a proposition he wants to put on the ballot. When the practitioners say, "This is not a game for amateurs,' they know whereof they speak.

But there is reason for far greater concern, I believe, on the second question—the impact of the initiative process on our system of representative government. I share the view expressed by former Senate Majority Leader George Mitchell. The Maine Democrat often told audiences that "democracy began with the creation of an independent and strong legislative branch. Throughout history, there have been strong executives—whether we called them kings or emperors or dictators. Democracy emerged with the development of legislative bodies—parliaments—able to assert their authority against the will of the executive." If that is the case, then the health of the legislative branch is critical to a functioning democracy.

The rise of the initiative process in the last two decades of this century has been accompanied, teeter-totter, by a decline in the standing of legislatures and Congress. To be sure, there is a chicken-and-egg problem. Disillusionment with legislatures in particular and politics in general feeds the demand for tools that can bypass the checks and balances of our tripartite system of government. When there is gridlock in Washington or the state capital, frustration grows and people search for escape routes. There is some evidence that divided government—a split in party control between the two houses of the legislature or between the legislature's majority and the governor's party—results in the increased use of the initiative.

But it is also the case that the impact of measures passed by initiative on those governing institutions has clearly weakened them. Through the initiative process, tax and expenditure limits have been enacted in almost half the states. As Caroline Tolbert observed in *Citizens as Legislators,* "The Colorado legislature can no longer enact tax increases—tax hikes can only become law if approved by the voters in a referendum election. The general assembly can declare an emergency by a two-thirds vote and raise emergency taxes subject to voter approval. Measures like these institutionally weaken the ability of legislatures to collect revenue and provide services, a fundamental responsibility of government." Peter Schrag made the same observation about California, where, he pointed out, initiatives have "sharply circumscribed the authority and discretion of the legislature, county boards of supervisors, school boards, city councils, and the courts"—the central agencies of representative government. "Each measure, because it further reduces governmental discretion, and because it moves control further from the public—from local to state government, from the legislature to the constitution, from simple majorities to supermajorities—makes it even harder to write budgets, respond to changing needs, and set reasonable priorities." These measures have, in effect, set up the government to fail in its basic responsibilities.

But none of the initiatives have affected legislatures more directly than term limits. In the 1990s eighteen states imposed term limits on their legislatures, almost always by initiative. (Limits were enacted in twenty-one states, but three were overturned by the courts.) The effect on individual careers is obvious; the impact on the institution may be argued. Term limits clearly deprive the legislature of experience and familiarity with the issues; the institutional memory disappears as if lobotomized. They foster more competition within the chamber, as people jostle to position themselves for the ever-present leadership openings. In theory, they reduce the pressures of fund-raising and the inclination to view each issue through the prism of the next election. In fact, they may make those pressures even worse, because members of the state house of representatives often are positioning themselves to run for the state senate when their terms expire, and senators are looking for opportunities in statewide office or Washington. And voters, far from expressing greater confidence in these term-limited legislatures, appear to scorn them or ignore them as much as they ever did.

George F. Will, among others, has lobbied for term limits, making the argument that if lawmakers' tenures are shorter, their approach to public policy will be more reflective and disinterested than if they are calculating constantly how to keep themselves in office. Will's argument for term limits is far removed from the populist impulse that has driven most of the movement. His goal is to make Congress "a deliberative body and [not] merely a ratifying body, one that exists only to affirm decisions made elsewhere." He rejects the idea that "the principal criterion of good government is responsiveness," and he laments that "Congress has lost the status and esteem—including the self-esteem—that went with its deliberative function." By Will's analysis, "the problem is legislative careerism," and the cure is term limits. "No one wants to purge from politics the traditional arts and crafts and skills of negotiating, conciliating, logrolling, and the rest," he writes. "However, term limitation is an attempt to enlarge the domain of deliberation, to improve government's 'aptitude and tendency' to behave reasonably."

When Will argues that members of the California Assembly, for example, are more likely to "behave reasonably" if every incumbent knows he or she will have to clean out his office and files for good no more than six years after arriving, he is, in a curious way, asserting that citizen-legislators—unlike professional politicians—would have the same ennobling characteristics that the Progressives at the beginning of this century ascribed to their idealized citizenry. They would think about and search out the public interest, unswayed by personal considerations. The nation's founders had a better grasp of human nature. Madison and the other authors of the Constitution knew that personal or economic or sectional interests were a constant in psychology and politics; they were at pains to find a way to counter their influence—thus our federal system and our elaborate system of checks and balances.

And the Founding Fathers recognized that the surest way to assure accountability in this system of government was by subjecting officeholders to the discipline of election, so that they could be judged by the results of their policies and not just by the rhetoric or arguments they were able to muster.

Term limits defeat that accountability by assuring today's officeholders that they will not be around when the consequences of their political decisions become clear. Why this would strike someone as sensible as George Will as being conducive to reflectiveness in government is a mystery to me. If bank loan officers, for example, knew that they would be relieved of their duties within a few years of deciding who is creditworthy, no one would expect them to become more prudent managers of the depositors' cash. But we are supposed to believe that term-limited legislators will take better care of the public purse than those who know they will have to face the electorate in the future.

Whatever their merits, term limits are an enormously popular idea. Their popularity reflects a culture that increasingly insists the criterion by which any legislature—or individual legislator—should be judged is the readiness to carry out whatever is currently favored by the constituents. That is not George Will's argument; quite the opposite. But a letter to the editor of the *Washington Post* during the impeachment trial of President Clinton demonstrated how strong is the view that public opinion ought to drive the decisions of government. A man named Bill Touchstone wrote:

> With all the talk of morality lately, it does disturb me that a president violated the sanctity of his marriage. But something else troubles me more than that.
>
> The message the people have been sending to Congress for the past year or more is that we like our president (yes, even many Republicans have said it). We have said that we do not want him impeached, that we do not want a trial—much less one with witnesses—and that we want this over.
>
> But we have been told over and over by these leaders that they know better than we do, that what we want isn't what's best for us.

> The Constitution, which they have been quoting so frequently, starts with "We the People," not "We the Congress" or "We the Republicans." It is a scary thing when our leaders make claims of superiority. We have fought many wars against nations whose leaders have said much the same thing. This is the morality with which we should be concerned.

Six days later, an answer came in a letter from Daniel J. Collins. "I recommend that Mr. Touchstone take the time to read beyond the first three words of the Constitution," he wrote. "If he did, he would find that 'We the People' establish in it a republican form of government, by which elected officials would be chosen locally to represent 'We the People' in the manner they saw best during their term of office. 'We the People' would be protected by voicing our opinion at the ballot box and through the process of impeachment.... I believe the Constitution is thriving and as energized as ever."

Collins may have had the last word in this exchange, but his was the minority viewpoint. The longer the impeachment process went on, the worse the ratings the public gave the Republican Congress. The paradox in the polls was that large majorities considered the president guilty of the charges on which the House had impeached him—lying to a grand jury and obstructing justice—but were adamantly opposed not only to his removal but to his being tried for those not insignificant matters.

The conventional explanation for this involved many factors: Clinton had brought good times and thereby purchased some immunity for himself. At bottom, the wrongdoing stemmed from a consensual sexual relationship with a woman who by her own testimony had sought the relationship. And the independent counsel, Kenneth Starr, who had pursued Clinton with single-minded zealotry for four years, was so off-putting that he had long ago lost public sympathy for his efforts.

All these may have been at work in shaping public opinion, but the Touchstone letter gave a hint of a deeper force at work. It was clarified for me by a down-home political wiseman named Mike McKeon, who lives and works close to his subject, running his polling business out of Joliet, Illinois, a gritty factory town as far removed from the sensibilities of Georgetown as any place I have known.

McKeon said to me, "When people go to vote now, they ask themselves a couple simple questions: Who's gonna work at the job? What kind of job has he done? It's just like hiring a guy to come in and fix up your house. You don't care about anything except whether he shows up to do the job and does it right. You hire him, and he works for you. And the idea that somebody else might come along and fire him for something that is of no importance to you is unacceptable to people."

McKeon's insight was confirmed by a poll taken toward the end of the long investigation-impeachment process. The Center on Policy Attitudes, a nonpartisan survey research organization in Washington, D.C., interviewed a cross section of twelve hundred people in the last week of January 1999. One question in the impeachment section of the poll was: "Do you think members of Congress should stick closely to American public opinion when deciding what steps to take next—including results of polls like this one—or should members of Congress do what they think is best, regardless of what the American public thinks?"

By almost a two-to-one margin, 63 percent to 34 percent, those polled said public opinion should rule over conscience and individual judgment. That finding was not an anomaly. The same poll found that only 31 percent thought most House members who had voted for impeachment were mainly trying to do what was best for the country, while 66 percent ascribed some other motive to them.

And more broadly, the survey measured growing impatience and dissatisfaction with the overall responsiveness of elected officials. Only one out of five said they thought the decisions Congress made were the same as they, or most people, would make even as much as half the time. Most of the time, the vast majority said, their representatives were not representing them.

The suspected culprits in all this were "money" and interest groups. By a four-to-one margin, they agreed with the statement that government "is pretty much run by a few big interests looking out for themselves," rather than "for the benefit of all the people."

These findings were not out of line with those of many other polls taken during the past decade, but the trend lines showed a steady increase in the sense of political impotence. "On virtually all measures," this report said, "the public felt far less marginalized in the early to mid-1960s. In the late 1960s, dissatisfaction began a sharp upward movement until the mid- to late 1970s. Thereafter the movement upward was more erratic, but it reached new heights in the 1990s."

At the news conference where these findings were announced, I asked its principal author, Steven Kull, if the results did not amount to a vote of no confidence in representative government and a call for direct democracy. He demurred. "This does not mean that most Americans want direct democracy," he said, citing a finding in his poll that when asked how much influence the public should have on government decisions, using a scale of zero to ten, "only 37 percent gave the answer of ten." But, when pressed, he conceded that the median response had been nine—a call for almost complete sovereignty for public opinion.

This poll did not ask how much support there is for referring national policy decisions to referendum or instituting a national initiative process. But earlier surveys, taken before public trust in government had eroded to the point it is today, showed these measures to have great popularity. A Field Poll in 1997 found California voters favoring a national initiative by a 67 percent to 30 percent margin. A national survey in 1994 by a group called Americans Talk Issues found 64 percent support for national referenda on major issues. And a third survey, by Rasmussen Research in 1998, found an identical 64 percent to 17 percent majority in a national sample asked whether it is a good idea for states to adopt the initiative process.

The fact is that there is a persistent and probably growing distrust of representative government. In 1964, 76 percent of Americans said they thought they could trust the government in Washington to do what was right nearly always or most of the time. In 1997, when the Pew Research Center asked the identical question, only half as many—38 percent—agreed, while 62 percent said they trusted the government only sometimes or never. When asked why, the most frequent responses were that politicians are dishonest, are only out for themselves, say one thing and do another, and don't represent the people. This, mind you, was the frame of mind in a time of long-continued prosperity and before the scandal broke that led to the impeachment and trial of President Clinton.

An in-depth study of the question of trust, conducted late in 1995 by the *Washington Post* in conjunction with Harvard University and the Henry J. Kaiser Family Foundation, found a linkage between declining trust in government and an erosion of personal trust among Americans. Ominously, it found that each generation was less trustful than the one before; grandparents had more confidence in government—and in strangers—than their grandchildren.

And the breach of trust cuts both ways; people in government are as skeptical of the citizenry as the citizens are of government. Another Pew Research Center study, this one in 1998, concluded that "public distrust of government is paralleled by a belief among members of Congress, presidential appointees, and senior civil servants that the American public is too ill-informed to make wise decisions about important issues." Questionnaires filled out by 81 members of Congress, 98 presidential appointees, and 151 members of the senior executive service revealed a fairly startling lack of confidence in the citizenry. Fewer than one third of the congressmen and fewer than one seventh of the presidential appointees and top civil servants said they think Americans know enough about the issues to form wise opinions. Asked if they think people in government give adequate attention to public opinion, they dissented strongly from the public's views recorded in the Steven Kull survey reported above. Only one quarter of the presidential appointees, one fifth of the top civil servants, and one sixth of the congressmen said that not enough attention is being paid to grassroots views.

Predictably, members of Congress were more prone than the bureaucrats or their political bosses to blame public disillusionment with government on the performance of federal agencies. But all three groups agreed that media coverage of government is a principal cause of its low reputation. Roughly seven out of ten in each category gave a negative rating to the press's job in explaining and analyzing what they do.

I have written in many newspaper columns and in a book on the press, *Behind the Front Page,* that this is much more than the familiar blame-the-messenger syndrome. I want to reemphasize that point here. Vietnam and Watergate had a shattering effect on the Washington press corps in general and White House reporters in particular. Journalists who had thought of themselves as the most skilled and prestigious in the business had to admit that, in both instances, they had been conned by the public officials they covered and had unwittingly misled their readers, listeners, and viewers. Subsequent White House events—the Iran-contra scandal, President Clinton's attempt to cover up his affair with a White House intern, and all the rest—fed the cynicism of journalists. And the tone of "this is what they say, but who knows if it's true," colored the way they report almost all the news of government.

Congress had its own quota of scandals, from members preying on interns to financial finagling by well-known committee chairmen. But equally corrosive was the portrayal of Capitol Hill as a snake pit of partisan and personal sniping. The last two decades have seen control of the House and Senate swing back and forth between Democrats and Republicans, with bitter quarrels leading to the defeat or forced resignations of three Speakers of the House—Jim Wright, Tom Foley, and Newt Gingrich—and the retirement of many respected senior members who became disgusted with the angry atmosphere and the gridlock it produced.

But the legislative branch is not nearly as bad as the media make it look. Indeed, in one respect, it is clearly better. The standards of ethics—including financial ethics—are far higher than they were when I started covering Congress in the mid-1950s. Outside income is now largely prohibited. Gifts are sharply restricted. And we have gone from an era of black bags filled with untraceable cash to virtually full disclosure of the sources and uses of campaign funds.

The legislation that has led to these changes has drawn far less coverage than the scandals and disputes that prompted the change. Reporters are fight promoters by nature, and conflict is the grist of the journalistic mill. The legislative moments most likely to make it onto the television screen or the front page are those when people on opposing sides of an issue rip into each other. When the legislative process works well, it produces consensus, but consensus does not make news. The patient, quiet work of legislation is time-consuming and boring. And when a bill is sent to the president with nearly unanimous votes in the House and Senate, few reporters go back and retrace the hours of staff work and political bargaining that went into the result. The battle over the "patients' bill of rights," which produced stalemate, drew far more attention than the agreement to extend health coverage to millions of previously uninsured youngsters. So the public understandably comes to view the work of the legislative branch as ugly and unproductive.

That is, if they are aware of it at all. The television broadcasters and many newspapers have cut back sharply on their coverage of Capitol Hill in the past decade. News directors and editors have concluded that excerpts from congressional hearings and incremental stories on the progress of bills are boring to their audience, so they have eliminated most of them from their menus. As for the state legislatures, a survey by the *American Journalism Review* in 1998 found that since the early 1990s, the number of reporters assigned to statehouses had declined in twenty-seven states, with nine unchanged and fourteen up. The three largest newspaper companies in terms of circulation had all cut their staffing in state capitols during a time when the resources and power of state government were growing rapidly. A year later the picture had improved somewhat, but over the decade, the voters in twenty-seven states, including Texas, New York, Florida, and Illinois, were getting less coverage. Governors and state legislative leaders complain, with justification, about the rapid rotation of reporters covering those statehouse beats. When I began covering national politics in the 1960s, almost every state capitol boasted a cadre of resident reporters who had been in the pressroom for years, who knew how issues had been handled, had sources throughout the building, and who knew where all the bodies were buried. They were not hero-worshipers by any means, but they loved the beat they covered and were eager to explain what was going on there. Sadly, that is a rarity now—and the coverage of legislatures is often compressed to the point of being unintelligible and is rarely informed by any historical perspective.

All of these forces—from scandals to partisanship to slanted or uninformed journalism—have helped to denigrate the reputation of representative government in this country. But that would not place the republic in jeopardy were there not an increasingly visible and technologically feasible alternative—the vision of what Ross Perot, the 1992 and 1996 independent presidential candidate, liked to call the electronic town meeting.

Perot, a fabulously successful Dallas businessman who made his fortune devising computerized information systems for processing Medicare claims and other government data, had the same scorn for people who wasted their lives in politics as the industrial tycoons who bought up legislators a century earlier and brought on the Populist and Progressive reforms—including the initiative. His model of public-policy making was partly mechanical—"look under the hood and see what needs fixing." And it was partly academic. "I'd get the best experts in the country together," he would say when asked how he would deal with the health care problems, "and have them hammer out a solution." The real work of governing—resolving conflicting interests and differences of opinion, building majority coalitions, negotiating agreements, and enlisting public support—did not interest him. His reputation as a manager was authoritarian, but his rhetoric was populist. And he argued that with the modern tools of communication, Americans did not have to delegate the responsibility for deciding government policy to the hacks he saw when he looked at Washington or the state capitols. Voters could examine the alternatives for themselves and record their judgments by pushing the buttons on their handheld computers—a contemporary version of the New England town meeting, expanded by the marvel of modern technology to work in a nation of 280 million people.

Perot was understandably a little vague about how this would operate in practice. But the technology on which it depends is available. Home computers are becoming as ubiquitous as television sets, and the Internet is growing by leaps and bounds. Voting is also becoming automated. When you go for your driver's license, the clerk asks if you would also like to be registered to vote, and with a few strokes of the computer keys, adds your name to the election rolls. Absentee voting is encouraged in many states, with a quarter or more of the ballots being cast in advance of election day in some of them. Oregon has decided (by initiative in 1998) to eliminate all its neighborhood polling places. Oregonians now vote by mail from the comfort of their own homes. They use snail mail, as the postal service's delivery system is derisively called. But Arizona Democrats decided in 2000 to elect national convention delegates by Internet voting. And it can be only a matter of time before our speed-and-convenience-prizing culture decrees that it would be a sensible policy everywhere.

That idea was very much on the table, along with more ambitious notions, at a meeting sponsored by the Initiative and Referendum Institute in Washington, D.C., one weekend in

May of 1999. M. Dane Waters, its president, cut his political teeth in the term-limits movement, and the group's membership includes firms in the initiative industry. But Waters strove to keep the weekend intellectually honest by inviting academic critics of the initiative process as well as supporters.

There was no doubt about the leanings of most of those in attendance. The keynote speaker was Governor Kirk Fordice of Mississippi, a Republican, who was cheered when he saluted the audience as "the greatest collection of mavericks in the world. The goal that unites us is to return a portion of the considerable power of government to individual citizens... and take control from the hands of professional politicians and bureaucrats." Fordice noted that his state was the most recent to adopt the initiative—in 1992—but lamented that in the six years since then, "only one initiative has made it onto the ballot," a term-limits measure that was rejected by the voters. "Thank God for California and those raggedy-looking California kids who came in and gathered the signatures," he said. "Now the legislature is trying to say we can't have them come in, and we're taking it to court."

A skeptical note was introduced early in the proceedings by Peter Schrag, whose views on the impact of the initiatives on California government have already been quoted, and by David Magleby, a Brigham Young University political scientist who has written extensively on the process. Magleby said it was no mystery why the initiative was well liked. "It is a powerful agenda-setting device," he noted. "The media love it, because it is easy to report. The politicians love it, because they can use it to advance their careers. The interest groups love it, because their dollars can buy more in the way of policy results than through any other expenditure. And the political consultants love it, because, as one of them told me, 'Initiatives don't have spouses.' Absent personalities, tactics prevail." The disadvantages are substantial, Magleby went on, but are easily overlooked. "Many initiatives are incomprehensible to most voters, especially the less educated. The power of organized interests is clearly enhanced. Courts are placed in jeopardy" by having to rule successful initiatives unconstitutional. "And the role of elected officials of the state is substantially reduced."

The audience listened politely to Magleby's arguments, but there was applause when Lloyd Marbet, the bearded Oregon antinuclear activist, recounted how he had been "repeatedly thwarted by the power company lobbyists" in the legislature in Salem but fortunately had been able to take his case to the people.

There were sharp debates between academics and practitioners on financial-disclosure requirements and the broader issues of the influence of money on initiative campaigns. But the excitement began to build as speakers outlined the bright future they see for direct democracy. Rick Arnold, the Nevada-based signature gatherer, said, "The United States is one of only four or five major nations that has never had a national referendum. We should have it."

Ted Becker, an Auburn University professor and "unabashed supporter of direct democracy," invited audience members to visit his web site, "where we are trying to synergize the global democracy movement." Becker said that at the national level, "the United States is still stuck back in the eighteenth century. The system of representative government is outmoded. That's the Cartesian theory of government. Citizen participation is quantum thinking." And then he pointed to a series of developments, which taken together could make our eighteenth-century Constitution irrelevant.

"First," he said, "we will soon have an integrated Internet-television-telephone connection in every home that will allow the unlimited distribution of information and interchange of ideas. Second, we have made great advances in our conflict resolution techniques that facilitate reaching consensus. Third, groups of all kinds are learning to use the Internet to organize like-minded people wherever they live. And fourth, the development of scientific, deliberative polling—where random samples of citizens actually discuss and debate alternatives—makes it far more feasible to formulate ballot initiatives without the distortion of money."

He was followed by Marc Strassman, the founder and leader of the Campaign for Electronic Democracy, an Internet-based national effort to persuade states to allow electronic voting and—where the initiative process is available—the collection of ballot-measure signatures via the Internet. If the legislatures see the beauty, simplicity, and economy of this scheme, and Congress does the same for the nation, "we can have initiatives, voting, politics, and government at the speed of thought," he said. "What about the people who don't have computers?" a member of the audience asked. "They will get cheaper and smaller," Strassman replied, "and a liberal government would want to give computers away" to those who need them. Some might be skeptical, but Rick Arnold assured the audience, "Democracy will be changed by this technology." He added with a smile, "I'm looking for another job myself."

Somewhat surprisingly, given his own use of the initiative, Ron Unz said he was skeptical of this vision. "We'd have eighteen hundred initiatives on the ballot in every election in California," he said, "and people would get sick of it, just like they're sick of government-by-polling today. We should raise the barrier, discourage people from putting up initiatives. There should be some kind of a merit test." But the proponents were not fazed. "The legitimacy of an idea would be measured by how much support it has," Strassman said. And

Becker said that conflict resolution techniques and deliberative democracy by small citizens assemblies would solve all the problems. Only the best ideas would make it to the ballot.

The second-day highlight was the panel on the need for a national initiative. Wendy Wentlandt, the national political director of U.S. Public Interest Research Group, a Ralph Nader organization better known as US PIRG, led off. *Do we need a national initiative?* she had asked herself. "Absolutely," she replied. "The increasing domination of a wealthy elite is making a mockery of the democratic process." As a person of the Left, she said, "I support initiative and referendum for the same reasons the Progressives did. We need to stop the robber barons of our day." Such a system should require signatures from 3 percent of the voters to qualify an initiative for the ballot, should ban any corporate contributions to initiative campaigns, require full disclosure of the financing on both sides, and provide for distribution of a free voters' guide and free radio and television time for the debate.

Having outlined this vision, Wentlandt disappointed some in the audience by saying, "We're not going to get a national initiative-and-referendum process soon." Dick Gephardt, the Democratic leader of the House, "once introduced a bill for three advisory referendums a year," but it went nowhere. Republican Representative Peter Hoekstra of Michigan had proposed various approaches to a limited national initiative-referendum process but had given up on finding support. But, she added, "a national campaign would put us on the offensive and help protect the initiative process in the states that have it."

Richard Parker, a Harvard Law School professor, began his talk by agreeing that "it would be very difficult to institute initiatives at the national level. The first step would be to get a presidential candidate or a national party to take it up." But, becoming personal, he said it was important to make the fight. "I see the governing class in its native habitat at Harvard," he said, "and I can put their assumptions on a grid. They think initiatives make for low-quality decision making, that people are unfocused and easily manipulated and use their power to enact measures harmful to minorities.

"These elitists are bigots," he said. "At bottom, they oppose popular sovereignty. As the last SDSer, who still believes in the Port Huron statement [the manifesto of the 1960s leftist group, Students for a Democratic Society, which condemned corporate power and especially the military-industrial complex], I say the Left must be called to account on its lack of faith in the people."

Finally came Mike Gravel, former Democratic senator from Alaska and head of an organization called Philadelphia II, which calls for essentially creating a new Constitution based on direct democracy. "I think we can have a national initiative in very short order," he told the audience, "but we'll never get it from Congress. You don't need a constitutional amendment. The people are sovereign, and if they can't legislate 100 percent of the law, who can?" Gravel's plan—simplicity itself—is to take a national poll and if 50 percent want to vote on an issue, it goes on the next general-election ballot. Then Congress would have to hold hearings on the issue and mark up a bill for submission to the voters. Once an issue was on the ballot, only individuals could contribute to the campaign for passing or defeating it. An information video would be played on prime-time television so voters would understand the arguments.

And how would all this come about? "We could get this enacted by going to the people," Gravel said. "It would be self-enacted, just like the Constitution. If 50 percent plus one of the voters put signatures on a petition saying they want a national initiative, it's in effect." A flyer handed me by Don Kemner, the secretary of Philadelphia II, explained the theory behind this "self-enactment" strategy.

> The difficulty for the electorate today in "just doing it" is no different from what it was for the founding generation in ratifying the piece of paper the Framers called the Constitution of the United States of America. There was no statute in the Articles of Confederation or in any state constitution to allow the self-enactment called for in its Article VII.... James Madison replied (in *Federalist 51*), "The people were in fact the fountain of all power, and by resorting to them, all difficulties were got over."... The people are sovereign and a majority of the people enjoy the inalienable power to self-enact law without a procedure in place by statute, just as the people have in this sovereign power the ability to alter or abolish their form of government or to change the Constitution itself whenever they deem fit. Strange as it may sound, this is quintessentially American.

Is such a development likely? Not by the method Senator Gravel describes. Many of those at the weekend meeting, including its organizer, Dane Waters, told me that they do not support a national initiative. Their strong view is that the initiative process is not an alternative to representative government, but a useful check on legislatures, which, they point out, can obstruct widely supported legislation for reasons that do not reflect credit on the politicians involved. They argue that the initiative process is nothing more than one more check in our system of checks and balances.

But I think it would be a mistake to dismiss the possibility that the initiative process could leapfrog from California—our pacesetter state—and the other twenty-three states and hundreds of cities where it exists today and become the preferred form of decision making for the nation. Communications revolutions often have spawned drastic political change, and the Internet is revolutionary.

Consider this. The defenders of representative government can claim only two advantages for it. One is that our elected officials are supposed to be able to distill the public will through the filter of greater experience, information, and wisdom, and produce legislation more aptly designed to further the public interest than the raw, untutored opinion of the people would yield.

The public has shown what it thinks of the experience factor in that argument by enacting term limits through initiative almost any place it can and overwhelmingly endorsing term limits for Congress in the polls.

As for information, the reality is that with the Internet, any citizen can be as well informed on any subject as the most conscientious member of Congress or state legislature. The details of legislation, the testimony of expert witnesses, the analyses of lawyers, economists, scientists, and other authorities are all available on many web sites. And who can seriously claim that legislators, busy with campaigning, fund-raising, meeting with lobbyists and constituents, and traveling between their homes and the capitols where they work have more time for study and reflection on these matters than other Americans?

As for their wisdom and conscience, we know what the public thinks. Overwhelmingly, polls and interviews demonstrate that most Americans believe their elected officials look out first for themselves, then for their contributors, and put serving the public well down on their list of priorities. To tell American voters today that a politician is better motivated, more civic minded, and a better custodian of the commonweal than the voters themselves might be is an insult to their intelligence.

That leaves only one possible justification for preferring representative government. If the public believes it knows best what is right for the country and distrusts those elected to office, then the case for representative government comes down to proving that the process of legislation itself—debate, deliberation, amendment, compromise, all the purposely cumbersome mechanisms the founders built into the Constitution when they ordained a bicameral legislature, elected from different bases, serving for different terms, and subject both to executive veto and judicial review—all of this extraordinarily complex machinery somehow adds value to the ultimate decision.

But as that process is communicated to the country, it looks anything but reassuring. Bismarck famously said that no one should watch either sausage or laws being made. And the coverage of today's legislative branches reinforces what is already an overwhelmingly negative impression.

I do not think it will be long before the converging forces of technology and public opinion coalesce in a political movement for a national initiative—to allow the public to substitute the simplicity of majority rule by referendum for what must seem to many frustrated Americans the arcane, ineffective, out-of-date model of the Constitution.

At the end of the convention in Independence Hall, Benjamin Franklin, according to legend, was asked by a woman in Philadelphia, "Dr. Franklin, what have you given us?" And he is supposed to have replied, "A Republic, if you can keep it." The challenge of his last five words is no longer just a theoretical test question. Ken Masterton, the head of one of the many initiative-qualifying firms, remarked to me that the people in his industry—and those who employ them—"are holding the pen that's writing history. What history would we like to write tonight?"

A fundamentally different form of government is not just a possibility; it exists in half the country already. Will we recognize what is happening? Do we really wish to keep this a republic? That question is coming at us with the speed of E-mail and with the explosive power of a political bombshell. It is for us and our children to decide what kind of history we want to write.

For myself, the choice is easy. I would choose James Madison's design over Mike Gravel's without a moment's hesitation, the Constitution and its checks and balances over the seductive simplicity of the up-or-down initiative vote. We should be able to learn from experience. And the experience with the initiative process at the state level in the last two decades is that wealthy individuals and special interests—the targets of the Populists and Progressives who brought us the initiative a century ago—have learned all too well how to subvert the process to their own purposes. Admittedly, representative government has acquired a dubious reputation today. But as citizens, the remedy to ineffective representation is in our hands each election day. And whatever its flaws, this Republic has consistently provided a government of laws. To discard it for a system that promises laws without government would be a tragic mistake.

AFTERWORD

What happened in the 2000 election cycle confirmed many of the fears expressed in this book, which was published in April of that year. Initiatives continued to proliferate. There were twenty-six on the November ballot in Oregon; an additional six on its primary election ballot in May. The Oregon Voters' Pamphlet for the general election was so large it had to be published in two volumes; the one describing the ballot measures and summarizing the pro-and-con arguments ran to 374 pages.

Interest groups continued to find direct appeals to the voters preferable to the hurdles of the legislative process. Environmentalists, animal rights groups, anti-gay organizations, opponents of bilingual education, and, of course, a variety of tax limitation movements were all active.

The pattern of extremely rich individuals self-financing initiative campaigns also expanded. High-tech and other millionaires sponsored vouchers and charter school measures in three states. And George Soros and his partners launched a whole new wave of drug-policy initiatives, moving beyond their victories in the medical marijuana fights.

The financial warfare escalated. A single battle on the March California primary ballot, pitting the insurance industry against the trial lawyers, brought out $60 million in spending. The advertising in that one was as deceptive as what I had seen in the 1998 battle over "paycheck protection," and represented, once again, a caricature of the original purposes of the sponsors of direct democracy.

A month later, I had a further learning experience in my study of initiatives: a book tour for the hardcover version of *Democracy Derailed*. When my editor, Jim Silberman, and the publicists at Harcourt began discussing the customary author's tour with me, there were two things I asked of them. First, I hoped they would schedule it for April, because I needed to be free to help cover the campaigns for the presidential nominations for the *Washington Post*. The fights for the GOP and Democratic nominations figured to be over on or soon after March 7, when more than a dozen states, including California, Ohio, and New York, held their primaries on a single day. The publisher agreed; the voters delivered victories to Al Gore and George W. Bush right on schedule; and the book tour followed.

My second request also worked out—better than I could have imagined. As I said to them, my purpose in expanding on the reporting I had done in 1998 and turning it into a small book was to help stir the public debate on a process that had gone, I thought, too long unexamined, outside the small world of political scientists who had dutifully and usefully studied it.

To that end, we arranged that the promotional tour be built around a number of public forums and debates on the initiative process, rather than the usual bookstore signing events. In the end, a good many bookstores offered their hospitality, for which I am grateful. But the public forums were even better than I had hoped and provided a whole new set of insights into the phenomenon of initiative politics and what is driving it.

It was at a public forum in Seattle sponsored by the University of Washington, for example, that I was on a panel with Tim Eyman, who has become perhaps my favorite character in the wonderful, wacky world of the initiative industry. He is an engaging young man, still in his thirties, with boundless energy and enthusiasm, and a born entrepreneur. While still in high school, he began buying candy bars for ten cents apiece from wholesalers and selling them to hungry classmates for a quarter. One year out of college, he developed a successful business selling wristwatches with the emblems of sororities and fraternities to college students.

Eyman told me that the possibilities of the initiative process came into his consciousness from watching Ward Connerly's success with Proposition 209—the anti-affirmative action measure—in California. He did some of the early work on its twin, Proposition 200, in Washington, but found the organizational challenge too much and turned it over to Connerly and John Carlson (see Chapter 4).

"I was looking for another issue," Eyman said, "and I noticed the enormous success Jim Gilmore had in Virginia with his promise to kill the car tax." Gilmore, then the Republican state attorney general, rode to victory in the 1997 governor's race with a pledge to phase out the annual property tax on motor vehicles, pegged to the retail value of the car.

In 1998, Eyman sponsored an initiative to end the car tax in Washington, but fell 20,000 signatures short of qualifying it for the ballot. "The Achilles heel was the public feeling that if we killed that tax, they'd just raise something else. That gave us the idea we used in 1999: To cap the annual car tax at $30 and, at the same time, require voter approval of any increases in other fees or taxes."

The idea proved to be enormously popular. It meant that whether you drove a ten-year-old Toyota or a brand-new Mercedes Benz, you would never pay more than $30 a year for property taxes on your car. Starting with a base of supporters from the 1998 campaigns, Eyman said it cost him only $50,000 to collect a half-million signatures—all by volunteers—that far exceeded the requirement of 180,000 valid names to qualify for the ballot. In the November 1999 election, "Big business, big labor, the big newspapers and the biggest politicians, starting with [Governor] Gary Locke, were all against us, and we were outspent 20–1. But they made it a David vs. Goliath campaign, and we beat them, 56 [percent] to 44."

The victory was short-lived. In March of 2000, a King County (Seattle) judge ruled it unconstitutional, for violating the single-subject rule. But the governor and the legislature, thoroughly on the defensive, wrote the $30 fee cap into law on their own. Meantime, local governments facing a $1.6 billion gap in their biennial budgets, rushed to enact other fee and tax increases.

And that prompted Eyman to place on the 2000 ballot a "son of 695" initiative, referring to the number assigned his $30 auto-fee measure, that rolled back all of the post-695 increases and capped future property tax increases at 2 percent a year. That one passed, 56 percent to 44 percent, in November, 2000, and once again a judge stopped it from going into effect, because of the single-subject rule.

When I last talked to Eyman, early in 2001, he was working on yet another initiative for the November 2001 ballot. This one, he said, would simply limit property-tax increases to 1 percent a year, unless voters in a community approved a higher figure. Noting that it was a tougher provision than the one passed in 2000, Eyman said, "We're sending a message to the politicians that it's better to listen to the people in the first place."

Eyman said he had learned some lessons along the way. In 2000, he ventured beyond the tax-limitation issues and sponsored a measure, loved by the highway lobby, that would dedicate 90 percent of all state transportation funds to building new roads or improving existing ones. Originally, it also included a provision opening the high occupancy vehicle lanes, restricted to use in rush hours by cars or buses carrying multiple occupants, to all cars at all hours. Eyman had come to believe that it was the HOV lanes that were causing congestion in the metropolitan areas and fueling the demand for mass transit, which he opposed. But he was persuaded to drop the anti-HOV provision. Even so, his highway measure lost, 58 percent to 42 percent, because of opposition in urban areas loath to see more highways slice through their communities.

Eyman told me he had decided to confine himself to tax issues and do only one initiative a year. Nonetheless, he said, he now spends about ten months a year promoting initiatives, and two months—from Election Day through Christmas—selling his wristwatches. He had come up with a wonderful name for his initiative company, he said—"Permanent Offense"—and an equally wonderful motto, "Solving problems the politicians won't."

At thirty-five, operating from a modest office in the tiny town of Mukilteo, without ever being elected to anything, Tim Eyman has made himself a major force in the government of Washington state. The politicians in Olympia and Seattle might rage at him, and the editorialists and corporation executives denounce him as a negative influence on the future of the state, but the initiative process and his instinct for conservative populism gave him a power they could not deny.

Eyman was the most colorful character I met in 2000, but there were others who stimulated my thinking. I recall a member of the audience at a Commonwealth Club event in Palo Alto who pointed out to me the growing popularity among the Silicon Valley millionaires of drafting and paying for their own initiatives, with their own names attached in all the subsequent publicity about the measures. "They have gone from having trophy wives to having trophy initiatives," he said.

And I recall, a young man in Arizona, at a forum sponsored by the Morrison Institute of Arizona State University, who rose during the question period and addressed me as follows: "I don't want to be rude, Mr. Broder, but you have been talking about the past, and we are going to live our lives in the future. This is not the eighteenth century and we don't have to live under rules and procedures created back then.

"This is a consumer-driven economy," he said. "This is a consumer-driven culture. And it is going to be consumer-driven politics, whether you like it or not. We are not going to let other people make our choices for us. We are going to make those choices for ourselves."

I was a bit taken aback, but I recovered quickly enough to thank him for the comment and observe that he may well be right. But before we abandon that "eighteenth century model" of representative government for a new form of direct democracy, I hoped we would look closely at how government-by-initiative was operating in states such as Arizona.

It was about the time the book tour reached Arizona—having already covered eight cities and about a dozen forums in Washington, Oregon, and California—that I realized I was hearing one particular phrase in audience comments at virtually every stop. After I had argued my case about the shortcomings and dangers in the initiative process, especially the absence of the checks and balances that are built into the normal process of lawmaking, someone would rise from his or her seat and utter the following words: "But you don't know our legislature."

The tone was always one of complaint—a complaint that clearly was echoing in the ears of legislators themselves. When I met with a group of Colorado representatives and senators, at the invitation of the retiring speaker and minority leader, they told me they were alarmed by the lack of confidence in them and their handiwork—and by the growing reliance on initiatives as a way of settling public policy in their state.

Early in 2001, the National Conference of State Legislatures, operating through its nonpartisan foundation, began a study of the impact of the challenge to representative government. The University of Virginia and academics in Oregon and Washington arranged conferences on the spread of the initiative movement and its implications. And a special task force of the California legislature began an examination of the effects of the initiative process on the government of our largest state.

It appeared as if the phenomenon of government by initiative might finally receive the attention it deserves.

Nothing, however, suggested that initiatives themselves were becoming less popular or less numerous or that the campaigns for and against them were becoming less mischievous and misleading.

Almost every effort to restrain the growth of initiatives as rejected by the voters. When I was in Oregon on the book tour, the City Club of Portland was debating a ballot measure, originated by the legislature, to increase by 50 percent the number of signatures required to place a constitutional amendment on the ballot. The proposal was a response to the growing number of initiatives reaching the Oregon ballot and, particularly, the use of constitutional amendments by Bill Sizemore and others to place their favorite ideas beyond the reach of the legislature.

The City Club debate was passionate. Proponents of the idea warned that the constitution was being cluttered with provisions which were really statutory law, and that it was wrong for today's majorities to write their policy preferences into the permanent charter of government. Opponents replied that while the club, as previously noted, had called for reforms in the initiative process, this proposal had not been one of its recommended solutions. Raising the signature requirement, the opponents said, would raise the cost of getting onto the ballot. It would put the initiative process further beyond the reach of average citizens but would not inhibit moneyed interests or wealthy individuals from exploiting it.

By a narrow vote, the club membership endorsed the proposal, but the public strongly disagreed. On the May primary ballot, it was rejected, 58 percent to 42 percent.

Another kind of restriction on the initiative process went down to defeat in Alaska. Sportsmen, trappers, and allied interest groups persuaded the legislature to submit a provision barring future initiatives or referendums on wildlife or hunting. Despite the popularity of hunting in Alaska, the voters rejected this infringement on direct democracy, 64 percent to 36 percent.

Something similar happened in Arizona. The legislature endorsed a measure that would require a two-thirds majority to pass any future initiative on hunting methods or seasons. It failed, 62 percent to 38 percent.

In Nebraska, the legislature tried to shorten the time period for qualifying ballot initiatives, and, in a separate measure, to require two approval votes in successive years before a constitutional amendment could take force. The voters told the unicameral, by nearly identical margins of 62 percent to 38 percent and 63 to 37 percent, to keep hands off the initiative process.

Because of the presidential campaign, I had relatively little time in 2000 to report on initiative battles. I did get a look at some of the more hotly contested struggles.

In Michigan and California, wealthy individuals paid for measures to institute school voucher programs in their states. The California effort was bankrolled by Tim Draper, a Silicon Valley millionaire who, after serving for a year on the state board of education, "came to understand," as his spokesman, Chris Bertelli, told me, "that you can't fix the problems of our public schools from the inside." He proposed a sweeping solution, a measure that would offer a $4,000-a-year tuition grant to every new private school student and phase in a similar stipend for those already in private schools. And he was unstinting in his support, putting more than $20 million of his own funds into the campaign. It paid for some highly inflammatory mailings and television ads, including one headlined "What do California's schools and prisons have in common? Guns, metal detectors, security guards and fear." Draper brought great promotional skills from his high-tech entrepreneurial background, but one of his initiative sales stunts backfired. Draper offered a set of prizes, ranging from computers to Hawaii vacations and a $2,000 Macy's shopping spree to volunteer "team leaders" who signed up the most supporters. He seemed surprised at criticisms that his offer came perilously close to buying votes.

In Michigan, the impetus came from Richard and Betsy DeVos, the heirs to the Amway fortune. Their "Putting Kids First" initiative was more incremental. They offered a \$3,300-a-year grant only to students in "failing" school districts, defined as those where fewer than half the ninth grade students graduate from high school in four years. Initially it would have affected seven districts with 200,000 students—Detroit being by far the largest. The initiative would permit other districts to join voluntarily, either by vote of the residents or of the school boards.

Members of the DeVos family contributed about \$2.5 million to the campaign. Their role caused a serious rift in the Michigan Republican Party. Betsy DeVos had been the state GOP chairman, as well as one of its leading financial supporters. The state's top Republican, Governor John Engler, tried to dissuade her from launching the initiative campaign in a year when close battles loomed both for the presidential race and for Senator Spencer Abraham's reelection bid. His fear, as he told me, was that the voucher issue would split Republicans but unite the Democrats in opposition. But the DeVoses would not be halted, and when Engler made it clear he would not get behind the initiative, Betsy DeVos quit as party chairman, taking most of the headquarters staff with her.

California Governor Gray Davis, a Democrat, was opposed to the Draper initiative substantively, and, unlike Engler, who made his opposition to the DeVos initiative known through his political lieutenants, Davis actually made the first television ad against the Draper initiative.

In both states, the powerful teachers' unions, recognizing a threat to their membership, assembled potent opposition coalitions and poured in big dollars to defeat the measures. In California, the opponents spent \$32.3 million, compared to \$51.6 million for the backers. In Michigan, the spending on the two sides totaled approximately $20.6 million, $14.3 million by supporters and $6.3 million by opponents.

The advertising on both sides was remarkably deceptive. In Michigan, most of the DeVos-financed ads did not use the word "vouchers." Instead, they focused on other provisions of the measure, one requiring competency tests of all teachers and the other guaranteeing that state spending on public schools, which had grown rapidly in recent good economic times, could never be reduced. But Ed Sarpolus, an independent Michigan pollster, told me the ads backfired, because "They just confused people about what it's actually about." Draper's ads were more straightforward and, with their pictures of winsome children of various races, were designed to tug at the heartstrings. "A real choice for every family," was their tag line, "A fair chance for every child."

Both Draper and the DeVoses found a credible spokesman for their ads in Senator John McCain, the Arizona Republican, who had carried Michigan in the GOP presidential primary and run a strong campaign in California as well. The DeVoses also had an ally in the Roman Catholic cardinal of Detroit, Adam Maida. The cardinal ordered priests in his diocese to deliver homilies on the issue every Sunday in October and pledged to provide slots for 10,000 students in Catholic schools, some of which had been closed for financial reasons.

But in the end none of this availed anything. As was the case with the "paycheck protection" battle described in Chapter 3, the opposition forces used any weapon that came to hand to discredit the initiative. In Michigan, where the DeVos proposal was narrowly targeted, the opposition ads said, "Proposition 1 subtracts millions of tax dollars from all of Michigan's public schools and gives them away to private schools serving only seven school districts in the entire state. So who's going to end up paying for them in higher taxes?" In

California, where the Draper plan offered a universal benefit, the opposition campaign, run by Gale Kaufman, the manager of the fight against Prop. 226, said Draper would "take money away from public schools and spend billions on private voucher schools, with no performance standards for students and no accountability for taxpayers...an expensive experiment our children can't afford."

It was no contest. Draper was defeated 71 percent to 29 percent. The DeVoses did only slightly better, losing 69 percent to 31 percent.

In Maine, voters were asked to deal with a variety of emotional issues. A maverick conservationist named Jonathan Carter had gathered signatures for the latest in a series of efforts to change forestry practices in the state. On its face, it would simply require "landowners to obtain a permit for all clear-cuts," and set "reasonable cutting levels" for other property. But opponents, including the Audubon Society, said that it was poorly crafted and went too far in restricting long-established livelihoods of small-lot owners who already practiced good conservation. Maine's popular second-term Independent governor, Angus King, who joined the opposition, complained to me that "Even if he [Carter] loses, he wins. By coming back every two years and forcing the forestry industry to spend hundreds of thousands of dollars, he is making them very wary of doing business in Maine."

But King was even more outraged by another initiative, financed by the owner of the Scarborough Downs race track, to get voter approval for placing video gambling machines at the track as a lure to more customers. The initiative required that 40 percent of the net profits go to property tax relief, allocated lesser shares to other causes but, if read closely, steered a quarter of the net profits to the track operators. King called it "a corrupt and deceptive effort to rewrite Maine laws for the benefit of one guy and his business."

The talk in the state when I went there in mid-October was about two other issues—gay rights and physician-assisted suicide. King himself bore some of the responsibility for the former being on the ballot.

The Maine legislature in 1997 passed a statute, similar to that of many other states, adding homosexuals and lesbians to the categories of people protected against discrimination in employment, housing, and other areas of commerce. Social conservatives forced a referendum vote in a 1998 special election and succeeded in overturning it. Because the turnout in that one-issue election was small, proponents reintroduced the bill in the 1999 legislative session.

But King, who supported the measure from the start, said he would sign the second bill only if it included a requirement for another referendum of the people. When I was there, supporters were optimistic about the outcome, not only because the turnout would be larger in a presidential election year, but because after the 1998 defeat, they had negotiated successfully for the support of the Roman Catholic diocese, whose churches numbered one-quarter of Maine's people as communicants.

Sponsors had rewritten the statute slightly, using language that reflected the distinction Catholic theologians draw between homosexual orientation and homosexual behavior. They also made more explicit the guarantee that no civil penalties would be enforced against the church or parochial schools for their employment policies, so long as no public funds were being used.

When I was there, gay rights advocates were quietly confident that this time, they would prevail. Michael Heath, the head of the Christian Civic League of Maine, the major opposition group, told me that it had been difficult to raise money for his effort, because "The people on our side are weary of the fight. They say, 'They [the supporters of gay rights] are just going to keep coming back.'"

But I heard a cautionary message from Dave Garrity, a practicing Catholic and homosexual who headed the effort to pass the measure. He said, "We're very hopeful, but we're not comforted by the polls. People don't like to admit they're for discrimination."

His caution proved to be well-merited. Even though turnout was much higher, the measure failed by 51 percent to 49 percent.

The gay-rights referendum was quiet compared to the pitched battle waged by both sides in the fight over physician-assisted suicide. It began with a promise made by Darlene Grover, a critical-care nurse, to her father, who was dying of cancer. She told friends that when he learned his colon cancer would take his life, he said he wanted to be able to end his suffering "when the bad days outnumber the good." But he was afraid his daughter might be prosecuted, if she helped him achieve his goal, and that his insurance money might be denied to his widow if he committed suicide. So, she said, he endured a death so painful that she promised him, before the end, that she would do all she could to provide others with the option he had wished.

The campaign drew financial support from "death-with-dignity" advocates from across the nation. Unlike the Michigan group described in Chapter 4, the Maine supporters had ample funds for their campaign. But they faced the same formidable coalition that sank the Michigan measure—the medical, hospital, and psychiatric associations, the hospice-care people, and, especially, the Catholic Church. Bishop Joseph

Gerry of Portland sent a pastoral letter to the faithful, condemning the measure, and saw to it that sermons were preached on the subject in all the churches in the diocese.

Meantime, social workers, nurses, and physicians on opposite sides of the issue debated its merits on television and in public forums across the state. In one public television debate that I watched, two cancer patients–a woman battling breast cancer and a man with terminal stomach cancer–argued passionately about whether they should or should not have access to physician-prescribed lethal drugs and whether legalizing that option would or would not improve what all the experts agreed was Maine's inadequate system of palliative or hospice care.

Knowing that public opinion supported the broad principle behind the measure, opponents concentrated—as their counterparts in Michigan had done—on arguing that the specifics of the ballot measure were poorly drawn. They claimed that it lacked adequate family notification procedures and that the safeguards it provided to assure that this was a deliberate, well-considered choice by the patient who was clearly terminally ill were insufficient. In the end, the doubts prevailed, and the measure was rejected, 51 percent to 49 percent.

The forestry and video gambling measures went down by wider margins, in what proved to be a tough year for winning approval from Maine voters. But Governor King, who stayed neutral on the assisted-suicide question, drew the ire of some constituents by raising doubts about the whole initiative process.

When I interviewed the governor, he showed me an e-mail he'd received from an angry constituent. "I am amazed at your position concerning citizens' ability to advance initiatives for a public vote," this man wrote. "I also resent your implications that our legislators are more effective in making laws. Public involvement in policy making is the basis of the democratic process. I think you need to study the Constitution. The people control our government. You work for us; we don't work for you. We are the boss. What we say goes. You are a prime example of what is wrong with America and Maine today."

Governor King, who has a sharp sense of humor, began his reply e-mail with the comment; "Wow! Quit beating around the bush and tell me what you really think." Then he made several points:

The U.S. Constitution has no provision for initiative and referendum. The Framers would have been appalled at the very idea. They created a representative democracy, where ideas were filtered through a complicated process of checks and balances because of their concern that "the people" acting directly could make mistakes, just as could some kind of absolute monarch.

The Maine Constitution, as originally adopted, had no provision for initiative and referendum. These sections were added around 1910. The expectation was that this process would be used very rarely—which was the case, until the last 15 years or so....

By and large, the referenda we have had recently have in no way come from "the people," but from small, often out-of-state special interest groups...or in-state special interest groups....

More and more, in Maine and across the country, this process is being used to "end run" our constitutional processes by well-financed, narrow interests....I know who's the boss, as do the legislators. We are all answerable directly to the people at regular intervals and if the people don't like what we're doing, they have the unfettered right to kick us out. That's the way our system is supposed to work."

In 2001, King sponsored a bill that would bar initiative signature-gatherers from working at polling places on Election Day, thus making it more difficult to qualify measures for the ballot. The proposal was denounced by Jonathan Carter and other initiative backers and faced steep odds in the legislature.

There were many other issues that also reached the ballot in 2000. A post-election survey by the Brookings Institution's Center on Urban and Metropolitan Policy found fifty-five citizen initiatives among the 553 state and local ballot measures dealing with some aspect of growth policy. The report said that "It is important to note that these initiatives are not necessarily placed on ballots by volunteer community groups. Increasingly, initiatives are the work of well-financed individuals or interest groups that hire people to gather signatures."

The Sierra Club sponsored statewide land-use measures in Arizona and Colorado, both of which started with broad public support but ended up being solidly beaten by campaigns financed by developers, the construction industry, and others who would have lost money-making opportunities had they passed. In both states, the opponents heavily outspent the sponsoring organizations, and, in both states, the negative campaigns stirred fears of rising housing prices, crowded schools, and other ills.

On the other hand, in Oregon, which already had a strong land-use law, Bill Sizemore's taxpayer organization won narrow approval (53 percent to 47 percent) of a constitutional amendment initiative requiring state compensation of landowners who can prove the value of their property has been diminished by such regulations. An anti-billboard initiative failed by the narrowest of margins, 51 percent to 49 percent, in Missouri, but a similar measure was approved in Reno, Nevada.

George Soros and his two fellow-millionaires, described in Chapter 4, had another successful year in their campaign to rewrite the drug laws. Medical marijuana initiatives were passed in Colorado and Nevada. Initiatives tightening the rules on confiscating the assets of drug offenders were approved in Oregon and Utah, and California voters approved a measure requiring treatment, rather than incarceration, for drug users. Their only defeat came in Massachusetts, where they narrowly lost a bid to create a state fund earmarked for drug treatment from the seized assets of drug dealers.

The animal-rights lobby scored victories on hunting and trapping issues in Alaska, Montana, and Washington but failed to ban dog-racing in Massachusetts and certain hunting practices in Oregon.

The education lobby had several victories beyond its success in defeating the voucher measures in California and Michigan. Microsoft millionaire Paul Allen sponsored a measure to expand charter schools in Washington and saw it fall to the teachers' union opposition, 52 percent to 48 percent. At the same time, Washington voters endorsed the union-backed measure to mandate higher teacher pay and smaller class sizes. Colorado and Oregon passed measures requiring expanded funding of the public schools and, on a second try, the California teachers' union, backed by Governor Gray Davis, eased the requirement for approval of school bond issues from two-thirds to 55 percent.

Other familiar issues were back on the ballots. Nebraska became the nineteenth state to impose term limits on legislators.

Arizona followed California in ending bilingual education. California, Nebraska, and Nevada banned same-sex marriages. In a mixed year for tax-limitation measures, Alaska, Colorado, and Oregon voters turned down initiatives that would have saved them money but reduced services, while Massachusetts, and South Dakota joined Washington and Tim Eyman in eliminating certain taxes.

Overall, the post-election summary by the Initiative and Referendum Institute noted thirty-five of the seventy-one voter initiatives on the November 2000 ballot were approved—a lower winning percentage than 1998's 61 percent but better than the historic average of 41 percent. Taking 1998, 1999, and 2000 together, just about half the initiatives that made it to the ballot were approved—making the process an attractive investment for those who want to fulfill their policy goals without the bother of going through the legislature and governor.

Meanwhile, the debate goes on, with growing intensity. In 2001, Dane Waters edited, and his Initiative and Referendum Institute published, a volume of essays titled *The Battle Over Citizen Initiatives.* Its theme is the illegitimacy of efforts by legislatures to regulate the initiative process in their states. In one chapter, Paul Jacob, the national director of U.S. Term Limits, takes direct issue with this book and argues that "The initiative process is arguably the only avenue for citizens to reassert their control over government. But Americans, already dissatisfied with the unrepresentative nature of legislators, are about to discover that the very career politicians voters seek to rein in are destroying this avenue to reform."

As Jacob sees it, "The goal of legislators and critics of the initiative process is clearly not to correct the perceived flaws but to kill the process in its entirety and to restore a legislative monopoly for the politicians who have fallen into such ill repute among the people. The war between the people and the politicians may well be decided by whether the initiative process survives the current legislative assault."

In reality, there is no threat of dislodging the initiative process from the states where it exists. The debate will be whether to expand it to other states and to the nation. And that, from what I have observed and reported, would be a fateful step.

The 24 States (Shaded) and Some of the Cities with the Initiative Process

ACKNOWLEDGMENTS

Much of the reporting on which this book is based was originally done for the *Washington Post,* my happy journalistic home for these past thirty-three years. I am grateful to Maralee Schwartz, our indefatigable political editor, and to Leonard Downie Jr., the executive editor, for their support and encouragement in letting me open up this area for readers of the *Post.*

I owe much to the players in these dramas—the sponsors and opponents of these initiatives, the owners and managers of the signature-collecting firms, the consultants in the initiative campaigns, and the state officials who monitor the action. They—and the academics who have studied the initiative process and whose work is cited here—have been generous with their time and insights.

Bill Leigh and Wes Neff of the W. Colston Leigh Agency handled the negotiations for the book contract with their usual skill and contributed useful ideas on the shaping of the project.

Three people were indispensable in bringing this book to fruition. M. Dane Waters, the head of the Initiative and Referendum Institute in Washington, D.C., provided reams of historical and current data on this form of direct democracy, offered valuable contacts in the states, and met every request for more information promptly and graciously. Dane has his own view of the merits of the initiative process, which is sharply different from some of my conclusions. But I hope he will feel that I have dealt fairly with the subject and helped achieve one of his goals, which is a greater public understanding of this arena of politics.

James H. Silberman, the veteran editor I worked with when Haynes Johnson and I published *The System,* our account of the battle over health care reform, once again proved to be a meticulous handler of the manuscript and the source of constant guidance on its structure and contents.

And, finally and most importantly, Ben White, the political researcher at the *Washington Post,* took time in the evening and on weekends to chase down elusive data. He screened the literature of the Populist and Progressive periods, identifying great sources for the origins of the initiative process, and he hounded secretaries of state and other officials for the elusive financial data collected in chapter 4. Ben has a wonderful career in political journalism ahead of him, and I owe him more than I can say for his partnership on this project.

DAVID S. BRODER
WASHINGTON, D.C.
NOVEMBER 1, 1999

BIBLIOGRAPHICAL NOTE

The political scientists have been as busy and conscientious in examining the initiative process as most of us in journalism have been neglectful. I found many useful books and articles in the academic literature.

Among those I would particularly recommend are:

Bowler, Shaun, Todd Donovan and Caroline J. Tolbert, eds. *Citizens as Legislators: Direct Democracy in the United States.* Columbus, Ohio: Ohio State University Press, 1998.

California Commission on Campaign Financing. *Democracy by Initiative: Shaping California's Fourth Branch of Government.* Los Angeles: Center for Responsive Government, 1992.

Cronin, Thomas. *Direct Democracy: The Politics of Initiative, Referendum, and Recall.* Cambridge, Mass.: Harvard University Press, 1989.

Gerber, Elisabeth R. *The Populist Paradox: Interest Group Influence and the Promise of Direct Election.* Princeton, N.J.: Princeton University Press, 1999.

Hofstadter, Richard. *The Age of Reform: From Bryan to F. D. R.* New York: Alfred A. Knopf, 1955.

Magleby, David. *Direct Legislation: Voting on Ballot Propositions in the United States.* Baltimore: Johns Hopkins University Press, 1984.

Ranney, Austin, and David Butler, eds. *Referendums around the World: The Growing Use of Direct Democracy.* Washington, D.C.: AEI Press, 1994.

Schrag, Peter. *Paradise Lost: California's Experience, America's Future.* New York: The New Press, 1998.

Zimmerman, Joseph F. *Participatory Democracy: Populism Revived.* New York: Praeger, 1986.

INDEX